STRATEGIC LEADERSHIP CONVERSATIONS

AUSTRALIAN UNIVERSITIES

1980-2020

Foreword by John Dawkins

Edited by
Tess Howes

Copyright © Tess Howes, 2020

Published by Connor Court Publishing.

ALL RIGHTS RESERVED. This book contains material protected under International and Federal Copyright Laws and Treaties. Any unauthorised reprint or use of this material is prohibited. No part of this book may be reproduced or transmitted in any form or by any means, electronic or mechanical, including photocopying, recording, or by any information storage and retrieval system without express written permission from the publisher.

CONNOR COURT PUBLISHING PTY LTD
PO Box 7257
Redland Bay QLD 4165
online@connorcourt.com

www.connorcourtpublishing.com.au

ISBN: 978-1-922449-06-1 (pbk.)

Cover design by Graeme Bland

Printed in Australia

CONTENTS

Acknowledgements
- Tess Howes   1

Foreword
- John Dawkins   9

Preface
- Tess Howes   15

Introduction
- Tess Howes   21

Chapter One
- Denise Bradley   39

Chapter Two
- Alan Robson   65

Chapter Three
- Ed Davis   89

Chapter Four
- Geoffrey Sherington   107

Chapter Five
- Ian Chubb   129

Chapter Six
- Jim Ife   151

Chapter Seven
- Lynn Meek   171

Chapter Eight
- Peter Coaldrake   191

Chapter Nine
- Simon Marginson   207

Chapter Ten
- Carolyn Noble   233

Concluding comments
- Tess Howes   255

Select Bibliography   287

This book is dedicated to

Emeritus Professor Denise Bradley AC

1942-2020

equity advocate – HE policy powerhouse

her legacy lives on

ACKNOWLEDGEMENTS

Compiling this edited collection of interviews has been a team effort. I offer my sincere thanks to the contributors who generously agreed to share their insights on the implementation of strategic leadership and strategic planning in the Australian higher education sector from a personal, academic and experiential perspective for publication in this book. Thank you Denise Bradley, Alan Robson, Ed Davis, Geoffrey Sherington, Ian Chubb, Jim Ife, Lynn Meek, Peter Coaldrake, Simon Marginson and Carolyn Noble. Thank you also for the assistance and guidance you provided to me as I was developing the framework for this writing project and thinking through some of the complex issues raised. I am very grateful to you all.

Sadly, Denise Bradley passed away in March 2020 while this publication was in press. The sector grieves her loss. This publication is dedicated to her memory and acknowledges her tireless attempts to build a more equitable higher education sector for all.

I would also like to thank John Dawkins, former Commonwealth Minister for Employment, Education and Training, the architect of the 'Dawkins Reforms' (1988), for agreeing to write the Foreword for this publication. I often thought of John Dawkins as I was conducting my research on the academic response to the Dawkins Reforms, particularly the impact of the introduction of strategic leadership and strategic planning on the Australian university sector. Therefore, it was both rewarding and insightful for me to open a line of communication with John Dawkins and invite him to contribute to this publication. Thank you, John Dawkins, for encouraging me to develop a broader perspective on the Dawkins

Reforms and an appreciation the foundations this reform agenda established for modern Australian universities. As Macintyre, Croucher, Davis and Marginson acknowledge (2013) "if you seek John Dawkins monument, look around you" (p.47). Although John Dawkins was aware that many higher education staff and commentators remain critical of some aspects of the Reforms, he agreed to open a symposium at the Royal Melbourne Institute of Technology held in 2012 on the twenty-fifth anniversary and write the Preface of the publication released the following year (Croucher, Marginson, Norton and Wells, 2013). When John Dawkins agreed to contribute to this publication he was also aware that several contributors were critical of key elements of the reforms. The fact that he remains willing to continue to engage with the sector and actively participate in contemporary conversations on this topic is a sign of his resilience and pragmatism. John Dawkins' chapter reminds us all that transformational structural reform with a strategic eye to the future does not happen without a long-term strategic vision and medium-term discomfort.

There are several comprehensive reviews of the Dawkins Reforms, particularly, Croucher, Marginson, Norton and Wells (2013) *The Dawkins Revolution 25 Years On* and Macintyre, Brett and Croucher, *No End of a Lesson: Australia's Unified National System of Higher Education* (2017). These seminal texts are cited extensively in this publication and recommended reading for those keen to know more about the Dawkins Reforms and the impact this large-scale structural, educational, ideological and cultural change has had on the Australian higher education sector. This publication does not offer another comprehensive analysis of the Dawkins Reforms. This edited collection of interviews brings to the discussion the insights of a small but representative cohort of academic leaders who led, or witnessed, the implementation of the Dawkins reforms and observed the impact the introduction of strategic leadership and strategic planning has had on the Australian university sector.

ACKNOWLEDGEMENTS

The contributors offer honest, interesting and authentic reflections on their lived experience. In so doing, they offer insights from a range of academic leadership experiences that span the pre and post Dawkins era as they reflect on their academic careers with the wisdom of hindsight.

The contributors

The contributors include four former Vice-Chancellors and Deputy Vice-Chancellors, Denise Bradley, Alan Robson, Ian Chubb and Peter Coaldrake; a former Acting Deputy Vice-Chancellor and Dean, Geoffrey Sherington; a former Executive Dean, Ed Davis; a former Deputy Chair of Academic Board and Head of School, V Lynn Meek and three senior members of the professoriate, Jim Ife, Simon Marginson and Carolyn Noble. Collectively, the contributors hold or have held a range of senior academic leadership and executive positions at more thirty-five universities, higher education institutions and research centres throughout their long careers.

Each chapter is prefaced with a brief biography and photo of the participant so that the reader can engage with these senior academic leaders at an individual, personal, level.

It is no coincidence that of the ten contributors, only two are women (20%). In 2013, a timeframe relevant to the career span of the contributors, there were 521,479 academic staff (full-time and fractional full-time) employed in Australian universities of which 56% were male and 44% were female academics. The highest proportion of women academics congregated on the second lowest academic level, lecturer (Level B) and were predominantly in the 30-54 age bracket. Of the 13,680 academic staff employed at Level C to Level E (senior lecturer to professor) male academics held 71% of these senior positions. Men were also more than 4½ times likely to still be employed at a senior academic level at age 64 or older (82%) whereas only 261 women aged 64 or older were employed as professors (18%). The 2013 academic staff data proves that both age and gender discrimination against women is endemic in the Australian university sector[1]. In order to draw attention to the gender imbalance in the Australian university sector over the timescale of this publication, the two women contributors are presented first and last giving them the opportunity to have the first and last word.

The eight male contributors are presented alphabetically according to their first name in a democratic non-hierarchical ordering process. The contributors provide a professionally informed contextually relevant overview of their personal experience of leading strategic planning, or witnessing the implementation of strategic planning, that will inform current executives and the next generation of university leaders before they assume strategic leadership and strategic planning responsibilities. Presenting the interview data from the contributors verbatim, all senior academic leaders in the Australian higher education sector with a wide range of experience, opens "the university 'black box' of experience to scrutiny" as Coaldrake and Stedman (2013, p.7) recommend. The findings will also contribute to the emerging field of 'strategy as practice' research which also recommends exploring the 'black box' of strategy in practice that once led the strategic management research agenda (see Golsorkhi, Rouleau, Seidl and Vaara, 2010; Mintzberg, 1973a, 1973b; Mintzberg and Waters, 1985). [Golsorkhi, Rouleau, Seidl and Vaara, 2010]

As the following chapters demonstrate, several contributors view strategic planning as an essential executive leadership function and welcomed the opportunity to implement modern management practices in their employer universities, such as Denise Bradley, Alan Robson, Ed Davis and Peter Coaldrake. Their chapters detail several different approaches to leading strategic planning that enabled their

---

[1] http://highereducationstatistics.education.gov.au/uCube - higher education statistics staff count by current duties classification

universities to reposition for success in a very competitive national and international higher education environment. Carolyn Noble and Jim Ife hold an opposing view, arguing that the introduction of strategic planning resulted in needless pressure on academic staff resulting in anxiety, workload issues, diminishing academic morale and decreasing student satisfaction. The impact centralised strategic planning had on traditional academic leadership roles is described by Geoffrey Sherington and Lynn Meek providing the "Uninversity 'black box' of experience to scrutiny" 2013, (p.7) insightful micro case studies of several Australian universities in the pre- and post-Dawkins periods. Ian Chubb views planning as a key executive leadership responsibility however advocates for "accountability with minimal intrusion" (p.147). Simon Marginson brings a scholarly perspective to the discussion, informed by four decades of research into the topic. One of the impacts of the Dawkins Reforms raised by Geoffrey Sherington and Jim Ife is the demise of the 'God professor', which in my view, has been replaced by the 'God Vice-Chancellor' in modern Australian universities.

Collectively the contributors bring more than three hundred and fifty years of academic leadership experience to this publication. They are therefore well qualified to explain when, and for what purpose strategic planning was introduced to the Australian university sector and offer advice to the next generation of Australian university leaders who will be tasked to lead the sector through the challenges and opportunities of the 21st century. University executives have a responsibility to act in the best interest of the university. They also have a responsibility to act in the best interests of their stakeholders, past, present and future, and these two primary leadership tasks should not be in conflict.

The editor
As an undergraduate university student in the discipline of history

in the immediate post-Dawkins years I personally witnessed the leadership tensions that arose between academic staff and university administrators as the Dawkins reform agenda was implemented, particularly the imposition of managerial practices in educational contexts. My classmates and I shared our teachers' concerns about long-term funding for the humanities and diminishing resources for public universities visible on the funding horizon. However, I also witnessed many benefits from the structural transformation of the sector and initiatives promoting growth and equity, including the enrolment of mature aged, part-time and evening students; the introduction of online and distance modes of study that made education accessible to full-time workers, students with full-time caring responsibilities, students with disabilities and students in regional and rural locations.

On-campus childcare centres and parent cooperatives provided child minding for students with childcare responsibilities and early childhood education for future generations of students. Student services staffed by qualified professionals made health and allied health services accessible to students on-campus. Career development sessions on interview techniques and resume writing skills assisted the transition to professional practice, and numeracy centres provided tutoring for students who did not have the foundation knowledge to meet enrolment prerequisites. Indigenous academic support centres were also established in universities across Australia. Warawara, at Macquarie University for example, strengthened connections with the Darug community and provided academic and cultural support to Aboriginal and Torres Strait Islander students enrolled at the university.

New universities were established in outer metropolitan and regional locations. Physical proximity to modern universities enabled connections with local businesses and working class and migrant communities, suggesting new career trajectories for current and future generations of university students. Programs of study were introduced that were more closely aligned with changing employment markets and emerging industries. A myriad of educational innovations changed the character of Australian universities and broadened national higher education aspirations.

As a professional member of staff in a range of middle and senior management positions in the 1990s and 2000s, primarily in student administration, I became increasingly aware of the burden borne by my academic colleagues from the rapidly increasing student enrolments, large teaching classes, and significant increases in marking and administrative responsibilities. However, I also witnessed the pride and joy of families attending the graduation of their parents, partners and children. Many of these graduates were the first members of their family to attend university. In this respect, the 'massification' of the Australian university sector in the post-Dawkins era was motivating and exciting professionally and personally. The higher education landscape was effectively transformed in terms of growth, access and flexibility.

When I moved into an executive strategic planning role I witnessed leadership tensions frequently expressed between the executive and academic staff, primarily as a result of a contest of power and loss of collegial authority at the highest level of leadership in the university. These observations inspired me to commence a doctorate and accept a research strategy and development role reporting to the Excellence in Research Australia 2010 initiative (ERA2010) where I came to appreciate the responsibilities borne by universities compelled to comply with ever changing legislative requirements and onerous reporting regimes. I also became concerned about the consequences that the quality journal ranking publishing regime was having on limiting the richness and breadth of academic work.

Simon Marginson's chapter reveals the pressures ERA's preferred quality journal publication list generates for academics engaged in applied research who think it is important to contribute to disciplinary conversations in lower-ERA ranked publication sources (p.222). Carolyn Noble publishes extensively in disciplinary publications that lie outside the ERA criteria to maintain connections with colleagues in social work departments in national and international contexts. This publication also lies outside the ERA specifications as I think it is important to pursue important lines of disciplinary enquiry in the national interest.

As a sessional academic at two Australian university Business Schools I am now teaching management and leadership subjects to postgraduate and undergraduate students in classrooms alive (hopefully) with the transfer of theoretical and applied knowledge. I would also like to thank my colleagues and students for helping me clarify some of the ideas expressed in this publication. I value the rich intellectual stimulation that is inherent in academic work. Thank you all, especially Lee Ridge. I feel very fortunate that my career has come full circle.

Finally, it would not have been possible for me to bring this publication together without the constant and unwavering support of my family. Thank you all for your encouragement and regular release from my large family responsibilities. Particularly Bill, my husband, support team and critical sounding-board; and Alice, daughter, teacher and writer.

However, I accept full responsibility for the views expressed in the following chapters and any errors or omissions contained herein.

Tess Howes

March 2020

FOREWORD

The 30th anniversary of the commencement of HECS and the associated changes to the Higher Education system has just passed. Yet once again a book dedicated to reviewing the effect of the changes (referred to as the Dawkins Reforms) concludes that the jury is still out.

Like the review at the time of the 25th anniversary this review 'neither condemns nor celebrates' the Dawkins Reforms. I wonder what extra evidence is required to make a judgement. The problem seems to be that what are referred to as the Dawkins Reforms seem to defy definition and indeed authorship.

I remain the longest serving minister for education (and, in my case employment and training) and there have been 13 ministers since with responsibility for higher education. All have to some extent adjusted the 1989 changes. There were 11 ministers during the 23 years since the office was created and preceding my term. The point being that many of the occupants of the office had short periods of service during which most left few indelible marks. My contribution looms large by comparison.

As well, from 1959 the role of the Commonwealth Government in higher education was intermediated by an independent body bearing various titles and was lastly named the Commonwealth Tertiary Education Commission (CTEC) until its abolition in 1988. The key role of these bodies was to recommend public funding for the sector and once determined by the Government, to allocate the funds between the various institutions. In effect the chair of this 'buffer' organisation was the minister for higher education.

CTEC for example allocated funding for recurrent, capital and to some extent research and in the process approved the establishment of new institutions, managed the growth of all institutions, approved the creation of new areas of study, approved new buildings, and for over a decade enforced the 'binary divide' through different funding models for universities and colleges of advance education.

Within the following pages there is reference to John Ward's criticism of the Dawkins reforms as 'strangulation by regulation' as if there was no previous regulation. The regulation by CTEC was conducted politely and often over the phone and mostly by commissioners who came from the higher education sector and talked the same language. Nevertheless, behind the politeness was the reality of a steely resolve.

The problem was CTEC lacked any authority besides the rather blunt instrument of funding. The then chair of CTEC led a committee that produced a report in September 1986, on Efficiency and Effectiveness in Higher Education. The excellent recommendations contained in the report were intended to provide guidance to the Government on its funding decisions in the 1987 budget, but it was quite unclear how these recommendations would be implemented other than through highly prescriptive legislative provisions attached to the funding of institutions. Even if the government was interested in going down this path, it is unlikely that a disagreeable Senate would follow.

A new approach was required as I set out in the 'Challenge for Higher Education in Australia' in September 1987 immediately following the Budget, in which I embraced many of the recommendations of the CTEC report. However, I also set out the government's ambition to increase participation in higher education not only from traditional sources but also from those groups locked out of higher education.

The Green Paper (or policy discussion paper as I was required by Cabinet rules to call it) set out the growth targets for both enrolments and graduates as well as embracing the reforms recommended by CTEC, reforms more easily accommodated in a growing sector. The 'efficiency and effectiveness' reforms were to be achieved not through heavy handed instructions from Canberra but by way the institutions adopting the reforms through the profiles that they would propose to the Commonwealth as a basis for their future (and greater) funding.

Strategic planning was an essential prerequisite in the development of profiles and hence the emphasis on this objective in the Green Paper and later the White Paper (or the higher education policy paper).

The suggestion of profiles – even though they were to be developed by universities themselves – was met with a chorus of complaints that saw profiles as an assault on university autonomy. David Penington – one of the very public critics of the Dawkins reforms – expressed a different view to me privately on a drama filled visit I made to Melbourne University. He applauded the profile process as it gave him the ability to actually understand what was going on in his university. So not only did the profiles allow universities to indicate their plans to the Government but required Faculties, Schools and Departments to report their activities to the Vice Chancellor, in some cases for the first time.

In this book Tess Howes explores how the process of strategic planning was adopted in several universities, sometimes before 1989 when the profile process was introduced but most often as a result of the profiles. Most of the other reviews of the Dawkins reforms have focussed on the macro policy issues of funding, participation, access, fairness, research activity, international education and so on.

This book hones in on the response to the reforms at the institutional level through the lens of strategic planning, and while not explicitly discussed, as a means of developing profiles to guide each university's future consistent with the broad objectives of the White Paper and as an accountability mechanism for the extensive public funding that the Commonwealth provides to the university. Strategic planning is also crucial in exploring new areas of revenue for teaching and research.

In 1988 the Commonwealth provided around 80% of a university's budget. By 2017 this had fallen to a little over 50% as other sources of revenue had grown. During the same period funding from the Commonwealth (including HECS) had also increased. What I found most refreshing (and affirming) was that institutions through their planning process were charting their own future.

Some of the critics of the Dawkins reforms complained that the Unified National System had become the Uniform National System – however I think the contributors to this book would disagree. In years immediately following 1989 and the start of the UNS, I did worry about the lack of diversity in the approach followed by universities however there is a distinction to be made between each university just emulating others and each university devising its own plan and that plan having similarities with others.

There appears little doubt that strategic planning processes necessary for the development of profiles, led to a more centralised approach to the management of universities. Some contributors lament the loss collegial decision making that accompanied this greater centralisation, while others felt that a consultative approach to strategic planning could capture the benefits of collegiality while avoiding its often, long winded pomposity.

Centralisation was also a consequence of the requirement for the Vice Chancellor to be the one taking responsibility on behalf of the university for the funding agreement with the Commonwealth. It is clear this requirement explains, at least in part, the fortification of the Vice Chancellor's office with managerial expertise which seems unremarkable when more than half of universities in Australia have annual revenues in excess of $500 million and some over $2 billion. Universities in Australia have negotiated an external environment of great change and challenge and have heard little applause for their heroic efforts.

Perhaps the greatest contribution has been the increase in the number of graduates processing from their great halls - an increase from less than 90,000 in 1987 to over 300,000 recently. Enrolments of domestic students have grown from 300,000 in 1987 to over 1 million now with another half million students from overseas. All this while the number of institutions reduced.

This increase in graduates entering the workforce has helped in the economic transition that Australia has so far successfully managed.

There are, no doubt more challenges ahead – perhaps immediately ahead.

This exploration by Dr Howes demonstrates how the adoption of strategic planning within universities has contributed to their success to date and how it will underpin their future fortunes.

J S Dawkins AO

March 2020

PREFACE

The British colony of New South Wales was established at Sydney Cove on the 26th of January 1788 as a transportation destination for criminals imprisoned in England's overcrowded gaols and prison hulks moored on the River Thames. By 1850 the colony comprised the entire eastern coastline and almost half the continental land mass of Terra Australis, claimed for Britain by Captain Cook in 1770 under the doctrine of *terra nullius* meaning 'land belonging to no one', ignoring the fact that more than one million Aboriginal and Torres Strait Islander people occupied the continent (Bourke, 1998, p.38). The first Australian university established by legislation in 1850, the University of Sydney, was modelled on the ancient universities of England and Scotland: Oxford (1167), Cambridge (1209-31), St Andrews (1413), Glasgow (1451) and Aberdeen (1495). Construction began on the landmark University of Sydney gothic revival quadrangle building in 1854, just four years after the last transport of convicts arrived in Sydney.

The rich history of education in Aboriginal and Torres Strait Islander cultures was not acknowledged in the establishment legislation of Australia's colonial universities, although as many as twenty-nine clans of the Gadigal people were living in Sydney when the cornerstone of the University of Sydney, Australia's first university, was laid on the territory of the Gadi (gal). The doctrine of *terra nullius* was not overturned until June 1992 when the High

Court of Australia ruled in favour of Eddie Koiki Mabo[2], in *Mabo v The State of Queensland*, resulting in the passing of the *Native Title Act 1993* (Commonwealth) more than two hundred years after the colony was established at Sydney Cove.

By 1899 the colony of New South Wales was comprised of six smaller colonies radiating from settlements located at strategic transport hubs on the Eastern, Southern and Western coastlines. The colonies were federated under the Commonwealth of Australia Constitution Act, a British Act of Parliament, that declared the former colonies, now the States of New South Wales, Victoria, South Australia, Queensland, Western Australia and Tasmania shall be known as the 'Commonwealth of Australia' from the 1st of January 1901. Twelve years later, the Commonwealth of Australia had six universities – one in each State: the University of Sydney (1850); the University of Melbourne (1852); the University of Adelaide (1874); the University of Tasmania (1890); the University of Queensland (1909) and the University of Western Australia (1911). This phase of expansion was temporarily interrupted by World War I and the Great Depression. However, soon after the end of World War II Australia had three new universities: the research-intensive Australian National University (1946), the University of New South Wales (1949), a former technical training institute for mechanics established in 1843, and Monash University (1958).

One of the first comprehensive reviews of the Australian higher education sector was commissioned by the second Menzies Commonwealth Government, chaired by Sir Keith A H Murray. The Murray Report, released in 1957, recommended an increase in Commonwealth investment in higher education to fund essential structural and teaching improvements and deliver the professional

---

[2] Eddie Koiki Mabo (1936-1992) was a Torres Strait Islander who fought for more than 10 years to change Commonwealth land ownership laws and overturn the doctrine of *terra nullius* on behalf of the Mer Island and other First Nation communities.

and technical services required to drive the Australian post-war economy. "Both governments and the public have come to be aware that the national community of our age cannot flourish without good universities" (p.7).

However, when the *Review of Tertiary Education in Australia* (1964) chaired by Sir Leslie H Martin released its report just seven years later, higher education was still only funded to the amount of 0.8% of the Australian Gross National Product (GDP). Arguing that this level of investment was inadequate to build a quality higher education system in Australia, the Martin Report recommended the establishment of Colleges of Advanced Education (CAEs), an initiative that commenced in 1965, followed by a rationalisation of technical education that was administered by the Technical and Further Education Commission (TAFEC) from the 1970s. The Martin Report stated that the Commonwealth of Australia would be best served by a 'binary' system of higher education in which universities, CAEs and TAFEs provided educational services relevant to different population classes, a precedent well established in Australian educational history (Campbell, 2010, p.107). However, the level of higher education funding did not significantly increase until the second Whitlam Government[3] budget in 1974. During the period 1969-70 to 1975-1976 Commonwealth funding for universities increased from $398 million to $1117 million and funding for CAEs more than sixfold (Marginson, 1997, pp.11-45). The Fraser Government[4] was elected in 1975 and effectively reduced funding on an annual basis by not factoring in rising costs (Macintyre, Croucher, Davis and Marginson, 2013, pp.14-15) a trend

---

3 The Australian Labor Party (ALP) Government led by Prime Minister E Gough Whitlam AC QC (1916-2014) held office from December 1972 to November 1975.
4 The Liberal Country Party Coalition Government led by Prime Minister J Malcolm Fraser AC CH GCL PC (1930-2015) held office from November 1975 to March 1983.

that continued and accelerated when the Howard Government[5] was elected to office.

Marginson and Considine (2000) position the establishment of Australian universities within the economic and historical development of the Commonwealth arguing that Australian universities developed unique characteristics that can be traced to the historical period in which they were founded, influencing their founding ideologies and institutional missions:

- The *Sandstone* universities, the oldest universities established in each State of the Commonwealth featuring grand sandstone architecture in the model of the Oxbridge Universities.
- The *Redbricks*, the most prestigious group of universities established in the post-second world war years.
- The Australian National University (ANU), a research-intensive university.
- The *Gumtrees*, founded during the second phase of the post-WWII period.
- The *Unitechs*, the largest of the former Colleges of Advanced Education (CAEs) with strong industry links and an applied emphasis in teaching and research.
- The *New Universities*, the large group of new universities established in the post-Dawkins era (Marginson and Considine, 2000, pp.189-197).

When Minister Dawkins released the 'Green (discussion) Paper' in December 1987, Australia had twenty universities, including Bond University, Australia's first private university. A massive period of growth and expansion continued through the late 1980s and 1990s in the post-Dawkins era, when an additional nineteen universities

---

5 The Liberal National Party Coalition Government led by Prime Minister John W Howard OM AC held office from March 1996 to December 2007.

were established.

The next chapter, Introduction, will outline the key features of the Dawkins Reforms and provide an overview of some of the current challenges of the Australian higher education sector to provide the context for the contributors' chapters to follow.

INTRODUCTION TO THE 'DAWKINS' REFORMS OF 1988

Soon after John Dawkins was sworn in as Minister for Employment, Education and Training in July 1987 as part of the second Hawke Government[6], he commissioned a review of the administrative arrangements of the Australian higher education sector and released *The Challenge of Higher Education in Australia.* The tone of this document made it clear that change was on the horizon. The 'Green' (discussion) Paper released a few months later in December 1987 that outlined the proposed reform agenda was contested by many higher education commentators, academic staff, the Vice-Chancellors of Australia's oldest universities, the University of Sydney and the University of Melbourne, and Peter Karmel[7], Vice-Chancellor of the ANU, considered a "perceptive critic" (Macintyre, Brett & Croucher, 2013, p.9).

The objections raised were overlooked and the legislative instrument that implemented the Unified National System (UNS), *Higher Education: a policy statement* the 'White Paper', was released six months later in July 1988. The White Paper conceded that "the Government's strategy for the development of the higher education system is part of a wider agenda of reform spanning all the elements of the employment, education and training

---
6 The Australian Labor Party (ALP) Government, led by Prime Minister Robert (Bob) JL Hawke AC GCL (1929-2019), held office from 1983-1991.
7 Professor Peter H Karmel AC CBE (1922-2008) was Vice-Chancellor of Flinders University (1966) and Vice-Chancellor of the Australian National University 1982-1987.

portfolio" (p.3). Several attachments outlining procedures for dispute resolution; staff development and staff assessment; serious misconduct; unsatisfactory performance; voluntary early retirement; redundancy; continuing employment and probation (pp.133-137) outlined procedures to mitigate the wide-spread staff dissent expected to follow. Appendices comparing recurrent grants, student load, and educational trend data (pp.115-131) evinced the case for change. The Commonwealth Tertiary Education Commission (CTEC) was also disestablished hereby transferring control and administration of the sector to the Minister and the Department of Employment, Education and Training. The Vice-Chancellor of the University of Sydney, John Ward[8], claimed that the Dawkins Reforms compromised the autonomy of universities and represented what he termed 'unprecedented political interference' in an editorial published in *The Australian* entitled 'Strangulation by Regulation' (1988). John Ward was the last Vice-Chancellor to agree to join the UNS (Macintyre et al., 2013, p.43).

The Dawkins Reforms resulted in many large and small-scale institutional mergers and amalgamations to enable institutions to achieve the minimum size of 8,000 effective full-time students (EFTSU) required for membership in the UNS as a comprehensive research and teaching university. In 1987 before the Dawkins Reforms were implemented there were nineteen universities and forty-six colleges in Australia with an average size of 5,212 students. A few years later there were thirty-six public universities and two small private universities with an average size of 16,166 students (Macintyre et al., 2013, p.44). A mass, unified, higher education system had been swiftly installed. Changes to the size and constitution of the governing body, Council or Senate, were also outlined in the 'White Paper' to provide Vice-Chancellors with the expertise to manage the new commercial activities of

---

[8] Professor John Manning Ward AO (1919-1990) was Vice-Chancellor, University of Sydney, 1981-1990. He was tragically killed with his wife and daughter in the Cowan Rail Accident in May 1990.

the universities. This progressively shifted institutional planning from an academic-collegial model to centralised and commercially focused, strategic planning. Aware that few Australian universities had Strategic Plans in 1988[9] the elements universities should include in their Strategic Plans were outlined in the 'Green' Paper:

- a broad statement of institutional goals and detailed objectives of its component elements.
- an overview of current educational provision.
- an analysis of the adequacy of current provision in view of institutional goals and objectives.
- planned changes in provision over the following three to five years.
- mechanisms to achieve the required reallocation of resources to make policy changes at each level of institutional decision making, including research and staffing policies.
- mechanisms to identify and maintain an effective response to employer and community needs; and
- appropriate monitoring and review procedures (1987, p.52).

Dawkins argued that "the Government's proposals for reform and reorientation of higher education *should not distort the system's traditional functions* [my emphasis] and intellectual inquiry and scholarship" (White Paper, 1988, p.5) although this appears to have been the outcome at several contributors' employer universities. While an extensive analysis of the origins of the Dawkins Reforms is beyond the scope of this publication (see Croucher, Marginson, Norton and Wells, 2013; and Macintyre, Brett and Croucher, 2017 for a comprehensive discussion), suffice to say that the Dawkins Reforms turned "colleges into universities, free education into HECS, elite education into mass education, local

---

[9] The first published, formal Strategic Plan so far located is *Looking to the Future* (1988) published by the University of Melbourne https://search.sl.nsw.gov.au/primo-explore/fulldisplay/SLNSW_ALMA211139665000002626/SLNSW

focuses into international outlooks, vice-chancellors into corporate leaders, teachers into teachers and researchers" (Croucher et al., 2013, p.1). However, although Dawkins introduced the reforms, the transformation agenda was implemented in a range of ways by individual Vice-Chancellors generating a significant number of internal leadership tensions (Howes, 2018; Howes, Gonczi and Hayes, 2015).

Several of the organisational challenges identified in the contributors' chapters resulted from a rapid increase in domestic and international student enrolments, rise of the professional executive and increase in the size of the professional portfolios, and shift of institutional authority to the Vice-Chancellor as Chief Executive Officer and their teams of Deputy Vice-Chancellors, Pro-Vice-Chancellors and Executive Deans. The latter consequence gradually but effectively marginalised the academic community from influencing the distribution of university resources that impacted all aspects of academic work.

An analysis of the strategic planning model and quantitative performance measures outlined in the 'Green' and 'White' papers demonstrates that the model recommended to guide the introduction of strategic planning in Australian universities, had been developed in the post-World War II period in North American Business Schools to improve organisational efficiency primarily in commercial, industrial and manufacturing contexts (Andrews, 1971). For example, Igor Ansoff's Rational Planning School 'Matrix', the generic Strengths, Weaknesses, Opportunities and Threats (SWOT) basic analysis, Michael Porter's 'Five Force's, 'Value Chain' and Porter's 'Diamond' and the Balanced Scorecard designed by Robert Kaplan and David Norton, Harvard Business School. Various strategic planning models proliferated in management literature, for example, the Ansoff Model of Strategic Planning (1965), Steiner Model of Strategic Planning (1969) and Porter's Competitive Analysis (1980). The literature was also replete with case studies celebrating strategic planning success, e.g. the Annual Planning Cycle at General Electric promoted in Rothschild (1980). In the management literature, strategic planning was increasingly positioned as an essential management function. Igor Ansoff, considered to be the 'father' of strategic planning, acknowledged that some early attempts ran into difficulties (1984), conceding that strategic planning is a complex activity and likely to fail unless an appropriate type of planning is used (p.460). However, as Mintzberg observed, Ansoff's response was to make the strategic planning process even more comprehensive (1994b, p.149) rather than allow it to take an intuitive and emerging approach recommended by Mintzberg.

> Through all the false starts and excessive rhetoric, we have certainly learned what planning is not and what it cannot do. But we have also learned what planning is and can do, and perhaps of greater use, what planners themselves can do beyond planning (Mintzberg, 1994b, p.416).

Mintzberg (1994b) also suggests that planning is inherently political, another common theme throughout the contributors' chapters.

> The implication in the pitfall literature is that political activity interferes with planning, that planning is an apolitical, objective exercise that is undermined by the pursuit of self-interest through confrontation and conflict. Here we wish to take this argument apart, showing first that planning is not as objective as its proponents claim, second that sometimes it may in fact breed certain kinds of political activity, and third that other kinds of political activity can sometimes prove more functional for organisations than planning" (p.188).

Academic leaders were well aware that institutional planning procedures were required to establish strategic institutional priorities, and that Australian Vice-Chancellors should be held accountable for performance. Peter Karmel however, urged the government not to impose a "business model of management" (cited Macintyre, 2017, p.70). Nevertheless, a business model of management was imposed which precipitated a 'shift of power' and strategic resourcing authority to "a small group of full-time managers, backed by the corporate managers on their governing council or boards" (Connell, 2019, p.126). Some critical management theorists have argued that rational strategic planning could be considered an example of what Nietzsche (1968) described as "will to control, predict and dominate the future" (cited Carter, Clegg and Kornberger, 2008, p.23).

A key point of contention raised by academics when the 'Green' and 'White' papers were released was that the documents were written in management jargon. Critics of the reforms argued that the language itself and the managerial tone of documents made the reforms incompatible with the educational purpose and functions of universities. As few participants in the Green Paper task force had experience in higher education (Macintyre, 2017, p.64) little consideration was perhaps given to the fact that the strategic planning model used to frame the reform agenda had not been developed for use in public institutions, not-for-profit organisations, higher education institutions or universities, particularly universities on the other side of the world with a unique Australian history and character.

One of the first influential publications on strategic planning in the higher education sector, is George Keller's *Academic Strategy* (1983). Keller proposed 'new management wine in old academic bottles', urging American university and college leaders to embrace modern management practices, particularly strategic planning, to improve institutional performance. Keller developed several Strategic Plans for a number of American universities and colleges throughout his career. The last Strategic Plan he developed for Lynn University [*Lynn: 2020 focusing on our future*] was released in 2005. Interestingly, Keller subsequently changed his approach to leading strategic planning in universities and colleges, arguing that *Academic Strategy* failed to consider the educational planning context. This is discussed in detail in his controversial final publication *Higher Education and the New Society* (2008) that was published posthumously (see also Thomas, 1980). A small collection of literature analysing the implementation of strategic planning in educational contexts was not available in 1987 when the Dawkins policy instruments were being drafted. However, this literature could have been used to guide strategic planning practice in educational institutions over the next three decades (see for example Anderson, Johnson, Milligan, 1999; Bosetti and Walker, 2010; Conway, Mackay and York, 1994; Keller, 1983; Kelly and Shaw, 1987; Lelong and Shirley, 1990; Maassen and Potman, 1990; Marshall, 2007; Rowley, 2001; Rowley, Lujan and Dolence, 1997; Shirley, 1988; and Zechlin, 2010).

Despite educational, cultural and ideological dissonance with Australian universities, the business model of strategic planning supported by inflexible, quantitative performance measures was progressively implemented and transformed all aspects of academic life (Macintyre et al., 2013, pp.46-47). An example of how the application of inflexible quantitative performance measures impacted on the nature of academic work and the careers of individual academics is illustrated in an editorial featuring Professor Helen Dunstan, a historian at Sydney University who appealed her retrenchment for unsatisfactory research performance, citing her strong teaching record and internationally recognised scholarship on 18th Century China. Professor Stephen Garton, Provost and Deputy Vice-Chancellor is quoted as saying "No one could approach this with any joy. We have a lot of good people everywhere – it's a budget issue, not a performance issue" (*The Australian*, HES, March 21, 2012). The following week Professor Garton confirmed that the staff-cuts were both a reputational and budgetary issue. "Some other Go8 universities are pulling ahead of us in terms of research performance … many of these poor research performers are also not making up teaching hours to compensate ... adding unnecessarily to the level of part-time teaching expenditure. Given our current budget situation, these are things we can ill afford to ignore" (*The Australian*, HES, "Performance puts uni's reputation at risk", March 28, 2012).

Another significant feature of the post-Dawkins era was a rapid increase in non-traditional domestic student enrolments, as there were multiple access barriers to universities in the colonial period (Davis, 2017, p.29). For example, in 2011 36% of young Australians were enrolled in a university or tertiary education institution, an increase from 32.6% in 2006 (Parr, 2015). By 2018 this number had increased to 27.3% of the population although the enrolment of Aboriginal and Torres Strait Islander students and students from rural communities did not increase in line with projections (Wells and Martin, 2013, p.203; Parr, 2015). This confirms Pusey's (1991) finding that if Australia's social policy, particularly educational policy, is shaped by economic principles, access and equity will not improve but be reproduced in a systemic reproduction of social inequities (see also Yeatman, 1990, 1994; Marginson, 2016a; Welch, 1996, 1998, 2010).

The 'White' Paper made it clear that new sources of revenue would be required to fund the growth outlined in the reforms. The Wran Committee in December 1987 recommended the reintroduction of student tuition fees returning the sector to a "user pay" framework, abolished by the Whitlam Government to increase access for non-traditional students including women. Legislated by the *Higher Education Contribution Act 1988* the tuition fees charged as part of the Higher Education Contribution Scheme (HECS) were subsidised for domestic students and supported by an income contingent part-repayment timeline to ease its passage through the Labor caucus, both houses of parliament and gain acceptance with the wider public.

Universities were also encouraged to enrol as many full-time full-fee-paying international students as they could to mitigate public funding decreases and help balance their multimillion-dollar operational budgets (Welch, 2002). In 1988 there were approximately 18,000 full fee-paying international students enrolled in Australian universities. By 2000 this figure was 95,000; in 2011 it was 330,000 (Krause and Reid, 2013, pp.149-151) and in 2019 there were 704,009 international students enrolled in Australian higher education institutions[10]. This is a staggering 38 times increase in just 21 years that has had a significant impact on the sector. The rich cultural exchange, the establishment of global graduate professional networks and the contributions hundreds of thousands of graduates continue to make in their home countries is extremely beneficial. However, the rapid growth of international student enrolments resulted in overcrowded classrooms, increasing pressures on standards and reliance on international students as 'cash generators' or 'financial lifelines' for public Australian universities that is not viewed in a positive light by several contributors in this publication.

The impact of these external forces has been considerable and continually exacerbated by a corresponding relative decline in public funding. As a result, Australia's higher education sector is fiercely competitive, consolidating institutional inequity in the national higher education framework. The Group of Eight (Go8) universities for example are generally able to successfully contest approximately 64% of the research block grants and 74% of competitive research funding (Marginson, 2016a, pp.256-258) leaving Australia's remaining 31 universities to complete for the remaining funds. The impact of this funding disparity on the sector is clearly illustrated by Pettigrew (2016) in French, Kelly and James (2017, p.9). Research income awarded by the Commonwealth Category 1 Competitive funding schemes, and schemes on the

---

10 Australian Government, Department of Education, International student data 2019 https://internationaleducation.gov.au/research/International-al-Student-Data/Pages/InternationalStudentData2019.aspx#Pivot_Table

Australian Competitive Grants Register (ACGR), important in peer prestige and world rankings, does not cover the full cost of the successful research project. Both the Australian Research Council (ARC) and the National Health and Medical Research Council (NHMRC) expect universities to provide the infrastructure to deliver the objectives outlined in the successful proposal. This poses a significant resource shortfall for universities, particularly research-intensive universities, an issue raised by Alan Robson and Ian Chubb. As a result, revenue from teaching and the enrolment of full fee-paying international students is used to subsidise research and other operational costs. Alan Robson explains "Unfortunately, in a sector that is under-funded these are the types of internal decisions that you need to make, and they are not always popular which is one of the key leadership challenges for Australian Vice-Chancellors" (p.88). Ian Chubb adds "The Group of Eight (Go8) used to say that we were the only country that put such a high price on success. We were in fact millions of dollars short" (p.145).

The financial circumstances of each university will impact on the level of investment Vice-Chancellors are able to direct to new or current strategic initiatives. Financial constraints therefore constantly influence the level of commitment that can be made to support institutional strategic initiatives, as well as the shape, scope and timeline of the university-wide Strategic Plan published at the conclusion of the strategic planning process. This has at times impacted on the level of support, or lack thereof, of core academic functions which can lead to resentment and discontent within the academic community. If, for example, financial constraints result in the imposition of funding cuts that are opposed by the academic community, the Vice-Chancellor must communicate the rationale behind the strategic funding decisions in ways that do not further alienate the university community (Sharrock, 2014). Carolyn Noble expresses what this felt like as a teaching and researching academic. "Every time a new Strategic Plan was released, we knew that money would be squeezed out of teaching and allocated to some other scheme or short-term consultant appointment. On the ground, at the teaching interface, all that changed was less money for teaching and more bureaucracy and decreasing student satisfaction" (p.243).

Some of the leadership tensions revealed in the following chapters are perhaps consequences that might have been difficult to foresee (Macintyre et al., 2013, pp.46-47) although the 'managerialisation' of the sector, a cause of ongoing friction, dissent and academic vexation, was one of the key reforms. However, as Denise Bradley, Ed Davis, Ian Chubb, Jim Ife and Simon Marginson attest, several institutions were already developing managerial and strategic planning capabilities prior to the implementation of the Dawkins Reforms. Denise Bradley observed a range of individual approaches to planning as part of her work on the Wilson Quality Committee, the Commonwealth Tertiary Education Commission and the Higher Education Council. She was particularly impressed with the planning process at the University of Melbourne led by David Penington who "established a fabulous formal planning process that had performance funding built into it as well as an annual review of every Faculty. It was terrific and I brought it straight back to the university (p.47). Jim Ife attributes the implementation of business practices in Australian universities to the prevailing neoliberal environment and the entrepreneurial capabilities of some academic leaders, such as Professor Don Watts at the Western Australian Institute of Technology "Professor Don Watts saw this as the future. And he was right – it was the future. I don't see the Dawkins Reforms themselves as being that important. They were more symptomatic of the times and similar things were happening in university systems in other countries" (p.157). Ed Davis agrees as competitive business schools were already operating as businesses in the late 1980s leading the development of a commercial mindset in some sections of the sector:

> So, although we were an academic department in a university, we were very conscious that the MGSM was also a business and we looked to implement business strategies in order to increase the revenue generated. This was in the late 1980s and beginning of the 1990s, so I don't think this commercialisation strategy had anything to do with the Dawkins Reforms; what we were doing at the MGSM was completely independent of that. And, it wasn't just the MGSM, other Business Schools were moving in the same direction ... This is an example of how universities, or parts of universities, started to morph into businesses from the mid-1980s well before Dawkins (pp.99-100).

Ian Chubb was Chair of the Higher Education Council in 1995. He confirms a finding of the Hoare Report (1995) that suggests the outcomes of the implementation process was still uneven across the sector seven years later. "I mean you would go to some places and wonder how they managed to open their doors each morning. You would also go to other places and ask them what was happening, and they would know" (p.138). It could therefore be argued that Dawkins was systemising a uniform managerial approach to ensure consistency across the Unified National System.

The Dawkins Reforms of 1988 are now fully integrated in the Australian university sector. Many of the current challenges can be dealt with by increased investment, series of policy adjustments and establishment of a coherent financing architecture that incorporates the VET sector. This was one of the recommendations of the *Review of Australian Higher Education* (2008), led by Denise Bradley and proposed recently in *Visions for Australian Tertiary Education* edited by James, French and Kelly (2017). Carolyn Noble helped to establish one of the first dual-sector higher education departments by co-locating the undergraduate social work program and TAFE programs (p.237) demonstrating that these initiates are possible but dependent upon ongoing collaboration and resourcing.

There are also a multitude of complex challenges on the global higher education horizon that we will not be able to meet without radical change and transformation. Higher education experts and policy analysts therefore should be encouraged to propose bold visionary and 'provocative' ideas that will help position Australian universities to meet the challenges of an uncertain future, such as those proposed by James et al. (2017). We should also listen to one of the foremost writers in higher education, Simon Marginson, who suggests that policies promoting greater horizontal diversity across the sector would increase strategic creativity, improve institutional performance and inspire democratic momentum for "transformation in an egalitarian direction" (2016a, p.265). As Glyn Davis[11] states, the Australian university sector has a "singular lack of diversity" (p.26). This will make it very difficult for individual universities and the higher education sector in general to respond to the cycles of innovation gaining momentum. And although the unitary model may have "served us well. It may also have run its course" (2017, p.8).

In organisational theory the forces that result in organisations developing similar organisational structures is termed *institutional isomorphism* (DiMaggio and Powell, 1983). There are three mechanisms that cause this to occur: mimetic, coercive and normative isomorphism. In environmental contexts that are both uncertain and complex as illustrated in Hrebiniak and Joyce's typology (1995), decisions made by management, or 'strategic choice' theory, enable organisations to respond to the forces of environmental determinism in a range of ways. One organisational mechanism that can be used to navigate this complexity and uncertainty in the external environment is by copying or imitating

---

11 Professor Glyn Davis AC was Vice-Chancellor of the University of Melbourne from 2005-2018.

successful organisations, *mimetic isomorphism*. Forces that arise from adherence to normative standards demanded by the general business environment, consumer groups and wider society, is *normative isomorphism*. External forces imposed by legislation, the government, regulatory agencies on which the organisation is dependent to maintain legitimacy, is *coercive isomorphism*. These external forces limit diversity and promote homogeneity in very powerful ways that is almost impossible for organisations to resist (Daft, 2016, pp.199-203; see also Marginson, 1999, 2000 who applied this theory to the Australian higher education sector).

The national higher education environment is complex and uncertain. Therefore, Australian universities competing for research funding and those attempting to increase their rankings in the world university league tables will naturally mimic the Go8 universities - *mimetic isomorphism*. As they have extensive connections with the professions and industry, the degrees offered must comply with professional requirements so as to facilitate accreditation as soon as possible after graduation, they are subject to the forces of *normative isomorphism*. The national higher education sector is highly regulated and centralised with a uniform funding architecture managed by the government, therefore Australian universities are also subject to the forces of *coercive isomorphism*. Under these circumstances, institutional diversity and differentiation will be very difficult, if not impossible, to achieve. Although Dawkins argued that the reforms should encourage greater diversity, the unitary structure of the sector, centralised regulation and a uniform funding model was, in fact, a "template for homogeneity' (Macintyre, 2017, p.80). Simon Marginson explains that "the competition for prestige in a hierarchical system ... results in universities trying to emulate their peers and move up the ladder" (p.219). This gives rise to a "very fluid discourse that linked everyone together around the planning process ... homogenising the sector ..." (Carolyn Noble, p.245).

Population ecology theory explains why organisations operating in a constantly changing and competitive environment must continually and purposefully adapt. If they are in a state of structural inertia and unable to adapt to meet the changing external environment they are likely to fail and new organisations structured to meet the changed external environment conditions will take their place (Daft, 2016, pp.183-154). Organisational history is replete with examples, Blockbuster -v- Netflix; Barnes & Noble -v- Amazon; the corner store -v- the supermarket giants. If the forces of institutional isomorphism that currently inhibit organisational adaptation and differentiation are eased, Australian higher education institutions may be able to adapt and adapt quickly to meet current and future challenges. Although Davis (2017) raises several significant challenges he concludes on a somewhat optimistic note. "Fortunately, we have a public university sector skilled at responding to profound challenge. With the right policy settings, Australia can trade a single history for diversity, one path for many. If we understand history, we need not be its victims" (p.128).

There are also many reasons to be optimistic about the future of the Australian higher education sector. In 2020 Australia's universities are successfully competing with leading world universities in the global university rankings. Seven Australian universities are ranked in the top 100 universities in the 2019 Academic Ranking of World Universities (ARWU): the University of Melbourne (41); the University of Queensland (54); Monash (73); the Australian National University (76); the University of Sydney (80); the University of New South Wales (94); the University of Western Australia (99); followed by the last Go8 the University of Adelaide (101-150 band). The same Australian universities were ranked in the top 100 universities in the 2019 QS World University rankings: the Australian National University (=29); the University of Melbourne (38); the University of Sydney (42); the University of New South Wales (43); the University of Queensland (47); Monash University (=58); and the University of Western Australia (86); followed by the last Go8 the University of Adelaide (106), and a very high performing new university, the University of Technology, Sydney (140). This is a remarkable achievement for a university sector that is just 170 years old.

John Dawkins achieved his mission, certainly. The sector has been transformed structurally and ideologically. Several contributors were supportive of the reforms as the following chapters will illustrate. Peter Coaldrake, for example, "welcomed these changes as I did not think that it was a problem for universities to be required to demonstrate modern management practices and be expected to achieve their Key Performance Indicators (KPIs) in order to receive public money" (p.198). Subsequent governments continued to adjust the higher education policy settings and presided over a relentless decline in investment. Individual Vice-Chancellors pursued institutional strategic initiatives in ways that contributed to some of the current academic discontent (see for example, Becher and Trowler, 2001; Bessant, 2002, 1995; Biggs and Davis, 2002; Coady, 2000; Connell, 2019; Davies, 2005; Hil, 2015, 2012; Lowe, 1994; Maslen and Slattery, 1994; Meyers, 2012). Geoffrey Sherington reflects that the "difficulty for executive leaders will be trying to keep the connection between themselves and their colleagues, while remaining clear about the direction they are heading" (p.127). Peter Coaldrake proposes this is "about building a citizen community, and that [is] of course linked to issues of pride and ownership" (p.202).

Lynn Meek highlights one of the sources of the growing discontent, a divide between the executive and the academic community. "Academic Board was supposed to promote academic wellbeing and academic values, particularly in the teaching, learning and research areas of the university. However, it often found itself in a difficult position between the dictates of management and the angst of the academic community" (p.176). And, although this tension is less obvious in 2020 it has still not been resolved.

Millions of domestic and international students hold Australian degrees, contributing to significant social and gender mobilisation and reform movements in Australia and communities around the world. Hundreds of thousands of university staff benefit from rewarding careers in a range of academic and professional roles. Current Vice-Chancellors and university executives view universities as large businesses and consider management expertise an essential requirement for academic leadership roles[12]. Large-scale structural change takes generations to fully implement and institutionalise. As this generational change occurs, many of the contested dimensions of the Dawkins 'revolution' will gradually be lost to the collective consciousness. This is hardly surprising as it is now thirty-two years since the Dawkins Reforms were enacted. It is therefore an opportune time for current Ministers of Education to work together with Australian Vice-Chancellors and their academic communities to lead the Australia higher education sector to prosperity in the 21st century. Particularly, as the consequences of COVID-19 on the Australian higher education sector are not currently known. Close co-operation between the government and the sector will be critical in ensuring the long-term viability and prosperity of the Australian higher education sector.

This edited collection seeks to enter this debate by presenting a collection of interviews with a small, representative cohort of former Vice-Chancellors and academic leaders with decades of experience in a vast number of higher education institutions across the sector. The contributors offer contrasting ideological and philosophical perspectives on this topic as they reflect on their academic careers and individual leadership experiences. Offering advice to the next generations of academic leaders tasked to lead the sector through the challenges of the 21st century, the contributors provide

---

12 A general sentiment frequently expressed and hypothesis to be tested in a future research study.

the framework for the recommendations for effective strategic leadership practice presented in the concluding discussion, as well as an outline of the key elements that should be reflected in an 'effective' Australian university Strategic Plan.[13]

This publication also neither 'celebrates nor condemns' the Dawkins Reforms and like Macintyre et al. (2017) occupies a 'middle ground' between the scholarly works and higher education reviews cited herein, bringing a collection of authentic first-person reflections, that are inherently personal, to the discussion.

I will now let the contributors speak for themselves.

---

[13] A documentary analysis that will explore this in more detail is currently in development.

CHAPTER ONE

Emeritus Professor Denise Bradley AC
(1942 - 2020)

Emeritus Professor Denise Bradley AC was an esteemed advocate for equity in education. She was extensively involved in national education policy groups for more than three decades and her contributions to higher education policy have changed the face of the Australian tertiary sector. She was Vice-Chancellor and President of the University of South Australia (1997-2007), Deputy Vice-Chancellor (1997-1991) and Principal of the South Australian College of Advanced Education (SACAE) in 1990. Denise began her career as a teacher, was instrumental in the establishment of the University of South Australia, and later led a national review of the higher education system which resulted in the Bradley Report and subsequent sweeping changes to Australia's educational landscape.

"Education offered me plenty to do but also something to care about and to put my efforts into, and I care deeply and profoundly about issues to do with access to a high-quality education for all," said Denise.

Central to Denise's ethos was a view of education as an investment rather than a cost, as well as the implementation of effective programs to service disadvantaged groups. "It's absolutely critical for society that we educate our citizens, for economic reasons as well as a whole set of good social reasons," she said. "All of my life experiences have led me to understand that the only way you can deal with questions of access to education for disadvantaged groups is through use of special programs," she said. "You have to change their world view about what's possible and you have to give them the means to do it." Denise has been recognised extensively for her significant contributions to Australia's tertiary sector. Among an impressive registry of accolades, she was made an Officer of the Order of Australia in 1995; awarded a Centenary Medal in 2003; named South Australian of the Year in 2005; was made a Companion of the Order of Australia in 2008; and conferred with the prestigious College Medal by the Australian College of Educators in 2011.

Tess Howes: Professor Bradley thank you very much for agreeing to participate in this study. Could you please start this interview with a brief summary of your career focusing on the various leadership positions you have held on your pathway to the role of Vice-Chancellor.

Denise Bradley: I started my career as a secondary school teacher. My first senior leadership role was Women's Adviser to the South Australian Education Department. I went from there to a role as Dean and from there through to a Vice-Chancellor eventually, so a conventional kind of path in that way. But simultaneously with that, I always had a strong connection to various policy implementation roles in Advisory and Statutory Bodies at both State and Commonwealth level. I have been involved in the education sector since 1975 across three sectors: schools, Vocational Education and Training (VET) and higher education in both a College of Advanced Education and the University of South Australia (UniSA).

Can you recall the first time you were involved in a strategic planning process?

Yes. The first strategic planning process I was involved in was at my employer institution, the South Australian College of Advanced Education (SACAE) in the mid-1980s and I was the instigator of it. The SACAE was formed in 1982 by a merger of the Adelaide College of the Arts and Education, the Hartley College of Advanced Education, the Sturt College of Advanced Education and the Salisbury College of Advanced Education. We had many internal problems resulting from the amalgamations and also needed get some agreement about the strategic direction of the institution. I was Deputy Principal at that stage and one of the reasons I was appointed to the job was because I was able to demonstrate that I was capable of leading centralised planning. So, we developed and published a formal Plan that was ratified by the College Council.

There was no formal amalgamation strategy – the various institutions were just co-existing?

Yes, as most of the amalgamations were driven out of financial necessity. We also knew that it was not possible to continue doing what we had always done, because we did not have sufficient resources to do all the things we wanted to do – or needed to do.

So, it was primarily a process of rationalisation?

Yes, but we were aware that the rationalisation needed to be guided by a strategy: such as what are the core values of the institution and what direction should it take? What should our programs look like and what kind of resources did we need to underpin those programs? That was the motivating factor when I took on the Deputy role – I had as a Dean been quite agitated by something that continues to worry me, which is the maintenance of arguments for the status quo in situations where it is abundantly clear that this is not sustainable with quality. After the Dawkins Reforms of 1988 we undertook the merger with the South Australian Institute of Technology (SAIT) that formed the University of South Australia (UniSA) in 1991. Both institutions had very strong internal planning processes which meant we had the skills to develop a Strategic Plan and sub-plans to anchor the amalgamation. And in the first year, the first year of the UniSA, I accepted a job that no one expected me to take which was Deputy Vice-Chancellor Planning. So, I established the process and was responsible for the development of the first Strategic Plan for the University of South Australia. The year before the amalgamation Professor David Lee who was Head of Research at the SAIT and I prepared a Research Management Plan for the new university – so there was actually a Research Management Plan for the UniSA a year before it was established! The Research Management Plan went through the Academic Boards of both amalgamating institutions to set the UniSA on the right foundations

- and basically the underlying assumptions of the Research Management Plan developed in 1990 provided the foundations for the first UniSA Strategic Plan. Those underlying assumptions were: you don't get any money unless you are conducting research, you don't get it for trying; and an intention to strengthen areas of performance. It was a very strong performance-based plan that made it clear that the UniSA focus would be on industry-based research and that we would work in research concentrations.

It showed great foresight to have a cohesive strategy across the research platform before you amalgamated two institutions to form the University of South Australia.

David and I didn't know each other before that time but we bonded in our understanding of the planning process. Very few people in those days took planning seriously. But it was abundantly clear to me, and to David, that once the new institution began, the only thing the Council would have would be the Research Management Plan. This is the reason why I wanted to be the Deputy Vice-Chancellor Planning when the UniSA was established. The strength of the Research Management Plan was that it contained a great deal of information about both institutions. We made it clear that when you looked at the history of the institutions they were connected by two things: one was the relationship with the professions and industry, as both institutions were born out of professional education, not general education; and secondly, a failure by the sector to look after whole groups of people, so there was an equity dimension. It is interesting to note that the SACAE had the first Aboriginal Teacher Education Program in Australia and the SAIT had the first Australian Business Administration program for Indigenous Australians. We recognised that both institutions had a focus on professional education and equity. Others might have said one is about teacher education and the other was about engineering and accounting, but we said no – the underpinning principles are the same and these principles will form the founding values of the UniSA. This also meant by implication we would not offer a general arts degree or a general science degree or do blue sky research. This was another aspect of the Research Management Plan – it made it clear what we would do, but also what we would not do. But then again, some people didn't see that part of it until much later.

Would you describe this strategic planning process as authoritarian, collaborative, or consultative – large scale or small scale?

It was consultative in the sense that it was a fairly standard process. We took our time, it took more than a year – we are now talking about the UniSA Strategic Plan, not the earlier Research Management Plan, but it was the same process in both cases. The first stage was to establish a remit to develop a Plan; we then circulated a discussion paper about the issues that needed to be addressed combined with the development of a vision and aims. On reflection, we probably put far too much information in the initial Strategic Plan so if you are thinking about how to do things better in the future this is something to keep in mind. The draft Plan was then circulated for consultation and the submissions received were looked at carefully. There were also campus wide meetings, meetings with external stakeholders which I thought were important, meetings with industry and the various professional bodies, plus meetings with people on our advisory committees, a conventional planning process. The draft Plan then went through the Academic Board and on to Council and it modified over that period.

Was Academic Board happy with the Plan and the strategic planning process?

Yes, everyone was happy with it. At the time, it was very, very popular. This was because it was a clear process when there was a high degree of chaos as a result of the amalgamation. I remember at the end of the first year, a member of the new Council who had been at the SAIT said in passing "the only thing that has come out of the whole year is this Plan. It is the only achievement of the year for the university". I took this as a compliment as most of the guys on the Board were horrified at my appointment as Deputy Vice-Chancellor because I was a feminist. And, because of its broad acceptance, the new UniSA Council seized on the Plan and used it very strongly. It was at that stage a fairly conventional sort of Strategic Plan; it was published and widely circulated. It was institution wide as well as academic and operational. It was also both high level and detailed and contained very specific objectives. Now, that is where I have changed my view because I now think it was far too detailed.

Was this Plan well received by the stakeholders? I imagine the answer is yes, as they were involved in the process.

Yes, it was. People largely accepted it but when it started to bite, not everybody saw it as a good thing. I think most people were relieved to have it. But perhaps, given the time, most people didn't expect it to have any impact on their lives … but it did! People would say we need to have a plan, the institution needs to have a plan but now we have a plan we don't need to change what we are doing - aren't we just going to leave everything alone? But it did have an impact as it was implemented.

I know that you were involved in the pre-Dawkins consultations – what did you think of the Dawkins 1988 Reforms?

I think that what Dawkins saw, remember he had previously been Minister for Trade, was that the university sector was stuck in the 19th century, particularly some of the Group of Eight (Go8) universities. They were communities of scholars and he felt that as they were receiving large amounts of Commonwealth funds they needed to be much more focused on serving the economic needs of the country - a concept I found extremely difficult to come to terms with. I objected to enrolling large numbers of international full fee-paying students which I saw as instrumentalism as did a significant number of people in the sector. However, it was clear to me, as I was working in a CAE, that the government was trying to deal with an obstinate group of Vice-Chancellors who were never going to let the sector transition to a new model and intended to use their power to stop change. When the Western Australian Institute of Technology (WAIT) became Curtin University[14] I was shocked on one hand, but on the other hand I was delighted because things were happening in some of the CAEs and Institutes, not all of them, which suggested that we needed a more dynamic sector. I thought Dawkins got this aspect right. I was also supportive of the overall notion of building a more entrepreneurial sector, one that was responsive to the needs of the country. The Dawkins Reforms also created an opportunity to open the sector up to a larger number of people - I liked this part. However, I think that they were naïve about what would happen if an increasing number of students from disadvantaged groups enrolled without providing programs to support them overcome obstacles to both their entry and their success. What Dawkins was also offering, and I am not saying that I saw this immediately, but as time went on I saw it, was that the changes provided opportunities for a broader group of institutions to have the status to enrol a diverse cross section of the community and graduate them with degrees that were actually valued.

---

14 In 1987 Curtin University of Technology became Western Australia's third university and Australia's first university of technology.

The Hoare committee stated in 1995 that universities had all made progress towards more contemporary management practices largely through the development of strategic planning with a focus on quality, however this progress was uneven throughout the sector. Do you agree with this statement?

I was on the Wilson Quality Committee so I participated in the institutional audits which were the pre-cursor to AUQA, so yes, I certainly would agree with that statement. The best developed planning process by a country mile was the process used at the University of Melbourne[15] so I borrowed it. David Penington was brilliant at railing against 'managerialism' and implementing it everywhere. He established a fabulous formal planning process that had performance funding built into it as well as an annual review of every Faculty. It was terrific and I brought it straight back to the university. I was also on the Commonwealth Tertiary Education Commission (CTEC) prior to that and later Deputy Chair of the Higher Education Council of the National Board of Employment, Education and Training (NBEET). Its legislation required a member of the Higher Education Council (HEC) to be present at all Profile meetings and report on the process in Parliament. This meant that from the late 1980s to the mid-1990s I was present at a large number of Profile Meetings and saw a range of internal university processes, so yes, I think this comment from the Hoare Report was correct.

Have you participated in a strategic planning exercise recently and did you approach it the same way?

Yes, once again, it was at the UniSA. One of the hallmarks of that institution was that it always operated from a relatively planned approach. We had a major reshaping of the Strategic Plan in the mid-1990s using a similar process except that we included a scenario planning workshop with members of Council, a cross

---

15 *Looking to the Future: The Strategic Plan for the University of Melbourne* (1988).

section of senior academic staff and student representatives and went away for a couple of days and looked at various scenarios for the university. We were very forward thinking at the time as our 1997 plan included graduate capabilities and a Statement of Commitment to Aboriginal Reconciliation. Another thing that we did at the UniSA which was probably unusual at the time, is we produced an Environmental Scan every year that was underpinned by very strong data. We looked at our own progress, analysed what was going on in the higher education sector nationally as well as internationally and this formed part of the UniSA annual planning process. We also accepted the Strategic Plan could not be a static document and it needed to be constantly recalibrated and reshaped as things changed. We introduced an annual 'lock up' for two or three days with senior staff including: the senior researchers, the Deans, the Heads of School, the senior management group and senior general staff too, so about 70 people in total. We considered a series of issue papers - this became a common model across the sector - and all that information would feed into our thinking about what kind of issues this raised for the university and what we needed to do in terms of longer-term planning. Between the late-1990s and 2007 when I left, we changed quite a few of these processes. Our approach then was to question our ideas every year and ask ourselves, is this still a good idea or should we have something different? We also conducted an annual review of the university. The senior management group would review every major academic and administrative unit, assess performance against their plan from the previous year and would quite often produce something which came out in the end, although not initially, with the budget. So, what you ended up with in September was a new Strategic Plan with a 3-year outlook with a larger 10-15-year vision and a 3-5-year planning horizon for capital, because you need that. Sometimes it was linked to new academic developments as well, plus a 1-year plan that was connected to the budget. So, all in all, a very extensive and comprehensive planning process.

The Heads of Departments and the Directors needed to explain where they were directing their funds, strategically? They had to demonstrate how the activities were aligned?

Yes, absolutely. I was not able to take leave until September when the Council approved the Budget as I needed to keep my eye on the process. It was procedural and very managerial. But most people agreed with it as they knew that an institution like ours, which did not have abundant resources, had to be driven by evidenced-based and performance-based planning. We also did space planning, space audits, and a whole range of things in the years 1998-1999 and managed to dissolve two campuses without much industrial trouble. I wasn't always loved, but when I retired most people would say I did a good job with UniSA as it really was a basket case in 1997 when I became Vice-Chancellor. This was largely because of a combination of determination, which you need to have, but also an appreciation that you are never going to get everyone to agree on everything, so you needed to have legitimate processes in place so that you could say, once a decision had been reached, whether people liked it or not, this is the decision we reached and this is the process we went through. Otherwise you can get locked in interminable fights – well, that was the way I did it.

We had some industrial trouble when I had to make three hundred staff redundant in my first year as Vice-Chancellor because of a large financial problem left by my predecessor. I spent the first three months reviewing every aspect of the university operations personally and prepared a document, 'Changing our Budget Profile'. I then locked everybody who had decision making authority in a room, made them read the document and identify whether these were the right savings decisions. I told them that this was the amount of money we have and in order to avoid intervention by the Commonwealth and keep control of our own future, we needed to make significant savings. After some small changes were made we agreed on a way forward which is when I said to them "now I am taking this to

Council and if I hear any of you saying that you didn't agree with this then I will either remove you to another part of the university or find a way for you to leave the university as you will be subject to formal disciplinary procedures. You agreed to this, there is no other option and the bottom line is clear". I made a speech which was quite famous at the time as I felt I had to. We needed to implement large-scale change and it would not be successful if senior people did not take responsibility for the decisions we needed to make. These people then had to own these decisions at the local level. I know I pushed them in many cases, but I needed them to produce savings and it was obvious it had to be people because that was the nature of the budget. There was no way you could save $18m in 6 months without getting rid of staff. It was horrible; but it worked. Because, I think, there was widespread acceptance of the situation at the university and although people didn't like what I said, they had to accept the power of the argument in the document. We all knew that UniSA was in dire financial circumstances and then South Australia had a 6% real cut on actuals, not on projections, as a result of the Vanstone cuts. We were also in Enterprise Bargaining mode and staff wanted a significant increase over two years that had not been factored into the financial forward plan. The Union knew that if they were going to get this pay rise, there was no other way. They didn't like it, they complained about it, and they complained about me, but it was not reported on the front page of the *Advertiser* – ever. I think this had to do with commitment in an odd kind of way. People felt strongly about the underlying mission of the university and had a loyalty to it. We stood for something important. We also felt that we were part of an institution that had always been at the bottom of the barrel and we wanted a different future. Many of these people wanted to leave anyway; but it was very difficult, and we remained in a challenging financial situation for years. But, we actually stopped doing a large number of things that we really shouldn't have been doing anyway. I also think the document, 'Changing the Budget Profile', was convincing. When

I showed it to one of our advisors he said, "this reads like it was written by one person". I said, "Yes, it was written by me. It had to be written by me as I led the consultations and had to bring all the information together". It was about making a judgement so it was not something I could delegate to someone else. You can't ask another person to draft a set of recommendations and decide which ones you were going to accept and which ones you weren't while remaining connected to what you thought was the fundamental mission of the institution.

If you were tasked to lead a strategic planning process now, would you follow the same model?

No, I would lead it differently – the way we were doing it towards the end of my term as Vice-Chancellor. I would have a high-level statement, because I think that is important, a statement of shared purpose with adjectives that described us, such as 'applied', because language matters. I would make sure we had some underlying broad statements about institutional direction and then move quite rapidly down to the strategic directions of the academic divisions and administrative areas depending on the university structure. Structure is important and what suits me is a flat structure as this means that all the tactical decisions can be made by me and my direct reports. In a flat structure you can have some fairly high-level statements about direction and strategic purpose. Then my direct reports would be responsible for implementing these strategies in a targeted way within their areas and report to me on their progress month by month. This is preferable to having strategic objectives for individual cost centres in the Strategic Plan that would have to be interpreted.

You would need to be very confident about your leadership team.

Absolutely, but we would also monitor performance on a regular basis. We were a very strongly data driven institution with a great deal of information about progression rates, retention rates of students etc that was systemised. I was always able to say to one of my Heads of School "I note that demand for your Bachelor of so and so has been on a downward trend since 1994" which they hated. We had reports on everything. We had reports on the retention rates of low-SES students in this particular school, for example, and these types of discussions were part of the annual review and planning process. However, there is another question about a data-driven planning process you need to consider – does data obscure things and become an end in itself? I think there is an endless tension between planning and review. We also used to do a formal review of the planning process every year and as a result we changed things. Not always, and not everything, but changes were continually made.

Was it difficult to achieve consensus?

I think we achieved consensus among the senior managers. The worry from year to year was that a gap might open up between the formal documentation and the actual operational planning. All of the areas had strong operational plans but quite often those two things would drift. Part of our review included asking the heads of the various areas if they had two plans. Quite often the answer would be yes, so we would ask them what issues in the university plan they were worried about, and what issues in their operations plan they were concerned about so that we could try to get them bring these things together. There was a constant attempt in the university when I was there, and I think it would be the same now, to keep the planning together with what the people were actually doing on the ground. One of the things that we did, which I am very proud of, is that I changed all the heads of the administrative units. I appointed quite young people, many of whom hadn't come from the higher education sector. They were experts in their area, of course, but I looked beyond their expertise for people who had a history of performance-based management, and a history of playing nicely with others in that they were co-operators, not empire builders. That worked very well and was one of our greatest strengths in my later years as Vice-Chancellor. This goes again to the leadership issue – I looked for people who could work in a team and work co-operatively to lead strategic change in the institution.

You were involved in the establishment of the Australian Universities Quality Agency (AUQA) in 2000 therefore you supported the 'fitness for purpose model'?

Yes, I was on the Australian Vice-Chancellors' Committee (AVCC) Standing Committee for Education and got the AVCC to gradually accept that we needed a national quality agency. The AVCC's formal position up until then was that quality was the responsibility of autonomous institutions and we did not need a national regulator. This was when the Liberal Minister David Kemp was appointed. I managed to persuade the AVCC to change its position and then together with Stuart Hamilton, Executive Director AVCC, we negotiated with the Commonwealth and the States to establish the governance model for AUQA because this was not originally what the Commonwealth Government wanted. They wanted their own Agency whereas I believed that we needed to maintain control over the model and the governance process, otherwise there was a real and present danger of the imposition of something quite draconian. So, I became a Foundation Director of AUQA. There were just three of us initially, then we appointed David Woodhouse as Executive Director and went through the process of establishing AUQA and commencing the 1st round of reviews.

A standards approach would not have been acceptable?

No, we were miles away from a standards framework at the time. I felt what we needed to do was gain acceptance from the sector about the need to conduct a public review of their processes. I knew what it was like; I had been an auditor and had also been on the receiving end of it at my institution. However, the notion of a public audit focuses the mind and I think it worked quite well. I read all the 1st round AUQA reports and many of the 2nd and I thought they were fair, even a bit kind at times.

I was critical of the fact that AUQA's fitness for purpose methodology used the strategic plans of the institution to measure performance as I was well aware that many institutions at the time were still developing capabilities in strategic planning.

Yes, but this was moderated by the process. I also think that if you go through the 1st round AUQA Reports and you look at institutions that have, one way or another, been in trouble, the signs were there, in those reports. Directly or indirectly. And part of what AUQA did was to make institutions think very clearly about what they spent their resources on. I also think that the AUQA Reports were fair, in some cases, in acknowledging at times that this all seems to be a bit of a shambles, but you do quite well. These things can be difficult because there is a serendipitous element to them. Audit panels, like all panels, can have people who have very fixed ideas about the way things should be and there were arguments at times between various panel members. We felt at the UniSA that the AUQA team largely identified where we had problems. You could say that the combination of peer review combined with a formal process, where the formal processes are mediated by peer review, works, in my view.

Do you think that organisational culture plays a role in this process?

Yes, it does. For example, it is not by chance that most of the Australian Technology Network (ATN) universities are strongly planned institutions. All of these institutions commenced with a notion that they are businesslike, and it is easier to plan strategically in an institution that sees itself as a business. Whereas it is much harder to do in an institution that thinks it is doing something grand and vague. I was a powerful Vice-Chancellor internally, however, I always ensured that the process was governed by sound procedures. If the organisation sees itself as engaged in a business-like activity, it is important that the senior leaders also see themselves bound by that same process, including the Vice-Chancellor and the DVC-Academic. You can't have one rule for the Vice-Chancellor and different rules for everyone else.

So, reflecting on your career, has the process of developing and implementing strategic plans had an impact on your understanding of leadership.

Yes, it has been central to my understanding of leadership although I have changed my view on what constitutes good strategic planning over that time. I have also been involved in quite a lot of planning at the national level too, where I think I have made a difference. Before I chaired the Bradley Review, I chaired the Committee that produced 'A Fair Chance for All' in 1990 which outlined a national equity strategy. Two central things about leadership are developing strategy and exercising judgement and the judgement should always be about what to do, whether it is about people or activities, and it must be connected to your overall understanding of what the strategy is. A number of people haven't made the right judgements; but you need to make decisions as a lot of things can go wrong if you don't. If you make a judgement and you then think it is wrong, you can retrieve it. Almost all the large problems I have seen during my long career came about because someone avoided making a decision when they needed to. Also, some critical decisions you make might not be right. I made some decisions that were wrong, but it is better to make a few wrong decisions than not to make any at all.

Isn't this the leadership test – what do you do when you know you made the wrong decision?

Yes. I still remember when I made a decision that involved a large structural change which everybody agreed to, but while it was still being implemented I decided it was wrong and told my staff that we should stop and reshape the change. One of my senior colleagues said at the time, "it is certainly the right thing to do however you will look like an idiot". I replied "well, I will have to look like an idiot, but everyone will forget about that eventually. It was a good idea at the time, but it is not working". Actually, this did me no harm. Some of my colleagues were concerned about the waste of money however I was more concerned about all the people who were impacted by the change as you don't get productivity from people who are unhappy.

So, do you think the introduction of centralised strategic planning has had any impact on the internal organisational dynamics of the institutions?

Yes, it has. This is what it is designed to do. Centralised strategic planning helped universities develop a concept of the whole institution which I don't think they did before – develop a shared vision. That is the good part of it. The bad part of it is when it doesn't work well, and I think this happened with some of the models we had in the early days ... as poor strategic planning can have a significant impact on innovation.

Yes, it does. Academic Boards got caught up in this, in the sense that they became disenfranchised as part of the process.

Academic Boards had considerable power in the institutions that I worked in. I remember in the College towards the end when the resources were so tight we needed to put a freeze on appointments, which was a fairly conventional thing to do. But in those days these decisions had to go through the Academic Board and they basically rejected that solution. When we asked them what they would do instead they said to us "well that is your problem, you are the managers". So, we moved to a completely different model of making decisions about appointments and thinking about whether we could or could not afford a position which is what most institutions do now. Why would you want to be on Academic Board if you were responsible for making decisions that will put colleagues out of work? Although I understand this, at the same time most of the curriculum decisions they made were decisions about resources.

As these decisions were increasingly made strategically this led to what people term the 'managerialisation' of Australian universities.

Yes, that is what happened. Universities just designed processes to go around Academic Board as these types of decisions needed to be made.

What was it like planning at the national level as Chair of the Review of Australian Higher Education that produced the report that came to be known as The Bradley Report[16] 21 years after Dawkins?

I was very surprised to be asked to Chair this panel. Some people thought it was because I knew the Minister, but I had only met

---

16 D Bradley, P Noonan, H Nugent, and B Scales. (2008). *Transforming Australia's Higher Education System* (Report of the Review of Australian Higher Education). Australian Government, Canberra.

her once or twice as part of a group. Other people thought that it was because she was a woman and I was a woman; I really don't know why the Minister asked me to lead this review as there was no history between us. However, I accepted, and it was a good panel, particularly as we had enough differences between us, both ideological and experiential, that led to some very robust debates. I did not know Bill Scales or Helen Nugent before we commenced, but I knew Peter Noonan as we had disagreed mightily on the working party that developed the relative funding model when I argued constantly that we needed to include some equity loading in the model. This was completely rejected by the panellists which was not surprising. I now have a much more realistic view of how to get things done than I did then. But, I kept having these interminable arguments on the various panels and consultation groups I was involved in. I also raised this issue during the consultation sessions for Dawkins' Green Paper and the White Paper arguing that we had to do more than just increase the number of students entering higher education as this would not do anything for working-class people. I can remember saying to Minister Dawkins at one meeting that all this would do was enrol more stupid middle-class people and would not do anything about the smart working-class people. So, I failed in this argument. I was on the CTEC at the time and then on the HEC where I kept raising this issue and then surprisingly, years later, Peter and I found ourselves on the Bradley committee.

Had he shifted position by then?

Yes, I think so. He is an evidence-driven person and in the meantime, we developed *A Fair Chance for All*[17] so we actually won that fight. But I think Peter also saw, as an economist, that we needed to find a larger pool of people to enrol in higher education to achieve the

---

17 Australia Department of Employment, Education and Training 1990, *A fair chance for all: national and institutional planning for equity in higher education: a discussion paper*, AGPS, Canberra.

participation targets. Bill Scales is an economist with a history in both public and private sector regulatory bodies, so the panel had profound differences which can be a good thing, however, as Chair I needed to be able to bring it all together. The interesting thing is that when Minister Gillard asked me to Chair the panel I said yes but only if it is a small panel as you can deal with this level of disagreement with 4 people but you can't deal with it if you have 12 people on the panel - apparently Bill Scales said the same thing to the Minister. I had previously been involved on the panel advising on *Our Universities: Backing Australia's Future*[18] with Minister Nelson. That panel was very large and mostly about the Minister getting what he wanted, so I knew from personal experience that this was not the way to develop an effective national educational strategy.

It was also an incredibly pressured process. I was invited in late November 2007 and we did not have our first meeting until February 2008 because it had to go through Cabinet and was delayed by the parliamentary recess. We also had to search for a secretariat and were extremely fortunate that Anne Baly was appointed as Executive Officer. She was utterly fabulous, thank goodness, as this is a critical appointment. It was also a very hands-on process. Three of us basically wrote and corrected the drafts; some of our email conversations extended until 2 am in the morning as we were constantly arguing and rewriting each other's work. The consultations with the higher education providers were also very interesting. I used to start all the meetings with the statement "I know that you want more money, you don't need to tell me about it. I know what the arguments are, I know you want the indexation rate fixed, but we need to talk about other things". Looking back on it now, the thing that I am most disappointed about, actually peeved about given that the government put it in the Terms of Reference, was that we expended a huge amount of effort discussing a single

---

18 Nelson, B, Australia Department of Education, Science and Training 2003, *Our universities: backing Australia's future*, DEST, Canberra.

tertiary sector. The chapters on this topic took a huge amount of work and there was a lot of internal disagreement about these chapters – it was an incredibly complex area particularly as we were addressing questions about the underpinning funding and where the legal responsibilities should be. The government itself said that it was going to address this issue, that it was in negotiation with the States, but then did nothing. And, of course, what we have now is what could have been predicted. A group of pirate kings and queens, the university Vice-Chancellors, claiming whatever resources they could because they had the market power to do so. This combined with the State Governments withdrawing their funding for the VET Sector has contributed to the terrible mess we are in today. And, I feel very, very concerned about it because it does not bode well for Australia's social and economic future as there is a terrible disjunction between the university and VET sectors which there should not be. I hope the new COAG process might be able to address it but at least universities now can see that something needs to be done. I sit on the NSW Skills Board and I am very worried about it.

The Recommendations outlined in the Bradley Review focused attention on equity and demand-driven funding. However, since 2017 there has been a movement away from this position.

Yes, we are moving back to the central planning model again. As I mentioned earlier, the Bradley panel came from very different perspectives and yet we were able to agree on the recommendations outlined in the Final Report. I see no evidence that the central planning model worked in the past unless the government put in place financial incentives for students to enrol in particular areas. I acknowledge that there are problems with over supply and it is inevitable, I think, that we will continue to see the gap between the earnings between people with university qualifications and some people from the VET sector narrow, but I don't necessarily think this is a bad thing. We are moving to a position where a majority of people have a higher education qualification therefore the premium for people with higher education qualifications will decrease. And, in a way, this might lead people to think more carefully about what they are going to do, and in some cases, consider completing an apprenticeship if they look at average earnings.

Of course, I would like more money to go into equity. But what we were able to do in the Bradley Review was demonstrate what was likely to work, evidenced by experience and research, and then recommend those initiatives be implemented. I know a lot about the issue; I have been involved since the early 1970s, first in schools, then in VET and then the university sector. I have also been lucky to work with people who are very good and very experienced. I was very fortunate to get Dr Lin Martin to work with us for three months on the Bradley Review. We were both across the research literature, she more so than I was, which really helped. Also, Anne Baly, Executive Officer, had been on the 'Fair Chance for All' working party, so given the experience we had on the committee I was sure that what we were recommending would work. What I was not sure about was whether it would be rejected or accepted by the sector. But we did give power to people in the institutions who were knowledgeable about these things to argue for action. In my experience, governance bodies are usually quite concerned about equity. Not so concerned that they want to invest billions of dollars in it, but they are keen to make sure the institution responds to the legislative requirements. The Department had also by then realised that they needed to find new cohorts of people to meet the participation requirements, this was our underpinning argument. In my opinion, the Bradley Review presented a coherent argument. However, in finding these new cohorts we will need to address some of the social and economic issues relating to regional and rural disadvantage. I think Dan Tehan, Minister for Education, is well qualified to deal with this challenge[19], however, the only way to respond to the regional problem is to increase the level of funding.

Regional education is a significant issue and I think the government is going to have to accept that they will need to spend more money to achieve the outcomes outlined – they have to do the same with training in rural and regional areas. We have made some small gains in Indigenous Education; the problem is very complex although some institutions have been trying very hard in this area for quite a long time. But, of course when Indigenous education is combined with regional issues the disadvantage becomes even more significant. Reflecting broadly on what Bradley achieved is that it made the issue of access and equity, to use the old terms, a mainstream issue in higher education. I don't think it was before then. Even the Go8 institutions know a token commitment will no longer be sufficient. When I started talking about equity years ago, and I wasn't the only one, people thought I was a lunatic. Whereas now it is seen as a much more mainstream issue.

So, it has been 10 years since Bradley, it is time for another Review?

No, I don't think so – what we need now is action. There are, of course, issues about the funding of the Australian Higher Education Sector and I personally don't think that it is in Australia's interest to return to a centralist model because it did not work. Anyone who has ever run an institution will tell you that - not necessarily publicly. I spent a great deal of time as Deputy Vice-Chancellor and Vice-Chancellor seeking 'forgiveness' from the Department for getting the overall student numbers but not in the areas the government wanted. We can, of course, encourage students to enrol in particular areas, but we can't make them. Year after year we would need to promise to do better next year to achieve the student projections in areas the

---

19 The Hon Dan Tehan MP, Minister for Education, released the National Regional and Remote Tertiary Education Strategy on 28 August 2019 https://ministers.education.gov.au/tehan/national-regional-rural-and-remote-tertiary-education-strategy

government wanted, even though we met our overall targets – I just don't think this type of approach works. Another key issue relating to funding is the fact that our entire system is being subsidised by International students which I don't agree with.

So, then, in closing, what advice do you have for the next generation of individuals who will be tasked to lead strategic planning in Australian universities?

All I would say is that there is no one right way to lead strategic planning. The approach needs to be crafted to the culture of the organisation and address the challenges of that particular time. It is not always easy to do but if you don't plan strategically, your institution will not do well in the long term. Many institutions keep bumbling along but in my view a stunning example of success of leading in a well-planned institution is the Queensland University of Technology (QUT), and among the Go8 the University of Queensland and the University of Melbourne are very good performers. One of the things these universities had was key reformers at the right time. For example, David Penington is very important in the history of Australian higher education; he did some excellent work at the University of Melbourne when it needed to be done.

You mentioned earlier that you have changed your mind about strategic planning?

When I was younger and less experienced, I thought there was a right way to plan strategically but I no longer hold this view. There are different ways of doing it but what you need to do is get the balance between people having a sense of where they are going, and what they will be judged against, combined with a process that allows you to take a good idea and run with it.

This is the great challenge of strategic planning and also of leadership.

CHAPTER TWO

Emeritus Professor Alan Robson AO CitWA

Professor Alan Robson was the Chair of the inaugural Higher Education Standards Panel and is a former Vice-Chancellor and Deputy Vice-Chancellor & Provost of The University of Western Australia. Professor Robson has been Chair of the Group of Eight Universities (2007-2010) and Deputy Chair of Universities Australia (2005-2011); Deputy Chair of the Council of the National Library (1998-2005); a member of the Western Australian Science Council (2003-2009) and the CSIRO Board (2003-2008). He is currently Chair of Trustees, The Western Australian Museum; Chair of Advisory Council, Science and Industry Endowment Foundation CSIRO; Chair of Board Perron Institute for Neurological and Translational Science

Professor Robson was awarded the Australian Medal of Agricultural

Science. In 2003 he was made a Member of the Order of Australia and awarded a Centenary Medal, and in 2009, Professor Robson was made a Citizen of Western Australia. In 2013, Professor Robson was made an Officer (AO) in the General Division for distinguished service to tertiary education through governance and administrative roles, to the advancement of scientific and medical research, and to the community.

Professor Robson is an eminent university leader who has a profound commitment to quality educational outcomes for students in our higher education system. He was a member of the TEQSA Advisory Council, the Quality Indicators for Learning and Teaching Working Group, and the Quality, Deregulation and Information Working Group, established by the Commonwealth Government. The education system of Western Australia has benefited from Professor Robson's expertise. In 2001, he chaired the Ministerial Taskforce on Structures, Services and Resources Supporting Government Schools. From 1998 until 2005 Professor Robson was Deputy Chair of the Council of the National Library of Australia.

Tess Howes: Professor Robson, thank you very much for agreeing to participate in this study. Could you please start this interview with a brief summary of your career focusing on the various leadership positions you held on your pathway to the role of Vice-Chancellor.

Alan Robson: I have been at the University of Western Australia (UWA) since I commenced as a lecturer in 1974. I am unusual in this regard as most of my colleagues have worked at a number of different institutions whereas I elected to stay at the UWA for my entire career. I became a Professor in 1983 and Dean of the Faculty of Agriculture in 1991-1992. I was then Foundation Director of the Cooperative Research Centre (CRC) for Legumes in Mediterranean Agriculture (CLIMA) before I was appointed Deputy Vice-Chancellor in 1993. From 1993 to 2004 I was either the sole Deputy Vice-Chancellor, or when there were other Deputy Vice-Chancellors, I was Deputy Vice-Chancellor and Provost, a new leadership position that Deryck Schreuder introduced when he commenced his term as Vice-Chancellor. This position essentially said that I ran the university internally so that Deryck Schreuder could be externally focused. I was appointed Vice-Chancellor in 2004 and stayed in this role until I retired in 2012. The first strategic planning process I was involved in was not for the UWA but as Chair of the Grain Legumes Research Council in about 1986. This was one of the rural industry organisations that subsequently became part of the Grains Research and Development Corporation. As part of this role, I had to prepare a strategic plan as John Kerin was a very forward-looking Minister for Agriculture who completely changed the approach to agricultural research and development. The next strategic plan I prepared was as Founding Director, CRC for Legumes in Mediterranean Agriculture (CLIMA) so before I was appointed Dean and Deputy Vice-Chancellor, I had experience in strategic planning. This too was unusual, as there was very little emphasis on strategic planning in the university sector at the time. This emphasis increased during the 1990s in the post-Dawkins period.

Strategic planning was a feature of the 1988 Dawkins Reforms, a centralised Commonwealth Government initiative. UWA is a long way away from Canberra – what did you think of the proposed reforms when the Green Paper was released?

Yes, Canberra is a long way away from Perth. Because of this, I deliberately took on a number of national higher education leadership roles during my career as the decision-making was always conducted in the East. I held leadership roles with the Group of Eight (Go8), Universities Australia and the Commonwealth Scientific and Industrial Research Organisation (CSIRO) throughout my career. I know John Dawkins reasonably well and have interacted with him on a number of occasions. He is, of course, a graduate of this university and the only student representative to be evicted from Senate by the Chancellor for objecting to a decision made by Senate. When the Dawkins Reforms were released the Vice-Chancellor of UWA was Robert Smith. As he was part of Dawkins 'Purple Circle'[20] we understood the thinking from him. I was a great supporter of Robert Smith as I felt he was the first person to introduce a new approach to the management of this university – this approach was consistent with the management agenda outlined in the Dawkins Reforms. When I first became a professor in the School of Agriculture, UWA had a Staffing Committee, Equipment Committee and Accommodation Committee. These committees were all sub-committees of Academic Board and Academic Board had control of the resources and made the resourcing decisions for the university. However, when Robert Smith was appointed Vice-Chancellor he pushed for devolution – he was in favour of one-line budgets. I was supportive and actually moved the motion for devolution of the

---

20 There were seven members of the Purple Circle: Don Watts, previously Head of the Western Australian Institute of Technology then Vice-Chancellor of Bond University Australia's first private university; Robert Smith, Vice-Chancellor of University of Western Australia; Mal Logan Vice-Chancellor of Monash; Brian Smith, director of the Royal Melbourne University of Technology; Jack Barker, recently retired head of Ballarat CAE; Helen Hughes, an economist at ANU and Don Aitkin, who often "directed his frequent public commentary against the universities" (Macintyre, 2017, p.63).

Budget at Academic Board as a very young professor.

At this time, Academic Board was like a very daunting, adversarial debating club, and the Executive seemed to be constantly locked in debate with dissident professors. Years later I did a Review of the Academic Board at the University of Sydney, when Gavin Brown was Vice-Chancellor, and it was exactly the same. After Smith resigned as Vice-Chancellor, we had some discussions with Murdoch University and agreed to amalgamate although this decision was subsequently defeated in the Upper House by the National Party. However, as a consequence of the amalgamation discussions, Murdoch was on the selection panel when we were looking to appoint a new Vice-Chancellor. They were not keen to appoint an internal UWA candidate, so Fay Gale was the successful applicant and appointed the new Vice-Chancellor for UWA.

I am a great admirer of Fay Gale however she had a very rocky period when she was first appointed as her three Deputy Vice-Chancellors had all applied unsuccessfully for the job which placed her in a tricky leadership situation. In the end, they all left UWA and Fay Gale appointed me originally as Coordinator, Academic Staffing, and then as Deputy Vice-Chancellor. I did not apply for the role of Deputy Vice-Chancellor because as I had the CRC, my research was going very well, and I wasn't sure I wanted to be a university administrator. I was only 48 at the time but I accepted the offer and am very pleased that I did. I was Fay Gale's Deputy Vice-Chancellor from 1993 until 1997 and during that time I helped her to press forward with the devolution process commenced by Robert Smith. I also worked very closely with the Executive Director (Academic Services) and Registrar, Peter Curtis, to establish the Planning and Budget Committee. I chaired this committee through Fay Gale's term as Vice-Chancellor, Deryck Schreuder's term as Vice-Chancellor and my term as Vice-Chancellor. Therefore, I actually led the strategic planning processes at UWA from about 1995 to 2012. We made sure that the resourcing decisions were also made by the Planning and Budget Committee – as these two responsibilities need to be linked. We realised that you could not plan effectively unless you were able to resource the planning initiatives – this is very important in terms of strategic planning.

The first Strategic Plan we developed at the UWA was during Fay Gale's term as Vice-Chancellor. It had a Vision, Mission, Priority, Objectives and Values as well as targets and responsibilities. It was both high level and detailed. When Deryck Schreuder commenced his term as Vice-Chancellor I proposed that we develop an Operational Priorities Plan to support the Strategic Plan – I still think that this is the right strategic framework to use. So, we had an overarching 10-year Strategic Plan, you could have a 5-year document if you want, with a 3-year Operational Priorities Plan and 1-year Management Plan underpinning the strategy. When I became Vice-Chancellor, I added an Annual Agenda to the strategic planning process. In my view, you need to constantly engage with the university community, so I visited every School and every Department at least once or twice a year to discuss the Annual Agenda. We also ran an annual senior leadership planning forum where I presented an analysis of institutional performance supported extensively by data. In Deryck Schreuder's time we produced a 2-year Operational Priorities Plan which linked the strategic priorities with the actions we needed to take. We also outlined who was responsible and the measures of success so that we could continually measure the institutional strategic performance.

This approach continued through Deryck Schreuder's term and my term as Vice-Chancellor. When Michael Chaney was appointed Chancellor, he was primarily interested in the performance data as he was a very experienced and astute businessman. So, he asked me to present a summary of the key performance indicators from the Operational Priorities Plan every Senate Meeting so that Senate had a very clear picture of our performance. He also made 20% of my salary dependent on achieving the institutional strategic key performance indicators and made sure we ran a performance-based budget. We commenced with a 0-sum budget every year, prior to that it had all been historical budgets which I don't agree with as I think you need to have an objective basis for distributing resources within the university. The other thing in strategic planning that I think is absolutely essential is that you have to have a discretionary fund so that you can fund good ideas when they are proposed. In my term it was about 5% of the budget, it used to be called 'The Vice-Chancellor's dead fish', however I think it was very important in attracting and keeping good people.

During my term as Vice-Chancellor, we operated strongly from a strategic management perspective and the UWA moved from 180 to 96 in the Jiao Tong Rankings which is a considerable improvement. Some of this was due to Barry Marshall and Robin Warren winning a Nobel Prize however this did not account for all of it. One of our key strategic initiatives was to be within the top 100 universities in the world – we achieved this at the end of my term as Vice-Chancellor. The other important thing in Strategic Planning is what I call 'confronting the brutal facts'. Don't guild the lily and tell yourself that you are doing really well – be honest and report actual performance. The first Operational Plan I led, and the subsequent plans were all called 'Achieving International Excellence'. Here in Perth it is easy to think that Western Australia is the centre of the universe. I did not agree with this nor was I interested in competing with the other Western Australian universities – I wanted to make sure UWA was recognised for international excellence. However, when I first started to articulate this strategy, I ran into some difficulties as the local community thought I was not interested in the Western Australian community. So, we had to refine the message and position UWA as a gate way for the rest of the world into Western Australia. We had an excellent institutional research unit with some very good data that was accessible to everyone. This data was presented in time trend format so that we knew exactly how we were performing. For example, we could monitor our research income and compare it with other Western Australian universities as well as universities throughout Australia – providing both a state and national perspective on our research performance. The other thing that you need to plan effectively, is very good data.

Do you think it was unusual for a Go8 university to have a comprehensive data capture and reporting system at the time? Many of the new universities did – particularly the former Institutes such as the Western Australian Institute of Technology (WAIT) which was a data-driven institution. But the UWA stands out in terms of its data collection and reporting capability as a Go8 in the pre and immediate post-Dawkins years.

We had an excellent individual running the institutional research unit, Robert McCormack, who was a statistician by training. I could say to Rob, for example, we want to increase the percentage of students with an ATAR of 95 who chose UWA and he could get that data for me immediately. All our planning discussions were supported by data. You cannot convince academics by rhetoric; this will not get you anywhere. Consistency is also very important. It is no good saying we are going to do this or going to do that and then change your mind. Deryck Schreuder had a very good analogy for this, he said "universities are like an ocean liner and if you move them a little bit, after a while they have moved a fair way". I think this is a good way to think about how strategic planning works in a university. It needs to be data-driven but I also think that this top-down versus bottom-up argument is not helpful. The strategic framework needs initially to be top-down, but you also must be responsive to everyone's view once you have outlined the strategic framework.

This leads us into a discussion of how consultative you need to be with the academic community. How engaged do you need to be?

You need an enormous amount of engagement as you need to socialise the ideas. You can start with a strategic framework but then after that you have to socialise these ideas with your Executive, the senior management team and with the university community. You must then be prepared to change the framework as you socialise it to fill in the gaps and add the detail. One of the things that we did was to form a Teaching and Learning Committee and a Research Committee. These committees were given responsibility for providing input into the Operational Priorities Plan and for preparing a Teaching and Learning Plan and a Research Management Plan that reflected the priorities in the Operational Priorities Plan. The Faculties also had to prepare plans that were aligned with the UWA Operational Priorities Plan. The Faculty Plans could be different in terms of specific content, but they needed to be consistent and aligned with the Operational Priorities Plan.

Deans were also required to report on Faculty progress to the Executive and to their Faculty colleagues each year. During my term as Vice-Chancellor, the Academic Board did not play a significant role in the Operational Priorities Plan except that the Chair of the Board met regularly with me initially as Deputy Vice-Chancellor and then as Vice-Chancellor so that if there were concerns about the direction of the university, these concerns could be raised and discussed. The Operational Priorities Plan was considered at Academic Board for noting, and I don't recall issues being raised.

When you commenced as a young academic in 1974 was the Academic Board's predecessor, The Professorial Board, responsible for making all the academic and resourcing decisions?

Yes, but this changed during the process of devolution led initially by Robert Smith. I think it was a hopeless system – it was still in place when I was Dean and the planning outcomes were very inconsistent. For example, you might get additional staff, but you would not get the accommodation; or you would get the research equipment but not the staff. Or you were given a small block grant, a teaching or research grant, which was so tiny that you couldn't do anything with it. This meant that the Head of School had no autonomy and was restrained in terms of the change that could be implemented at the local level. As part of the devolution process the Budget shifted to a performance-based budget. We would also run a Planning and Budget workshop and hold Planning and Budget meetings throughout the year, so we were constantly building the Budget based on our institutional performance data. In October we would bring down a Budget so the Deans and other senior administrative staff knew how much they could spend in their areas of responsibility. The senior professional staff were also involved in this process and the Budget was published – it was a public document. The agenda, minutes and associated paperwork were published and available.

I believe absolutely in transparency. Prior to this time, we used to have a model that I called the 'helicopter model', where if you made a lot of noise someone would fly over you in a helicopter and drop a bundle of money on you to keep you quiet. I used to get very cross with Deans who did not have explicit budget models so I made sure the Deans explained why they were distributing the money in this particular way - they had to be accountable for the money the Faculty was spending across the academic and administrative areas. I don't think people should be treated with ignorance. The resource distribution process needs to be open, explicit, performance-based and the Deans had to be able to defend the resourcing decisions they made.

Thinking about institutional performance - what did you think about the introduction of the Australian Universities Quality Agency (AUQA)?

I think that the AUQA Reports and the preceding Wilson Reports contain a great deal of useful information. I was delighted with the last AUQA Report of the UWA published when I was Vice-Chancellor because it said that the UWA was a very well managed university functioning at a high level. The AUQA Reports were useful and informative objective assessments. I can remember attending a meeting at the University of Sydney as part of the Wilson Quality Audits. At this meeting we discussed which Go8 universities would not make it into the top band and the consensus was, Monash and Sydney, which is exactly what happened. We all knew what was happening in the individual institutions and what was going in the sector. For example, when Fay Gale commenced her term as Vice-Chancellor here, there was no question that Adelaide University was doing much better than we were. But, by the end of my term, there was no question that UWA was doing much better than Adelaide. They are going ahead in leaps and bounds now … and it is interesting to think about why this is the case.

Are you suggesting that institutional performance is leadership dependent?
My experience suggests this it is. After I retired, the Chancellor of the University of Sydney, Belinda Hutchinson, invited me to be a member of their Strategic Committee along with Thomas Barlow and our Report made it clear that the university was underperforming. When you contrasted this with the performance of Melbourne which had excellent leadership under David Penington and Glyn Davis, in my view, it is interesting to think about leadership across the university sector. I can remember attending the very first Go8 meeting because Fay Gale was Chair of the AVCC and we thought it was a conflict of interest for her to attend the Go8 meetings as well as Chair the AVCC so she asked me to represent her at the Go8 meetings. I couldn't get over the fact that the Vice-Chancellors did not like each other at all.

Do any of the Vice-Chancellors like each other?
There is intense competition in the sector, but I am friends with quite a few Vice-Chancellors although they are a very interesting mix of personalities. I did a review of the Academic Board at the University of Sydney for Judyth Sachs, who was Chair of Academic Board at the time, and I could not believe the attitude of some of

the academics and was also surprised at the lack of connectiveness between the Executive and the rest of the university community. I am proud of the fact that I know people's names at this university, but then again, I have been here since 1974! I am always amazed that universities do not engage internally as much as they should, particularly when they are appointing Vice-Chancellors. I was the first internal appointment as Vice-Chancellor at UWA since Sir George Currie was appointed in 1940 and the only UWA graduate ever to be appointed Vice-Chancellor.

Shouldn't effective leaders who are nearing the end of their term as Vice-Chancellor implement a succession plan and look internally at an individual or potential individuals who could assume the role of Vice-Chancellor as well as look externally? They could then mentor these individuals, develop their leadership capabilities and prepare them for the leadership role?

I have been on a number of Vice-Chancellor selection committees at a number of Australian universities and, yes, very few of the successful applicants are internal applicants. Lance Twomey was very good at developing Vice-Chancellors, a few members of his executive team moved into leadership roles – the University of Sydney also tends to appoint Sydney graduates. It is certainly an interesting discussion, as the Vice-Chancellor leaves a significant leadership mark on a university. The other thing that is really important for Vice-Chancellors to consider is that they need to have strong people working with them. Do not select friends who will just reinforce your thinking and support your decisions. You need people who will challenge you and tell you when they think you are making a mistake. When I was Vice-Chancellor, the Executive Meetings were very robust and at times fierce – respectful, polite, but very strong. I think that my leadership benefited from this. The other thing that is important is when we left the room we left in agreement. The decisions made were decisions of the Executive and everyone held this position. There was no leaking and no backstabbing. It was very positive in this sense.

You have provided some excellent guidance on how Vice-Chancellors should lead, specifically how they should lead strategic planning. So, in thinking again about the first Strategic Plan you developed with Fay Gale and the Strategic Plans developed under your leadership which were extensively collaborative, can you comment on how well the Strategic Plans were received by the stakeholders?

I think they were very well received. I can remember some things that were not well received, and I learned a great deal from this experience. I decided that we needed to have research priorities and we would pick a few areas in which we would strive for excellence and talked about this as 'Peaks on the Plateau'. I found out later that it was being referred to by staff in a derogatory way as 'Pigs on a Platter'. Eventually we sorted it out and agreed a set of research priorities, however, this made me realise that I moved too quickly from the idea that we needed some research priorities to identifying the research priorities without sufficiently engaging the community. I received some very good advice from an experienced Dean when I commenced my term as Vice-Chancellor. He said that I was doing quite well however recommended that I would do a lot better if, before I announced the bad news, I shared some good news. Frame the communication and commence it with the things that are going well and suggest that if we did more of this our performance would improve. If you deliver the bad news first, you will have a room full of folded arms and feel the resentment building, resistance mounting. These people will then shut down and won't listen to the next part of the presentation.

I don't remember a great deal of opposition to the strategic plans – I do remember some opposition to the idea of strategic planning and the idea of operational planning and there was certainly resistance to the idea that someone should tell me what to do in my classroom. Originally, here, what happened in the classroom was between the academic and the class and when I shut the door, I was in control. So, there was a bit of resistance to the establishment of the Teaching and Learning Committee which was established in Fay Gale's time. Interestingly no one minded the Research Committee as they saw this as a way to increasing access to research resources. Once the Teaching and Learning Committee started saying … "you must have a proper subject outline and you have to have specific graduate outcomes" … people were not happy as they saw it as a loss of autonomy.

Did the movement towards centralisation and the implementation of strategic planning happen at UWA in the mid-1980s before the Dawkins Reforms of 1988?

No, it did not happen at the UWA until the 1990s – after the Dawkins Reforms.

What did you think of the Dawkins Reforms?

I thought it was ridiculous at the time, but I have since changed my mind. I have had this discussion with John Dawkins who I know quite well – I thought they were converting quite good Teachers' Colleges and Institutes of Technology into rather poor universities. And, of course, this discussion is still going on as Peter Coaldrake just completed a Review of the Higher Education Category Standards and the Final Report suggested that all universities should be able to demonstrate world-class research in at least three fields. The paper identified a couple of universities they thought might not meet this criterion but, in my view, I think it might be more than that. I would suggest that in Australia, about one third of universities are what we call research intensive, a third would have some research strengths in certain areas, and the remainder are not doing much research at all.

At the end of 2011 I was invited to chair the Higher Education Standards Panel to outline the new thresholds that would underpin quality in higher education.[21] We deliberately did not address the provider categories as I regard this as a political decision, not a standards decision. We did a great deal of work on this and invited six experts throughout the world to write papers on what standards we need to shape higher education in the 21st Century. Leo Goedegebuure helped us to get the report into shape for release as a Discussion Paper but by then the Minister did not want to have this discussion with us. This was during the Abbott Government who were pursing deregulation initiatives and so our paper was put aside and has never seen the light of day. I chaired the panel for the first three years, and we wrote the standards. I was then a member of the panel for the next three years, but nothing ever came of it.

It must be difficult if experienced sector representatives, such as yourself, who have a very clear idea of what we need to do, are not able to gain any traction with the Minister.

The Department also did not want to open the discussion. Our paper did not have a political position and if I had done the Coaldrake review I would probably have gone the other way and moved away from applying the term 'university' for all higher education institutions. In my view all university teachers should be scholars; but being a scholar does not mean that they are engaged in research by discovery.

I looked at a few Liberal Arts Colleges in the United States because I thought at one stage that a comprehensive research-intensive university could establish a Liberal Arts College as an alternative to the current university model which is very broad. At times, I am not sure you should call some institutions a university. I went to Colgate University, a leading liberal arts university in New York State. It is a very good university; and although they don't

---

21 https://ministers.employment.gov.au/evans/professor-alan-robson-take-key-higher-education-quality-role

do any research, they are scholars. I would have been prepared to argue this point, but I think Peter Coaldrake has taken a more pragmatic approach. The private institutions are a bit dark on this because they say the less research-intensive universities are given an advantage as they are able to call themselves universities.

This leads us into a discussion about the differentiation of institutions that Dawkins proposed which we could argue has not been realised.

Dawkins is vindicated in that a large number of these new universities have developed strong research profiles and in 20-years' time may even be research leaders. I think that Dawkins has been proved right, although at the time, I did not think it was a good idea. When I was Vice-Chancellor at UWA I introduced a variation of the 'Melbourne Model' in our undergraduate degree program to bring some differentiation to the sector – students who do not want to follow the UWA model could go to Curtin or another university. I embarked on this strategy as I thought universities should primarily be concerned with educating people which I did not think was happening. We were producing humanities graduates who knew no science; and science students who knew no humanities. In my view, this is not the mark of an educated person.

Critical thinking is also important, for example, when I was teaching, I used to set an exercise in 4th year where I would give my students 6 papers to read, 3 of which held one view and the other 3 held another view, and I would ask them to design a series of experiments to test the opposing views. I would tell them that if you can identify how the views are different, you will be awarded a C (pass), if you can get beyond that you will achieve a higher grade. I used to think that all science is empirical; all knowledge is empirical. All knowledge has all been derived by experimentation, so I approached my teaching in this way.

Leadership, particularly strategic leadership, is my area of interest. To me, leadership is an interpersonal relationship between individuals that is dynamic, multi-dimensional and complex. It is very difficult to measure these types of relationships in empirical terms.

Yes, leadership is difficult to measure in empirical terms. Leadership is also informed by your life experience. After I finished my PhD I was conscripted and spent two years in the army as a national serviceman. I went to Officer Training Unit at Scheyville and I learnt a great deal about leadership in the army. We were taught the three things that a leader needs to do was: 1) maintain the group; 2) achieve the task; and 3) meet individual needs. We were also told that these three things must be kept in balance. I have found this very valuable resolving difficulties in the university. When I graduated as an officer, I graduated with the Commandant's award as the cadet most determined to graduate which meant that I was at the bottom of the class. I had never fired a rifle before I went into the army, I hate camping and I was hopeless at drills. But after I graduated, I was sent to replace an Adjunct/Quartermaster who had lost control. I could see for myself that if you lose control, people will do whatever they want to as soon as your back is turned unless you have managed to get them onside. I learned this lesson early and took it with me to the university – I also came to the realisation that leadership is about winning hearts and minds.

Leadership is not about telling people what to do – if you just rely on this leadership approach you won't get anywhere. I think I am the only Vice-Chancellor who had military training, so I am also unusual in this regard. I did not tell anyone in the army that I had a PhD however one day the Drill Sergeant stood about an inch from my face saying "Robson, I don't care if you have an f...ing PhD; in here, you are an absolute nothing!"

That certainly let you know how the system worked! Getting back to the topic of strategic planning, have you led a strategic planning process recently? And, if so, have you changed your mind about the most effective approach? You said earlier in this interview that you didn't think an umbrella approach worked but some universities are moving back to a higher-level, strategic planning approach.

I chair the Board of Trustees of the Western Australian Museum and have recently been involved in a strategic planning process as part of this role. I was not responsible for leading the process; the CEO is leading it with his strategy people. That has been an interesting exercise and I think they have done a very good job.

No, I haven't really changed my mind about this and still think that detail is important. Effective strategic planning in a university should go right down to the unit level – to the Faculty level - not beyond that. The Deans should then be responsible for developing the operational performance indicators relevant to their discipline and the planning context and include Key Performance Indicators (KPIs) in the position descriptions.

This relies on an effective strategic planning culture at all levels of the leadership hierarchy. Do you think that organisational culture plays a role in enhancing or impeding strategic planning?

Absolutely. A culture that enables strategic planning is a culture that is open, transparent, frank and communicative. People need to take ideas and engage with others to refine these ideas – the engagement process is critical. The other thing that is important is that the message needs to be reinforced constantly. I have always believed that unless you were prepared to face people and argue your case, you will not win over their hearts and minds. Circulating a memo or talking to large groups of people as part of an information exchange without meaningful interaction will not achieve this. You need to give everyone the chance to have their say – this is not about achieving consensus but about listening to people and being genuine about it.

This takes courage and not everyone is willing to engage at this level. So, reflecting on your career, do you think that your experience leading strategic planning has had an impact on your understanding of leadership?

Yes, definitely. Although I used the army model of leadership I discussed earlier consistently throughout my career, I have also learned a lot from the people I have worked with. I learned a great deal about leadership from Fay Gale and from Deryck Schreuder that I found useful later on and I would like to think that my leadership skills improved throughout my career.

I believe you can improve and enhance your leadership skills however in order to achieve this you need to be reflective and think about the things that went well and the things that did not go as well. I had a dog and used to take him for long walks early in the morning. I used this time to reflect on the meetings that were scheduled that day and reflect on the difficult meetings and think about how I could have handled the situation better. I found this quiet reflective time very useful and very few members of the Executive resigned during my term as Vice-Chancellor; the turnover was very low although the times were difficult. So, I think being a reflective leader is important in helping you to deal with the leadership difficulties that constantly arise.

Were there any periods when you had very compelling issues to deal with, for example, financial difficulties which required you to make decisions that would be unpopular with your staff?

I used to say when I brought down the Budget each year that everyone was equally unhappy! In all honesty, there was never enough money. It was a lot more comfortable financially earlier in my career, but the financial pressures definitely increased over the years, and as the funding per student declined, we had to all work a lot harder. When I first became an academic, which was immediately after Whitlam, there was sufficient money for us to do what we needed to do. But over the years, we constantly had to make difficult decisions based on resource limitations which is not an easy thing to do. I was responsible for making quite a few people redundant in Fay Gale's term as we needed to let low-performing people go. I tried to do this in a way that made people feel good about the process and we gave quite good payouts. I always tried to handle this in a sensitive way. I once had a conversation with a professor and asked him what was going on as he had a good record but was no longer performing. He told me that he lost his enthusiasm and when I offered him two years' salary he agreed to leave.

I am a sessional member of staff and it is tough, really tough at times to maintain the enthusiasm.

This is one of the key problems of the sector as I do not believe that having large numbers of casual staff is consistent with research-intensity. How can it be? And, it is not consistent with quality. What you tend to see is senior, mainly male tenured academics managing an army of casual, mostly women casual teaching staff doing all the work so that the tenured male professor can do the more privileged research. I don't think this is a fair model – it is not equitable. And, as a result, very few Australian students are doing postgraduate work or pursuing academic jobs; certainly, this is the case in agricultural science. I don't know where the next generation of agriculture academics will come from. They won't have agriculture backgrounds; they will probably come from science. So, I don't think the casualisation of the teaching staff is the right model.

In my time as Vice-Chancellor we had very few casual academics – the only casuals we employed were postgraduate students while they were postgraduate students. Very few university staff were employed on casual contracts when I was Vice-Chancellor – the employment data will show that we were the lowest in the sector. And, instead of paying them as casuals we gave them a 0.3 contract. The insecurity of the teaching staff is a problem, a real problem. Why would people commit to an institution when the institution is not prepared to commit to them?

Yes, I agree, this is a problem that needs to be addressed. However, in thinking about strategic planning again, what impact has the introduction of centralised strategic planning has had on the internal organisational dynamics. For example, you discussed how the Professorial Board morphed into Academic Board and the strategic decisions were increasingly made by the Vice-Chancellor and Executive from the mid-1990s.

The Academic Board in my time as Vice-Chancellor did not have much of a strategic decision-making role and was poorly attended. The academic decisions were made by Academic Council which was a sub-set of Academic Board. However, since I retired, the Academic Board has had a bit of a resurgence and become more involved in the leadership process. The Academic Board has always had an important leadership role and made the academic decisions. However, I don't think the Academic Board should decide where we advertise professorial appointments – this is not the role for an Academic Board. You need to first decide on the strategic shape of the university, where are our strengths, where do we want to excel? These are strategic issues that should be made by the Deans and by the Executive, in my view.

Yes, but then the university becomes dependent on the leadership of the Vice-Chancellor and small teams of executives and perhaps vulnerable to leadership variances.

Don't get me wrong, Academic Boards are very important and when things are not going well the Academic Board tends to strengthen to fill the leadership vacuum. This helps to protect against the Executive running away with the show and going in the wrong strategic direction. I can remember some very fierce discussions at Academic Board. For example, the UWA had to deal with the Rindos Affair. David Rindos was an archaeologist who fell out with the Head of Department Professor Bowdler. She offended the mining community over native title rights, and it all got out of hand. The Academic Board took an interest in this matter as they believed that Rindos had been wrongfully denied tenure based on his research performance. The case was further complicated by allegations of sexual misconduct between staff and students in the Archaeology Department. There was also dissent when I discussed the potential appointment of Sally Morgan as a professor if she met the criteria and if we won a Centre for Indigenous History. We went through the proper procedure, but this caused a lot of disagreement. I believe in checks and balances and a separation of powers and robust discussions about contentious issues between Academic Senate and the Executive.

Do you think it is a problem that, as Academic Boards lost control of the resources, they became marginalised from the centre of power?

Yes, this did change and the role of the 'God professor' changed as well. When I first came here in 1974 the 'God professors' made all the decisions but that changed over time. I do not recommend that you marginalise the academic community, you should keep them involved but in a positive way if you can.

There was a period here when the Academic Board was a bit like Parliament – you had constant arguments between 'the Opposition' and 'the Executive' and of course this was counter-productive. We did not have this in my time, but we did have good, robust discussions. I would present the budget to the Academic Board so all the Professors could attend to hear the Budget presentation and some of them challenged parts of it.

Did the Budget change shape as a result of these discussions?

Not really, but I could explain why we made these decisions.

I am sure you were very convincing! Is it possible to run a modern university on a collegial basis – in the model of a traditional university? Are these things compatible? The tensions reconcilable?

I always say that universities are not businesses and have to be managed in a collegiate way and yes, I think you can manage universities in a collegiate way. You need to remember that you are managing people; highly educated, very talented, clever people. The Chancellor, Michael Chaney, was at times amazed how much criticism I was prepared to take from the staff. But, in my view, you need to manage the voice of dissent and this requires you to have broad shoulders.

The UWA ran a Working Life survey every three years and I read all the comments, every year, so I knew what people were thinking. This is how you get a sense of what is going on in the institution. If you know your institution, if you know your people and where the 'hot spots' are you know when to give these areas attention.

What approach to you do think will enable Australia to deliver a quality, sustainable, viable, quality higher education system?

I don't think that growth should be constrained. I prefer the demand-driven model so that universities can grow in areas where they are building strength. It often seemed that when the government was allocating additional places, we didn't receive any. This meant that we were too small to be comprehensive. I thought the Bradley Review was an excellent document and am disappointed that we are moving away from this model. As a result, I think we are already seeing a downturn in enrolment in low-SES students and Indigenous students.

Student contributions in Australia are the third highest in the world which is too high in my view. The Technical and Further Education (TAFE) sector needs to be properly funded so that we can produce a technical workforce of sufficient quality. I don't recommend a dual-sector model, I recommend we keep TAFE separate but fund the institutions properly and make sure they are well organised.

I don't think we have too many universities – International students will keep coming and sustain our universities financially. However, the university sector needs more funding and expenditure on Research and Development needs to be increased. I also think that research funding should be separate from funding for teaching but many of my colleagues do not agree with me – I hold a minority view on this. We would often say, first prize is one CRC, second prize is two – as you do not receive sufficient resources to fund one, let alone two.

I also don't think that it is wrong for teaching to subsidise research. We applied an internal funding model at UWA, and the Business School was always unhappy with me as I took some of their income to fund other areas of the university. My reasoning was that the Business School benefited from the research reputation of the university and are able to attract all these International students therefore they should help to fund the research that maintains our standards of excellence. As long as it is transparent, and people know what you are doing.

We have a relative funding model at UWA and weighted the different areas so that, for example, medicine received more funding than science as it is more expensive to teach, and you also have to fund the practical classes. Unfortunately, in a sector that is under-funded these are the types of internal decisions that you need to make, and they are not always popular which is one of the key leadership challenges for Australian Vice-Chancellors.

CHAPTER THREE

Emeritus Professor Ed Davis AM

Professor Ed Davis is Emeritus Professor in the Faculty of Business and Economics at Macquarie University. He was Dean of the Faculty of Economic and Financial Studies at Macquarie University from 2002 to 2008. From 1988-2002 he was a Professor at the Macquarie Graduate School of Management and was Deputy Director from 1996-2002.

Much of Professor Davis' research has focused on the management of workplace performance. He co-edited several books with Professor Russell Lansbury including *Technology, Work and Industrial Relations* (1984); *Democracy and Control in the Workplace* (1986); and, *Managing Together: Consultation and Participation in the Workplace* (1996). He established and co-edited the *Making the Link; Affirmative Action and Employment Relations* series (1990-2008). He has been honoured with Macquarie University awards for Outstanding Teaching (1997) and

Outstanding Service (2004).

In 2000 Professor Davis was National President of the Industrial Relations Society of Australia and awarded Life Membership in 2002. In 2004 he won the Lifetime Achievement in HR Award at the National Human Resources Awards.

In 2005 he was made a Fellow of the Australian Human Resources Institute. He was appointed a Member in the General Division of the Order of Australia in 2006 for "service to education and to the community in the areas of equity in employment, industrial relations and human resource management".

Since his retirement from Macquarie University in 2008, Professor Davis has focused on executive coaching and mentoring with clients across a range of industries. He has assisted several universities with conflict resolution as a facilitator, mediator and investigator. He is National Vice President and NSW President of ABC Friends.

Tess Howes: Professor Davis, thank you very much for agreeing to participate in this study. Could you please start this interview with a brief summary of your career focusing on the various leadership positions you held on your pathway to Executive Dean.

Ed Davis: I became an academic in 1974 as a tutor at Monash University then worked full-time at a number of institutions until 2008 when I completed my term as Dean of the Division of Economic and Financial Studies (EFS) at Macquarie University. In the years since then, I have remained involved in Australian universities; as a mentor, a member of Academic Boards and a Complaint Officer dealing with a range of issues. This has been interesting and fascinating, providing insights into the changes that have been happening in Australian universities.

Thinking more broadly about my experience in Australian universities, there are a few issues worth commenting on: firstly, funding. In my early years as an academic, I was not aware that funding was an issue. My students sat in lecture rooms or tutorials funded by the government from the mid-1970s until the mid-1980s. From 1980, I was teaching in the Faculty of Commerce at the University of New South Wales (UNSW). We had an extraordinarily competent Head of Department, John Niland, who went on to become Vice-Chancellor, a very good Vice-Chancellor. So, I may have been quarantined from funding issues as I was employed in workplaces that were well funded and well resourced. I moved from the UNSW to the Graduate School of Management at Macquarie University (MGSM) which was also very well resourced. When I was appointed Dean of the Division of Economic and Financial Studies at Macquarie University in 2002, now the Macquarie Business School, we taught 40% of the university's students including the bulk of the fee-paying students and made significant surpluses each year. The other Deans used to say that we were underwriting the rest of the university.

Secondly, when I started as an academic, the gap between the salaries and the financial rewards for a professor and university leaders was very small. For example, when I was on a committee looking at the salary of the Vice-Chancellor at Macquarie in the early 1990s it was barely above the salary of a Level E Professor. Now, we have Vice-Chancellors earning $1million plus which reflects the pressures on universities to operate as businesses, resulting in appointments of Vice-Chancellors at salary levels similar to those in parts of the corporate world. This has also happened at the faculty leadership level. A Dean of a Commerce faculty, for example, might earn about $500,000 today. I am not sure that these developments and possible repercussions have been properly considered. Of course, there is a case to pay university leaders high salaries because universities want to attract people with the range of skills regarded as essential for these positions, skills that attract a market premium. Key researchers also attract a market premium. In my faculty before I left in 2008, we had significant market loadings for our high performing people, perhaps as much as a 70% salary loading, for example. Good candidates were, at times, few and far between.

Do you think that this salary increase became an enabler of the increasing 'strategic' role of the Vice-Chancellor and separation of the Vice-Chancellor from rank and file academic staff?

Yes, both. A sense of the importance of the strategic priorities of the institution and the skills held by the individual to pursue these priorities. At the same time, leaders can still inform, consult, and engage respectfully with the academic community to bring them along to achieve the university's priorities.

So, they are not mutually exclusive?

No, they are not. To some extent Vice-Chancellors have 'floated away' from their academic peers and might also have consultants who coach them on their strategic communications. But, yes, there is inevitably a greater gap between our university leaders and their academic communities than there was in the 1970s. In the old days, you never saw a Vice-Chancellor, but then again, the Vice-Chancellor's role was different – we never went to see our Vice-Chancellor about an issue of concern. Although, I can recall a colleague, a lecturer, who called to make an appointment with his Vice-Chancellor and was surprised when the secretary said, "are you free this afternoon"? So, he went to see him and was given a cup of tea and had an amicable chat with a man who wore a jacket with leather elbow patches. I am not aware of similar stories now.

Interestingly, people could always make an appointment to see Professor Di Yerbury, Vice-Chancellor, Macquarie University. She walked through the campus, talked to the students and gave lectures on areas of interest - I attended a lecture she delivered on Lachlan Macquarie when I was an undergraduate student. She chatted with prospective students and their families during Macquarie's Open Days and was the most connected and approachable Vice-Chancellor I worked with during my career in the sector.

Yes, Professor Di Yerbury[22] was very approachable and consultative. She was a role model for many people who assumed academic leadership positions – she certainly was for me when I became Dean. I was particularly impressed by the way she handled selection interviews. She did whatever she could as Chair of the Committee to reassure people and make the process less tense. She then undertook the difficult task herself afterwards, which was to call the unsuccessful applicants and explain why they were not successful.

---

22 Professor Di Yerbury AO was Vice-Chancellor of Macquarie University from 1987 to 2006. She was the first woman appointed to the position of Vice-Chancellor and the longest serving Vice-Chancellor in Australia.

What leadership opportunities became available to you that enabled you to move from a young tutor to a Dean of a significant and financially successful faculty?

I had no leadership ambitions at all early in my career. I enjoyed Industrial Relations which was the subject I was researching and teaching. I think I did see myself as being in an upward stream, but I didn't have specific goals and career objectives. I was fortunate in many ways. My research went well, and various people took notice of my research and, as a result, I received job offers. I arrived at Macquarie in my late 30s as an Associate Professor to be a Director of a Foundation. It was a very small Foundation and for the first time in my career, I had the support of an executive assistant which helped me greatly.

I then started working at the Graduate School of Management at Macquarie University (MGSM) and I thought that if the role of Director became available, I might put my hand up. This did happen; but I wasn't successful. I also had the opportunity to chair assorted university committees including the Equal Opportunity Committee and the Probation Committee, which developed my leadership skills. I was Deputy Director at the MGSM from 1996-2002 and then successfully applied to become the first Dean of the Division of Economic and Financial Studies (EFS) in 2002. This was my first major leadership role.

I enjoyed this position very much, however, it was also an unusual experience in many ways. Macquarie, under Professor Di Yerbury, had moved very slowly away from the tradition of academics electing their own Heads of Departments and Heads of Schools. But eventually it became clear to Di, and other Vice-Chancellors, that they were being held accountable by the government and they needed their departments and faculties to produce the results required. Under the old model academics were more likely to appoint known friends who would defend the faculty from the university's Executive. It was not until the end of the 1990s and beginning of the 2000s that Macquarie joined the rest of the sector and started to appoint Deans.

In 2002, I assumed leadership responsibility for a Faculty that had never had an appointed Head. I was viewed very much as an outsider and was under pressure to deliver for the university. There was also no infrastructure in the Dean's Office. At Sydney and UNSW there were large floors of Associate Deans and Deputy-Deans – whereas all I had was a Faculty Manager, a Faculty Human Resource (HR) Officer and five academic department heads who did not talk much to each other.

When I informed my Heads of Departments that we were going to meet every week and share information on what we were doing and how we were going to respond to the university's expectations, they all looked at me suspiciously. I told them that I saw my role as helping them do their work. I certainly did not want to do their job, but I wanted to be better informed and in a position to help if they ran into problems. By and large I think this approach worked well after my Heads of Department got over the shock. I then started appointing people on a part-time basis to positions such as Associate Dean Research, Associate Dean Teaching and Learning, and Associate Dean International, but we were probably 10-years behind comparable faculties in other universities. I also said, to the horror of some of my staff, that we would publish the agenda and minutes of our meetings. A few people told me that this had never happened before but after a few months nobody read them – they just disappeared into a vacuum. I knew I had to work very hard to keep people informed and engaged. There was an enormous distance to travel.

In my view, this is the foundation of developing collaborative leadership foundations – to build interpersonal relationships.

I wanted to respect the authority of my Heads of Departments. I also wanted to be seen in the Faculty, in the university, have my lunch in the canteen, sit next to people and start a conversation with them. Perhaps this came out of my Industrial Relations background, but I found it enjoyable and always got something out of it. I also asked the lecturers of the largest classes to find 5-10 minutes for me to introduce myself to the students, tell them a little bit about the Faculty, say that we really appreciated them studying at Macquarie and wanted them to have a fantastic student experience. I also told the students that if something wasn't working we wanted to know about it. They should talk to their lecturer or Head of Department and if all else failed they should come and see me. And I tried to do this regularly and asked my Heads of Department to do it, so we had coverage across the Faculty. This 'open-door' approach may unearth issues that make you very uncomfortable; at the same time, it affords the opportunity to tackle issues that may have festered.

One of the participants I interviewed for my doctorate also stressed the importance of maintaining connections with the students. Interestingly, she also has an Industrial Relations background.

One of the problems with the way people are selected for university leadership and management positions is that they are appointed usually because of their research competence; but this does not necessarily mean they are good leaders. We have moved towards appointing people to some leadership positions who have business experience but there are very few senior leaders who have deep experience in managing people. This is true of universities, but the same thing happens in major private and public sector organisations. Management is about connecting with people, building relationships – good managers and leaders need very good interpersonal skills and a willingness to communicate and engage with others.

I agree! I would now like you to talk about your experience with strategic planning. Can you recall the first time you were involved in a strategic planning process?

When I started teaching at the MGSM in about 1988 we discussed strategy all the time. That was the jargon of business leadership so you would expect this to have an impact on the MGSM as we were teaching aspiring business leaders and business leadership subjects. We also had some very good strategic thinkers who transformed the MGSM from being a small department with about 300 part-time students who were all from Sydney and an older demographic, to a much larger business school with a diverse cohort of students enrolled in a wide range of study options. This was done in a deliberate, strategic way. We originally started with the Master of Business Administration (MBA) but increasingly thought that there were a lot of people in managerial positions who did not have undergraduate degrees and would not be eligible to enrol in the MBA.

We knew that these people were bright and had the ability to study at the postgraduate level, so we opened the program up and invited them to complete three postgraduate units to achieve a Postgraduate Certificate in Management. If they performed well, they could continue and complete another three units to be awarded a Diploma of Management, take another four units to achieve a Master of Management or continue to complete the final six units to graduate with an MBA. This really appealed to many people working in management positions and our programs grew rapidly which increased the flow of students.

It also changed the way we taught the various programs. For example, instead of two 13-week semesters in the traditional Macquarie model we moved to four 10-week terms which was very radical at the time. We also opened campuses in Hong Kong and Singapore taking our graduate business education to students in Asia and introduced short, compressed courses with lectures over the weekends. So, at the leadership level, we were exploring a range of strategies that shaped the MGSM model.

So, it was a very specific strategy?

Yes, it was very specific but as far as I am aware the rest of the university was not interested in following this type of model at the time. Di Yerbury as Vice-Chancellor was interested and said she would keep an eye on it. However, she left us alone to pursue this strategy and it was very successful. It wasn't until much later that other parts of the university started to be more strategic in their approach. MGSM was always strategic and ran a very different race to the rest of the university.

Was this an internal planning process or was it formalised and published as a Strategic Plan?

It was a bit of both. From memory we had a couple of Directors who were not highly consultative, but they were effective in developing and implementing strategy. The sense of buzz in the MGSM was very strong. We were highly ranked – even number one for a little while – and were financially well rewarded. But, at the same time, it was highly pressured, and we had to manage large numbers of part-time staff, adjunct appointments, who were responsible for at least half of the teaching. We were fortunate in that we were able to attract some high-quality adjuncts but if they didn't do well the students would let us know straight away. The students were paying a great deal of money for their units of study and if they told us that a lecturer was not able to teach, then, generally the adjunct appointment was not renewed.

So, you listened to the students as a primary stakeholder?

Absolutely. Students in the MBA program would always let you know if they were not happy. I was the leader of the Human Resources group and would encourage my colleagues to sit-in on each other's lectures to give feedback on performance. If I was going to introduce a new adjunct, I would generally invite them to give a lecture in my course and see how they interacted with the students. I would try to help them as much as I could. We had some great people teaching for us who held senior management positions in banks, retail and other organisations. The students loved this because they brought all their 'war stories' into the classroom.

These appointments also bring a sense of gravitas and connections to industry that are very attractive to the students.
Yes, and all of this was key to the MGSM doing as well as it did.

You seem to be suggesting that the transformation of the university as a community of scholars to a 'strategic' entrepreneurial university was more of a natural process, emerging from the sector, not necessarily imposed by the Dawkins Reforms. We know that funding was a pressure point in the 1980s, are you suggesting that this was the driver of the 'entrepreneurial' university?
As I mentioned earlier, funding did not become an issue until the mid to late 1980s. When I started working at the MGSM it was quite small. We soon realised that the MGSM could expand its market offerings by offering a range of degree programs including certificates, diplomas, masters as well as the MBA, and generate a large amount of money from charging full fees for these programs. So, although we were an academic department in a university, we were very conscious that the MGSM was also a business and we looked to implement business strategies in order to increase the revenue generated. This was in the late 1980s and beginning of the 1990s, so I don't think this commercialisation strategy had anything

to do with the Dawkins Reforms; what we were doing at the MGSM was completely independent of that. And, it wasn't just the MGSM, other Business Schools were moving in the same direction. We were in direct competition with the Australian Graduate School of Management and the Melbourne Business School which all set very high fees for MBAs and other associated programs. All three Schools were able to generate large amounts of money from their teaching and the MGSM went from about 5 full-time academic staff in the 1980s to probably about 30 full-time academics within 10 years. We were also able to pay salary loadings to retain key staff and attract new talented staff. This is an example of how universities, or parts of universities, started to morph into businesses from the mid-1980s well before Dawkins.

I suppose it should not be surprising that it was Business Schools that led the way.

Yes, although other areas of the university permitted flexible reward packages, directly or indirectly. If you were an academic in a medical faculty, you might also be involved in medical practice. Some legal academics were engaged in legal practices. When I became Dean of EFS in 2002, it was becoming sensitive to its market opportunities, in this case International student enrolments. In 2002 we had about 8,000 students; six years later we had about 13,000 students and the growth mostly came from International students undertaking undergraduate and postgraduate degrees in Accounting, Finance and Business. The rapid growth in size resulted in significant changes to the Faculty and in the academic decisions we made. Academic staff teaching large units of study often had to give several lectures: one lecture and three or four repeats in Macquarie's largest lecture theatre.

One of the things that worried me then, and worries me still, is the 'massification' of the sector – the sheer increase in the number of students. I completed my PhD and did some part-time tutoring at La Trobe University in the 1970s and at the time there were only about 3,000-4,000 students in the whole university. When I first came to Macquarie at the end of the 1980s there were about 13,000 students but when I left Macquarie in 2008 my faculty alone had more than 13,000 students. Macquarie had approximately 40,000 students at the end of 2019. The increase in student numbers put pressure on universities and departments within universities, particularly Business Schools, to generate money. This had a significant impact on universities as organisations and on internal leadership tensions. I have a friend who is a Dean of Commerce and she has 50,000 students in her faculty!

Do you think organisational culture and ideas of academic leadership changed as a result of the movement towards entrepreneurialism?

I know there was suspicion and resistance to the changes I needed to implement when I was appointed Dean of EFS in 2002. I had to make significant changes as approximately 70% of EFS staff were research inactive at a time when the university had to report on its research outputs: PhD students, research grants and publications. I appointed a very good Associate Dean Research who told me that we had a problem with the research culture of the Faculty that needed to be addressed. We also had a performance management system with salary loadings, but I could find no evidence that any staff had ever been found to be unsatisfactory on the basis of their research performance – even if their research output was nil.

Was it no longer possible to have a good teaching career without building a research profile?

The conventional expectation is that an academic will excel in both research and teaching; however, this does not always work out. Some outstanding teachers are poor at research and some great researchers are poor teachers. There is, of course, a cohort who are very good at both. In my Faculty we had a top cohort of academics who loved what they did and were producing most of the research, but at the bottom level there were people who were just not interested and did very little research. And, all too often, they were just left to muddle along in their positions.

This was a residual of the high trust environment that prevailed in universities when I commenced my academic career in the 1970s. At MGSM, if we were talking about high trust workplaces I would always talk about the traditional university. For example, when I started working at Monash in 1974 and wanted to take leave over Christmas, I asked how to apply for leave. The response was - just go away and come back again. I did not fill in a leave form between 1974 until the early 1990s when Enterprise Bargaining changed the way universities managed things like staff leave. Before this time, the university deemed you to have taken your leave, you could not accrue it.

Reflecting on your career, do you think that your experience leading strategic planning has impacted on your understanding of leadership?

I was fortunate that I taught Industrial Relations and Managing People which involves a lot of strategy. For example, what recruitment strategy do we need to put in place? What training programs do we need for our managers? How should performance management work? How did all this align with pursuit of the organisation's goals? I had been teaching these subjects for years when I took on the role of Dean, so I approached my leadership responsibilities influenced by what I had read and taught. I wanted to see good information flows, opportunities for consultation, and opportunities for people to be involved in decision-making, particularly decisions that impacted on them. I also wanted to see very good recruitment and selection processes as I was aware how badly these things were often done.

We had a good Human Resources (HR) officer who had been in the role for 25 years who signalled that she was planning to retire. I wanted to use this opportunity to reshape HR so that it was a dynamic part of the faculty. My aim was to appoint a group of people leading HR who were very experienced. We had to recruit approximately 30 staff in my first year as Dean to bring the staff-student ratio in line and we had funds to spend. I wanted to appoint a HR Director who could implement staff training and performance management.

I then involved my Heads of the Department in an extensive strategic planning exercise and asked them to consult with their staff, look at their research and teaching outcomes and tell me what was working and what was not working. If they needed help, I authorised the employment of consultants and we worked together to produce a Division of EFS Strategic Plan. We then invited Professor Di Yerbury, Vice-Chancellor, and Professor John Loxton, Deputy Vice-Chancellor Academic, my immediate boss, to attend the presentations. These presentations highlighted the current challenges in teaching and research and outlined what the Heads of Department planned to do about it; strategic recruitment was high on their agenda. Di and John were delighted at the discussions we were having. Di gave us permission to appoint our own HR Director; a decision not immediately welcomed by the university's central HR office!

You were able to apply the knowledge you had as an academic to your leadership practice?

Yes, but I had also been employed as a consultant for many different organisations facilitating strategic planning and I knew that it needed to be an engaging process in which each staff member had the opportunity to contribute.

In closing, what advice would you give to the next generation of university leaders who are or will be tasked to lead the sector?

My general advice to younger academics is to be very focused on research and try to dodge administrative responsibilities; at the same time put effort into and enjoy teaching. Academics must be very strategic about their research. Don't publish in the easy journals, publish in the high-status journals and win some research grants. Because if you want an academic career you need to build a strong research profile. If I was talking to people looking at an academic leadership career, depending on the person and the thickness of their hide I would say that mentoring is very important. Mentoring can help you develop skills to respond to challenges more effectively and not take it all too personally or get upset. I know from my complaint work that the stress that goes on behind the scenes can be very tough.

I was lucky because I had a superb mentor. This came about because I went to Di not long after I became Dean and asked her if she would consider bringing a mentor in to work with the Executive Group. She appointed Jeff Jarratt and although I wasn't interested in mentoring at the time, I organised it for my Heads of Departments. After I while I became curious and met with him and he helped me to work through some very difficult challenges. I feel very fortunate to have had a wise, experienced and unflappable mentor. Mentoring is critical however it must be good mentoring.

Are you suggesting two pathways for potential academic leaders?

In universities it is still primarily research. You will also find people recruited into leadership positions with managerial backgrounds. I have been on selection panels in universities that will not even short-list people who do not have a strong research profile even if they are very experienced in leadership which I thought was crazy. I realised when I became Dean that it was a full-time leadership role and decided not to do any teaching. I was involved in a few research projects, but this part of my role was not significant. If I was recruiting for leadership roles now, I would put more emphasis on the candidate's leadership ability than on their research competence although there needs to be a balance.

Shouldn't we look for people with both disciplinary expertise and leadership ability?

My leaning would be to ensure that people appointed to university leadership positions have a demonstrable record of high-quality leadership as well as a very strong record in teaching and research. Leaders should understand the people systems required for the effective running of their department, school, faculty or university.

They must also be highly skilled in how they communicate with, and lead, their peers, staff, students and stakeholders. Getting this wrong can be disastrous.

CHAPTER FOUR

Emeritus Professor Geoffrey Sherington

Professor in History of Education, University of Sydney

Former Dean of the Faculty of Education (1997-2003) and then Acting Deputy Vice Chancellor (2003), Emeritus Professor Geoffrey Sherington has been a member of the University of Sydney for over 35 years.

Having graduated with Bachelor of Arts with Honours in History from the University of Sydney and then a Master of Arts from the University of New South Wales, he then studied overseas in Canada and England graduating from McMaster University with a PhD. On return to Australia he was appointed a Lecturer in Education at the University of Wollongong before taking up an appointment at the University of Sydney.

After a career as lecturer, senior lecturer and Associate Professor he was appointed to a personal chair in the history of education in 1997 just prior to becoming Dean of the Faculty. Over the past 30 years he has been the author and co-author of 15 books and numerous articles in the history of education.

Professor Sherington has been the recipient of a number of competitive research grants. His current interests include the fate of the comprehensive public high school and the history of universities as public institutions.

Tess Howes: Professor Sherington, thank you very much for agreeing to participate in this study. Could you please start this interview with a brief summary of your career focusing on the various leadership positions you held on your pathway to the role of Dean and Acting Deputy Vice-Chancellor.

Geoffrey Sherington: After completing my Bachelor of Arts (Honours) at Sydney University I undertook a Master of Arts at the University of New South Wales. I then completed a PhD at McMaster University in Ontario, Canada. When I first came back to Australia I worked at the University of Wollongong as a lecturer, then in the early 1980s I returned to the University of Sydney when Professor John Ward[23] was Vice-Chancellor. He was a traditional type of academic who had been at the University of Sydney since 1948. He was a member of university staff for 47 years; he came up through the ranks so to speak. I knew him in the 1970s when he was Challis Professor of History and personally witnessed how he responded to the Dawkins Reform agenda. I was a lecturer when I first came to the University of Sydney, but by the end of the 1980s I was promoted to Associate Professor. At the time there were about 18,000 students and 2,000-3,000 staff so fewer people proportionally were promoted to Associate Professor at the time. In my year, for instance, I think it was in 1989, there were just twelve people across the university promoted to Associate Professor, whereas there were seven last year just in this Faculty.

Being promoted to Associate Professor put you into a leadership position in two areas: potentially as Head of Department, since many of the professors had given away that role in the 1970s-1980s; and it also provided a leadership perspective across the institution. You would not have had access to that perspective if you were below the level of Associate Professor. So, although the promotion

---

23 Professor John Manning Ward AO (1919-1990) was Vice-Chancellor of the University of Sydney from 1981-1990. He was tragically killed with his wife and daughter in the Cowan Rail Accident in May 1990.

was on academic grounds, principally on research although some consideration was given to teaching, you were then promoted to an administrative leadership position. No administrative experience was required, nor any understanding of how the institution functioned. However, once you were promoted to Associate Professor you were expected to assume a leadership position in the university. Within a few years I was one of the Deputy Chairs of the Academic Board which brought additional leadership responsibilities as the Academic Board was responsible for planning and policy making in the 1980s and 1990s. There were a few reasons for this: first, it was the only body centralised sufficiently to have an overview of what was going on in each of the Faculties. For example, I chaired a committee that looked at, for example, growing coursework, but it still had an academic focus. Secondly, Don McNicol[24] was appointed Vice-Chancellor in 1990. Don McNicol was a very experienced tertiary administrator however he had no prior experience at the University of Sydney. The Academic Board and the Committee of Deans, the Deans in those days were still elected however there was a movement towards appointed Deans, started to exercise authority over the distribution of resources although responsibility for the quality audits remained with Academic Board. So, things were starting to change. This was significant in the early 1990s for two reasons: first, we were still dealing with the amalgamations with the Sydney Teachers' College, the Conservatorium of Music, the Institute of Education, the Institute of Nursing, the College of Health Sciences and the Sydney College of the Arts at Glebe, White Bay and Balmain. These post-Dawkins amalgamations rapidly expanded the University of Sydney – we took as many as 10,000 students in a very short period of time. No other Group of Eight (Go8) university

---

24 Professor Don McNicol was Commissioner for Universities with the Commonwealth Tertiary Education Commission 1986-1988, Vice-Chancellor of the University of New England 1988-1990, Vice-Chancellor of the University of Sydney 1990-1996, and Vice-Chancellor of the University of Tasmania 1996-2002.

took as many students as Sydney did, and it immediately brought issues of standards and the merging of different academic cultures. The rapid growth of student numbers had a huge impact on the Faculty of Education which meant we experienced problems with quality as a result. Also, we did not have a strong research culture in those days, only the more traditional faculties had a strong research culture. So, yes, the Dawkins amalgamations had a significant impact on this university, however, the other impact came from the quality audits. Leadership for the quality audits was assumed by Associate Professor John Mack, who was Chair of the Academic Board. Many of the professors did not want this type of responsibility, so John Mack put together a small ad hoc working party when we knew we were going to be audited. The first audit was on teaching and Sydney ended up in the second division that year, the only Go8 to be in the second division. I don't think this was because of the amalgamations; it was possibly more about 'disturbings' about some of the teaching programs in some of the older, more traditional faculties. The second audit in 1995 was on research and this time Sydney went up to first division. The approach to the audits was very ad hoc as Sydney wasn't used to being held accountable. We used to say well the Colleges used to be accountable at the State level to the old Higher Education Board (HEB) for their programs, but we, the Academic Board, were not. We were responsible to the Senate and through the legislation, technically to Parliament.

The change that came with the emergence of Department of Education Employment Training and Youth Affairs (DEETYA) was a cultural shock at the University of Sydney. We did not welcome being subjected to these external scrutinies at a time when we were still dealing with the internal changes resulting from the amalgamations. This caused some resentment at the older universities … I am not saying that this also didn't happen at the newer universities, but I just don't know. Actually, the problem was much broader than that as we were also suddenly thrust into policy making. I don't think it was so much strategic planning, but policy making at the centre. I also had to make a choice in 1996-1997 because Ken Eltis became Dean of this Faculty and as he had experience in the Curriculum Directorate, soon moved into central administration leaving the position of Dean vacant. As a result, I became Dean for the next 6 years and I could see that the power was shifting away from the Academic Board towards strategic planning in terms of resource distribution, ideas of market competition and how we needed to position ourselves to attract the best students.

Gavin Brown[25] was Vice-Chancellor by this time and what he decided to do, was devolve power to the Deans. As the government devolved down to universities saying, 'you are not going to get your funds unless you perform in a certain way', Gavin said, 'The Deans want money; well they can compete for it in various ways'. He then established the Colleges and a Senior Executive Group comprised of the Deputy Vice-Chancellors and the Deans. So, I became more involved in the university leadership in 1997 as I was Dean of my Faculty. Gavin also made a number of new internal appointments and external appointments so from 1997-1998 the university started to think strategically.

In a commercial sense?

Yes, partly. Actually, I think Gavin would argue that it was more in an academic sense – redefining what the academic mission was because in his view this would satisfy the commercial side of things. His argument was that we needed to be the best academically to position ourselves strategically. He asked the Deans to develop their own strategic plans, think strategically about what their objectives would be for the next five years and outline how they were going to

---

25 Professor Gavin Brown AO (1942-2010) was Vice-Chancellor of the University of Adelaide 1994-1996 and Vice-Chancellor at the University of Sydney 1996-2008.

achieve them. This was basically what I did from about 1997 until about 2002 or 2003 when I stepped aside for a year when I was Acting Deputy Vice-Chancellor. Things were really happening by then as these strategies were implemented in the Faculties and to some extent in the Colleges.

I am interested in when universities started to think strategically and of course the shift of power to the centre is a really important part of that process. However, as far as I can tell, the universities complained and protested about these changes however they all went along with it and so the Dawkins Reforms were enacted in various ways throughout the sector.

I think that part of the problem is, the trap is, that when you start to think strategically you start to think corporately. John Ward was an older style academic Vice-Chancellor. He would not have had a performance bonus, performance objectives, or a specific strategy for the university. That was part of the problem as some people believed that we were drifting in the 1980s. This was also when the slow emergence of the Deans as so called 'robber barons' began as they were fighting over a 'shrinking pot' and they wanted to make sure they got as many resources as they could. How they got these resources didn't matter. So, they often used to make special pleadings to the Vice-Chancellor which further strengthened the centre as the Vice-Chancellor would say 'I can't give you more money, you have got to perform against the criteria so that we have rational ways of distributing the resources'. What is also interesting about this period of time, is that many of us were working in the old academic culture, which we thought was the pursuit of knowledge, teaching and research in its best aspects. But the new breed of people who were becoming Vice-Chancellors, or Deputy Vice-Chancellors, tended to think, that is all very well, but we have to achieve the corporate mission so that we can do all this academic work. The argument we used to have is that the government won't give us enough resources, but they won't let us practice the free market and also imposed restrictions on the number of students we could take. Gavin Brown argued that we were constantly caught between these two worlds. The so called 'privatisation' of the student body that took place in the 1990s was crucial. The Vice-Chancellor of Melbourne University, Alan Gilbert[26], created Melbourne Private as he could see that this was a way that he could minimise the control of Canberra. However, Gavin Brown never did that. Other institutions decided to establish overseas campuses to help them move away from the restrictions of Canberra, such as Monash. International student fees were not regulated at the time and you could basically do what you wanted.

Yes, and some universities got themselves into hot water as a result.
Yes, because we all forgot that the Commonwealth government controlled student visas, which is where they basically pulled the plug on us! Critics used to say 'well what do you want to do? It is all very well to stand up and criticise but where are your policies? What direction do you want to take?' We were more constrained here at Sydney whereas the opposition was quite open at Melbourne to what Gilbert was doing. Gavin produced the results at Sydney because he lifted the research performance and enrolled some very good students, so it looked like he was producing like a CEO and this satisfied both the governing body and the academics. Academics want to teach good students and have the opportunity to conduct good research.

So, we did not have the open debate and discussion at Sydney like there was in Melbourne[27], because Gavin was very successful in this way.

---

26 Professor Alan D Gilbert AO (1944-2010) was Vice-Chancellor of the University of Melbourne 1996-2004, then Vice-Chancellor of the University of Manchester UK, 2004-2010.
27 There was strong opposition to the establishment of Melbourne University Private which eventually failed. Professor Alan Gilbert was described by Davis (2002) as "the doyen of economically rationalist Vice-Chancellors" at the time (in Briggs and Davis, 2002).

And as you mentioned earlier, it was change on every front. It wasn't just change in legislative instruments, there were compliance issues, ventures overseas, student growth and diversity, non-traditional students, evening students ...

Yes, it was ... it had a big impact. It started before the Dawkins Reforms were implemented in the 1980s. We could see there were problems in the sector; that there was a drift. Surprisingly, this occurred at the time tertiary education was free. At the time we enrolled students who were not very interested and participation rates were not that high. There were also campaigns by *The Australian* and other groups that argued that universities were not efficient and not able to produce the national knowledge base that we need, so you could see change was coming. If the government was going to restructure the economy as the Hawke-Keating government did, why would they leave aside a big publicly funded sector like tertiary education which was so important to economic growth? However, we did not know what form it would take and initially thought we could handle it in our traditional ways, through the Academic Board. But by this time the Academic Board did not have any control over the resources. Increasingly, the funds were distributed from the centre, so the university started to create funding formulas based on enrolments and performance.

Most of the strategic planning I saw during this period was of two shapes: there was what you might call the 'institutional' planning during the enrolment weeks after the Higher School Certificate (HSC) results were released. We organised meetings to review the enrolments which was strategic, but it was a very ad hoc type of strategy. We would say 'right, how many people are enrolled in Health Sciences? Not enough. How many are enrolled in Engineering? Not enough. Right transfer your resources over'. It was strategic and it was important because if we didn't enrol enough students, we had to pay back millions of dollars to the government. This happened to us in the mid-1990s and we suffered accordingly. So, this was the commercial imperative and it was difficult as the institution was growing rapidly. We also needed to keep the standards up, but at the same time making sure that Science, for example, had enough students. Economics always did well but it was a very delicate balancing act. So, we started to employ statisticians, Tim Evans and others, for example who started to build a collective memory. Tim used to ask the Deans in August how many students we thought we would be able to enrol and would look at the September initial preference data and then talk to us again to ensure the projections were as accurate as possible. Then in January after the students had changed their preferences, which is pretty similar to what they do now, there would be meetings of the Deans, and everyone was either shamed or named if they didn't achieve their projections. As a result, the resources had to be shifted and this was an example of how the institution used to come together to plan because we all had a vested interest in the distribution of the resources. If you didn't enrol enough students, you didn't get the resources, so we were all in competition with each other.

The other type of strategic planning was conducted in off-campus strategy sessions that took place once or twice a year ... favourite spots were Coogee, or down near the beach at Rockdale, at Brighton-Le-Sands. But this was a bit close to campus, so we decided to go to Terrigal. Sometimes we had mini strategy sessions as well but what is interesting about the mid to late 1990s is that these strategy sessions started to change the dynamics of who was a 'significant person' at the university. In the 1980s, what you would now call professional staff had much lower status than academics. They were considered support staff, helping the academics, although they could make a career out of this, primarily in the Registrar's Office in those days.

The Registrar was the most senior non-academic position?

Yes, and the Registrar held a great deal of status because he was responsible for the welfare of the students. But when universities started to create new units like Planning and Strategy etc, these appointments gave new status and power to people in the Planning Office. As a result, the retreats became more inclusive, it was no longer just the Deans and a few members of staff from the Faculty, but increasingly people from the Centre. Probably as many as 20% from areas such as planning, marketing, and the International Office. This started to change the culture as we began to talk more about strategies and the corporate mission. Each planning retreat was themed. It might have been 'Internationalisation' or 'our research strategies' and the planning staff would produce figures to say, 'look this is what is happening ... Sydney is being well funded for medical research, but not for something else'. This started a new conversation which impacted on the way the University monitored performance. I am not saying it was good or bad; this is just what happened. So, by the 2000s university expertise and knowledge was being transformed. The Faculties still held the traditional knowledge base in terms of teaching and research, and that continued obviously, but the status of the 'God professor' – the person who represented his or her discipline and was a fountain of knowledge in that discipline - was becoming increasingly eroded and redundant in some respects because the sorts of knowledge you now needed in order to make the corporation work was different. There was also a great deal of growth occurring in the Centre, which was becoming bigger, even though at the same time there was decentralisation towards the notion of Faculty performance. For example, when I became Dean, we had a University Solicitor. This person did a very good job but the Chancellor who was legally trained said we need a Legal Counsel because we are such a complex organisation and we need expert advice about things like Enterprise Bargaining and so on and so forth. So, the Office of the General Counsel was established and continued to expand.

There are also lawyers and contract experts employed in the commercial arms of universities, such as Sydnovate, who work hand in hand with the Office of General Counsel as there are a number of complex legal issues associated with Intellectual Property and contracts etc.

Yes, and the point that I am making is that once you start thinking in a corporate way, then you need to protect the corporation in different ways ... so this is where it started. And although it didn't really have an impact on us, the academics, it meant that you needed different forms of expertise and knowledge to lead the university which you would never have thought about 20 years prior to that. So, in many ways, the university became top-heavy with experienced professional managers and academics couldn't do anything about it because we did not have that expertise.

I didn't have any training in strategic planning when I became Dean, yet I had a major issue I had to deal with. We had a program that was very small; it only had 10 staff in it – so what do you do? Somehow, I had to come to come up with an arrangement and let these people go. This is probably why you need a Legal Counsel. At the time we had people in Industrial Relations who would advise us on a case by case basis. But the point I am making is that academics were promoted on the basis of their research and teaching in their discipline, the 'God professor', and they didn't have the knowledge or expertise for dealing with this type of challenge. And, people resented it! They still do. Also, some of the change was not done well, for example the restructure of Human Resources (HR) was not done well however I won't go into the politics of that. The other reason for the off-campus strategy sessions, I think, was to try to create morale. Just as the meetings at the beginning of the year were to say to us, well we have some problems – and we need to work out how we were going to deal with them. The off-campus strategy sessions during the year served the purpose of building collegiality between the academic staff and new professional staff, although I am not sure it worked. The old divisions to some extent were still there, because people would say ... 'well you know, we are the true university people because we do the research and we do the teaching'.

They could not find a commonality of purpose?
No, there was not much commonality. The other interesting thing is that Gavin Brown said when he was appointed Vice-Chancellor that he would always have academics as Deputy Vice-Chancellors. But then he broke his own rule and appointed Bob Kotic as Deputy Vice-Chancellor. This was a bit of a shock to us and we said, 'you can appoint someone as a Finance Officer, employ them for their expertise, and pay them what you need to pay them, pay them a banker's salary if you like, but don't include them in the executive structure'. However, once the university becomes even more complex it will become increasingly difficult to manage all these specialised functions. Academics are not going to take on these roles; they are not going to do it. It is not within their area of interest or expertise.

It is interesting that the university did not recognise these types of disconnects. I suppose there always had been interdisciplinary rivalry, but I find it interesting that universities found it difficult to find a way to resolve these leadership tensions.
I think the pace of change made it more difficult. When I first came to this university in 1963 there were 12,000 students. It was a different world and our lives were fairly measured. Not necessarily harmonious but measured. Certainly, it was less stressful than things are today and the relationship between staff and students was more collegial. I am not saying things were perfect in the old days, but everything has changed. Current students are more demanding and look at university education in a much more instrumentalist way. And at the same time there are these complex

relationships between different parts of the university ... well probably because the place is so large. I think this Vice-Chancellor's view that all we have to do is tell people to get together, but I don't think this will work frankly. He has a big task in front of him but a lot of it is because we adopted a corporate model. The interviews in Marginson and Considine's study (2000)[28] suggested that some people thought these changes were inevitable. I am the last of a generation of people who built academic careers and then moved into senior executive leadership positions. This is changing. The notion that a Deputy Vice-Chancellor can be someone who has not had an academic career or even an academic interest has become more common. We then need to work out how these two parts of the university can come together and still preserve academic values.

Yes, and that leads us to one of the other questions – talking about how organisational culture plays a role in the strategic planning process? In higher education institutions, particularly universities, which are not mono-cultural, they are multi-cultural, and culture is one of the biggest change drivers and change resisters.

I think part of this process at Sydney was driven by size, but on the other hand we had the advantage of size, because it meant that although some of the changes were pushed from the centre it could be diffused because of the size and complexity and history of the university. In smaller universities, I think things were much more top down and forced because they had to be. But at Sydney, even that remnant group I mentioned earlier, the 'God professors', still tend to be mainly from the sciences and are concerned that something has gone wrong and we need to protect the role of the professor. There were many countervailing forces in terms of tradition and resistance to what was happening. To some extent it was ad hoc and somewhat pragmatic in the way it happened, but it

---

28 Marginson, S., Considine, M. (2000) *The Enterprise University: Power, Governance and Reinvention in Australia*. Cambridge University Press.

was more accentuated towards a corporate model and away from the old organisational notion of Sydney as an academic institution than it was over the last decade. If John Ward came back, he was tragically killed in a terrible train accident at Cowan in 1990, I don't think he would recognise the institution because it is so different to what it used to be.

The Hoare committee stated that by 1995 universities had all made progress towards more contemporary management practices, largely through the development of strategic planning, with a focus on improving quality however this progress was uneven throughout the sector. Do you agree with this statement?

David Hoare was on Senate at Sydney and used to say 'well, I understand your problems, but I think you need to do this'.

Did this make any sense at the time?

I am not sure as I was not involved in Senate at the time. But I think people at that stage were not quite sure of where the changes would take us. Some of them said 'well, OK we can accept some of these changes. I mean we dealt with Dawkins and the first years of amalgamations and the first periods of review so we can deal with this'. A year later the Howard Government was elected, and Howard said we could generate income from student fees, so we were able to operate more in a free market. But one of my colleagues, Ken Eltis, argued that there were actually more restrictions placed on universities during this time including a reduction in the amount of money distributed so we had to compete for the funds available. As a result, part of the new planning came out in the Budget process. I can remember a strategic planning process in the College of Humanities and Social Sciences years ago. We went away to plan but we were constrained as the main planning was taking place at the 'Centre' in the Strategic Planning Office and we had to work within those parameters. But, again, this tended to be because the budget had been devolved to the Colleges. Budget issues came first; strategic planning came second. It was only later on that we started to develop an overall planning notion. The first strategic planning process I can recall participating in was in 1994. We went away on a planning retreat where we were presented with the plan and each Faculty was required to respond to it. And from what I can remember, this by-passed the Academic Board, which would not have happed prior to that, and the information was finalised in the Planning Office. There was another process I was involved in when I was acting Deputy Vice-Chancellor that resulted in the publication of *The University of Sydney Strategic Plan 1999-2004 Ambition inspired by achievement.* However, it was highly centralised and often it would be planning in response to changing government requirements rather than a genuine attempt to engage in strategic planning. Actually, I don't think that Gavin Brown believed in strategic planning; he was not that sort of person. We needed a strategic plan – and everyone needed to know where we were going – so Gavin just went along with it.

And, that was reasonable?

Yes, it was reasonable in an institution of this size. The Faculties needed a plan so that they could refer back to it and check what they had agreed to do. When I was Deputy Vice-Chancellor we had meetings with the Vice-Chancellor Gavin Brown every Tuesday at 8 am – only about 4 or 5 people. It did not include the Registrar, but Gavin eventually let the Chief Financial Officer attend. Membership was restricted to the Deputy Vice-Chancellors and some of the Pro-Vice-Chancellors, particularly the three College Pro-Vice-Chancellors, but it was a bit chaotic. There would be an 8-point agenda which covered planning but also serious issues that needed to be discussed, such as Enterprise Bargaining. These serious issues might very well have had planning implications however the conversation was convoluted and three hours later we were still on point 2. This was an open secret. But the Vice-Chancellor would always achieve a resolution. He looked like he might have been asleep, but he was thinking through things with his eyes closed and would suddenly say 'I think we should do this … or I think we should do that'. He was certainly planning in his mind, but it was not always thought out for the rest of us.

What impact did this have on your academic life in terms of your teaching and research?

It certainly had an impact on the role of the Deans because we had to look at the Strategic Plan and then develop a plan for the Faculty to work out what we should be doing. We also had planning committees in the Faculty that would consider matters raised at the Faculty Boards. However, in reality, our lives changed from day to day, not just in teaching and research, but because of the money you were allocated, or the crises we were facing because the government was going to do this or going to do that. For the Deans most of it related to how our student enrolments were progressing – did we have enough students to pay ourselves and how were we going in research? These two issues were crucial. So, it was difficult for a Faculty to suddenly redirect themselves and say that we are going to take a new direction.

The most significant change I had to deal with when I was Dean, strategically, was when we took on Social Work. This was not in the Faculty of Education Strategic Plan when I was elected Dean in 1997; I don't think we had even thought about it but, by the end of that year we were incorporated as the Faculty of Education and Social Work. This came about partly because of a shared interest but also a crisis in Social Work itself because Arts could not fund a Chair. Without a Chair, Social Work could not train students or keep their accreditation. They were not a big group and have been a great addition to this Faculty, but the interesting thing is that this was a response to a resource problem not an intention to change the orientation of the Faculty. There were also planning implications and it changed the structure of the Faculty, but we had to make it work and reorient our programs. The amalgamation had academic foundations, it certainly did for me as my area of interest is in youth and youth policy, but it was circumstances, not strategic planning that brought it about. Another example was a program that we needed to close which was Technical and Applied Studies (TAS). We tried a number of strategies to keep TAS going, but they just didn't work. We tried enrolment strategies to attract more students, but, in the end, we had to close it as you can't have a viable program with only 35 students and 10 staff. Most of the staff took redundancy packages but it wasn't easy.

No, it is never easy getting rid of good people. The Australian Universities Quality Agency (AUQA) was established in 2000. What did you think when it was announced and AUQA teams started to audit universities in 2001 and publish the reports on the internet for everyone to see?

There was resistance in this institution about being subject to public scrutiny by people who didn't understand exactly what was going on. Some of the older professional Faculties were even more opposed than we were in Education. I remember there was some discussion about this in the College of Humanities and Social Sciences (CHASS) at that particular time however I don't recall the detail as I was not involved in any of the AUQA reviews.

The other thing about AUQA that I found interesting is that the university's own strategy documents were used to assess their quality. Some institutions had very ambitious aspirations and stretch targets, so they ran the risk of performing poorly against these outcomes, whereas other institutions were more 'strategic' in their approach and put forward targets they had already achieved which does not necessarily represent good practice.

Yes, it is interesting that you raise this. What has happened since is that the audit culture moved into research as part of the Excellence in Research Australia initiative, in which I refused to take part in 2010. What I think is occurring, is that academics are writing these things like clever research reports so that they are only judged on what they have achieved, in order to defeat the game. Whereas in the 1990s when I was on the Academic Board, we were more honest and told the auditors everything that was going on and what we were trying to do. But then again, this was not necessarily what they were looking for. They were interested in what we said we were going to do but also what we had achieved. And this is where we got caught short, because we hadn't always achieved very much because our goals were aspirational. In more recent years there has been a rewriting and reordering of that process. The interesting thing is that planning for a very long time in this university was ad hoc but the central authorities seem to be taking the view now that planning is and should be highly institutionalised and rational. For example, if this Faculty said it is going to do this, then three years later it should have done it. But this is very hard to do, particularly the way academics live their lives. So, I think it wasn't just AUQA, but the audit culture that has created this feeling of … constantly taking time away from what we really want to do. For example, in the first research audit, Research Excellence in Australia 2010 (ERA10) we were assured that all they were looking at was disciplines, not institutions. They wanted to know how good a discipline was, in say Neurological Science or Veterinary Science. And then they ranked us! They ranked the disciplines and the institutions, but the results were not reliable. For example, there was one area that was ranked very highly but we later found out that it was just one person, a Professor, in a Research Centre that had no teaching staff. Whereas other research centres had as many as ten teaching staff which meant that the institutional context was destroyed. Academics do not want to be unfairly judged on what they do or criticised in the media.

In my view it is taking something that is essentially qualitative and shaping it into quantitative metrics that do not tell the whole story. Do you think that centralised strategic planning has changed your ideas about leadership in Australian universities?

As I said before, leadership was foisted on academics depending on their academic careers in the early in 1990s and at Sydney it was the Academic Board that assumed this leadership role. In the following years this was replaced by more intervention by the governing bodies and a growing strategic role for the Vice-Chancellor and his associated academics and professional staff. But now the leadership is shifting even further to specialised notions of how to strategically manage your resources which are never sufficient. The current Vice-Chancellor is interesting because he is of a younger generation. These changes began when he was just finishing his studies and commencing his academic career. And it seems to me that what he is trying to do is still think like an academic, and then more directly, strategically. Whereas the previous Vice-Chancellor and I suspect other older academics acted more pragmatically as academics while thinking strategically. It is a bit like … I think you could look at the changes and compare them with another realm that has also changed significantly which is the role of the Minister. In the 1980s the Minister took advice from the public service, from people who had years of experience. Whereas now increasingly the Minister takes advice from a small group of advisors who have been put together for strategic purposes to help manage certain situations and think in a political way. This is occurring more within universities although there are institutional differences and dimensions in terms of size and traditions. There are also countervailing forces such as the old traditional ideas here at Sydney and the role of the Vice-Chancellor which has been transformed in ways that are much more diverse. This means that Vice-Chancellors need to think strategically about the outside world, how the university is represented in the public domain, how and who they negotiate with, and who advises them. This has been a major shift. And probably this is why we are still not sure what the current Vice-Chancellor is trying to do. His message to the people is 'this is the way I want us to communicate and we are a much larger organisation and we should do these things and do them much more efficiently' but we are not always sure of the strategic mission.

Finally, there is a new generation of people coming through the sector who did not personally experience Dawkins or the growth and all those changes and the influences on the sector ... what advice do have for them, to help them lead these great institutions?

I think the thing is that people now have to make a choice about the different academic leadership paths. I fell into a leadership role because that was how things were then. People now have to decide whether they want to follow a research path, or a teaching path, or a research and teaching path, or a path in executive leadership. Most executive leaders will be expected to have academic foundations, but not all of them. These leadership paths may also open to people earlier in their careers. The real difficulty for executive leaders will be trying to keep the connection between themselves and their colleagues, while remaining clear about the direction they are heading. In climbing the corporate ladder, you can easily lose connections with your peers unless you are very careful and maintain connections to the things you are interested in. Some people still want to pursue academic careers, whether they are interested in teaching or research, or the involvement with students, but for some reason, they continue to choose this career path over the more commercial side of life.

Universities are not what they used to be, but they still have certain features which make them different, such as the quest for knowledge and the collegial aspects of it. And my view is ... that old men should not give advice. That is my view!

CHAPTER FIVE

Emeritus Professor Ian Chubb AC FAA

Professor Ian Chubb was Chief Scientist for Australia from May 2011 to January 2016. Prior to this appointment, Professor Chubb was Vice-Chancellor of the Australian National University from 2001 to 2011; Vice-Chancellor of Flinders University of South Australia for six years and the Senior Deputy Vice-Chancellor (Provost) of Monash University for two years. He was Chair of the Commonwealth's Higher Education Council 1990 to 1994 and was, until mid-1994, Deputy Chair of the National Board of Employment, Education and Training (the Commonwealth's peak advisory body for the Employment, Education and Training portfolio).

Ian Chubb was President of the Australian Vice-Chancellors' Committee (AVCC) for 2000 and 2001, Vice-President for 1999-1998 and a member of the Board from 1996-2006. He serves, or has served, on numerous other Boards and Committees related to his university or Commonwealth responsibilities – in universities and in the public and private sectors.

In 1999 Ian Chubb was made an Officer of the Order of Australia (AO) for "service to the development of higher education policy and its implementation at state, national and international levels, as an administrator in the tertiary education sector, and to research particularly in the field of neuroscience". In 2006 he was made a Companion (AC) in the order for "service to higher education, including research and development policy in the pursuit of advancing the national interest socially, economically, culturally and environmentally, and to the facilitation of a knowledge-based global economy".

Ian Chubb's research focused on the neurosciences and was supported by the National Health and Medical Research Council, the Australian Research Grants Scheme and by various Foundations. Ian Chubb was the ACT's Australian of the Year in 2011. He has been awarded six honorary doctorates; a Centenary Medal (2001) and Thomas Hart Benton Mural Medallion by Indiana University (2011).

Tess Howes: Professor Chubb, thank you very much for agreeing to participate in this study. Could you please start this interview with a brief summary of your career focusing on the various leadership positions you held on your pathway to the role of Vice-Chancellor.

Ian Chubb: I came back to Australia from The University of Oxford as a lecturer and commenced a standard academic career. I was given various administrative roles by the then Dean but the most significant position I held during that period was Chair of the Research Committee at Flinders Medical School and subsequently, perhaps consequently, Chair of the University Research Committee. These days you would call that role Pro-Vice-Chancellor (Research). This was the first position that gave me a whole of university experience. During my time at Flinders, my team and I won a number of research grants, a sizeable amount of funding and developed a lab full of people. I suppose I wanted a different challenge, so I applied successfully for the position of Deputy Vice-Chancellor at the University of Wollongong. This led to the further development of my management skills but also skills in strategic planning because Wollongong in those days was over-enrolled, underfunded and in many ways a small institution trying to find its way in the world. It had to plan. I learned a great deal from the then Vice-Chancellor, Professor Ken McKinnon[29], who was a master at managing people and institutions but did not have a traditional academic background; he had not followed a traditional academic pathway. So, as a consequence I was very engaged with the academic side of things.

In 1990 it was time for another challenge, so I moved to Canberra to be the Chair of the Higher Education Council and soon after that became Deputy Chair of the National Board of Employment, Education and Training (NBEET). So, my full-time job was looking at the higher education sector from a strategic perspective,

---

29 Emeritus Professor Ken McKinnon AO was Vice-Chancellor, University of Wollongong, 1981-1995.

contributing to its future path as it were, as well as the rest of the education, employment and training portfolio held at the time by John Dawkins, then Peter Baldwin. This gave me the opportunity to think about the big picture rather than having just a single university focus. The Chair of NBEET changed to a part-time basis which meant that I became the resident Deputy in addition to being Chair of the Higher Education Council. I then became involved at a higher level because the Chair was part-time and lived in another city. However, in 1993 there was a Federal election on the horizon, and everyone thought that the Coalition was going to win. It was made quite clear to me by members of the Coalition that, if they did win, my job would be gone – to be generous to them. I had a very young family at the time and did not want to take the risk, so I went to Monash as Senior Deputy Vice-Chancellor. The Vice-Chancellor announced that it would be a role akin to the role of the Provost in American universities. I had been a Deputy Vice-Chancellor before at Wollongong, but Monash was different – it was a much bigger institution and dealing with a lot of challenges because it was an amalgamation of multiple and very different institutions.

When I arrived there had been no real 'merging' - they were coexisting and not necessarily easily. The Academic Board was the aggregate of it all and it was big – I recall that it had about 170 people on it – at least that's how it seemed. I was inclined to stay there, as it was one of the more interesting experiences in life, but about 18 months or so later the then Chancellor of Flinders came to see me to talk about some people who might be contenders for the Vice-Chancellor's job at Flinders.

I had an interesting role at Monash at the time and I was also part-time Chair of the HEC for two or three years until they replaced me in about 1995. Anyway, we talked through a list of names and at the end she said to me "what about you"? I said, "I am not interested, I am here now, my kids are at school and we have just settled in after our last move". However, a few months later, she rang me and told me I could have the job if I wanted it. I discovered it is a lot harder to say no to an offer like that, harder than it is to say no to an invitation to apply. So, I went to Flinders and I was there for six years and was then appointed Vice Chancellor, Australian National University (ANU). So, I have worked in four quite different types of institutions at four different stages of development and all different needs.

The ANU went from strength to strength under your leadership.

ANU was different then but also had to change – that was what Council wanted. My two immediate predecessors were very competent people, but they were both from the ANU, so I think Council made a deliberate decision to get someone from outside to make the necessary change. During this period the larger universities tended to take people who had been Vice-Chancellor somewhere else and I think that is a good strategy because nobody knows what the job is like until you've done it. The things that fazed me when I first went to Flinders did not faze me at ANU, or not as much, which meant I could focus on different things, maybe the right things, with that experience.

Are you able to recall the first time you were involved in a strategic planning exercise that produced something that we would notionally call a Strategic Plan, or a formal plan or research plan?

It would have been at Flinders, but I don't remember much about it in my first pass through that place. The first strategic planning process I can remember well was at Wollongong. By then I was a Deputy Vice Chancellor and we had to decide what we were going to be good at. We knew that we could not be good at everything. And I guess this is the motivation behind the whole concept of good strategic planning as it should help you make the choices you have to make, and more times than not you have to prioritise.

At Wollongong we developed a resourcing plan that was based around a small number of key areas of existing strength. So, in a way, we were picking winners, or we thought we were. While economists might rail at the very notion, very few of them have had to manage an institution with many different aspirations but thin resources. Not all theory makes practical sense – especially not in management and certainly not in economics. We decided to put our energy behind youth and vitality; behind groups of people who would make a difference to their fields as well as to the region. Wollongong was a very pleasant place to live and work, and I enjoyed it very much, but it was at a time in the history of the region where the university had to grow and develop for the benefit of the Illawarra. So we picked a few key areas to build a research foundation and some people would tell you that the ripples of that are still being felt at Wollongong. Some of the areas we invested in are still areas of research concentration. They have a larger number now because it is a much bigger institution and much better resourced than it was in those early days, but the same principles apply. That probably also happened at Flinders though I don't remember it as well.

Did you lead this strategic planning exercise or were you a member of a small planning committee? Was it top-down or bottom up, or collegial?

Top down? Bottom up? Well, most people who were involved would have a different view!

Of course!

I don't think senior leaders should stand back for fear of being labelled top-down people. You hold leadership positions to lead and that means that some of what you do is top-down. The real question is, how do you negotiate, discuss, debate and evolve broader agreement than if it was simply and purely top-down?

Equally, if the individual who is responsible for leadership doesn't have some ideas about where the university needs to go, then you will get nowhere. I would describe it as a collegial process driven from the top. The decisions we made were not all made by me alone but ultimately the responsibility was mine. I would walk into a room and say, "today we are going to decide on X, Y, Z" and we would stay with it until we had agreed on the outcomes. But it might not be X as I took it in – it might be a substantial component of X with some variations which comes about when you incorporate input from people who in a lot of cases know a lot more than you about some topic or other.

And you welcomed their input – you took their suggestions on board?

Yes. I don't know how people would describe me; they can worry about that themselves. But I think if they were fair, they would say that I did talk to a lot to people and that over the years I accumulated enough confidence to admit when I was wrong and seek advice when I needed it. I am not always tolerant of some ideas, that's true. For example, I do not agree with people who criticise processes and claim they were not collegial unless everyone's opinion is obvious in the outcome. This is sector wide; this is not peculiar to ANU. The first Strategic Plan I developed at ANU was initially drafted by me and a small number of colleagues, but we kept circulating it for discussion and debate. We took it to focus group meetings and did all the things that you would normally do but, no, I did not speak to every member of staff.

No, but you invited feedback. Did it change shape at all in response to the feedback?

Yes. I can't tell you exactly the extent of the change, but I don't think I could ever be accused of saying 'no' to a good idea, simply because it was somebody else's, not mine. I have spent my professional life listening to clever people and accepting the fact that there are some people in some areas who are a lot more knowledgeable than me, and I would be a fool to ignore their input. But equally I know how universities work and as I have said many times, while there may be smarter people than me in the university very few of them could do my job. The occasionally amusing thing is that so many can tell you what you should have done. It must be easy – I can't imagine how I missed this or that over all those years. But a Vice-Chancellor needs certain and particular skills and they are not all that common even in the most learned professors. You can't be a leader if nobody wants to follow you. In a university you can't issue an edict and expect the line to form behind you. You have to work hard to earn the respect and the trust you need to lead. I think that good leaders have particular characteristics wherever they are. They have vision, courage, principles and values. Consistency. They are consultative, decisive, and are listeners who hear and are committed to evidence-based planning. You can earn, you have to earn trust, but you can't demand it. Leaders in universities need those characteristics; they are not miners or people working in car companies or banks. Universities are replete with people whose professional training is based on a finely-honed capacity to critique. That's how academic work is conducted – deconstructing ideas and putting them back together in the same form or a different one. So a university leader has to be able to operate in a particular environment: a senior staff member once said to me 'Ian we all think we are self-employed… but we want a leader'. It can be tricky, it can be hard, but it can be fantastic. Shortly after I retired from ANU I was appointed Chief Scientist for Australia. It was an interesting and different experience. I don't think a day of my professional life passed without me learning something, and that includes when I was Chief Scientist. The big difference was that I met people in science or with some responsibility for science from all around the world. But the same principles applied. The best and most effective leaders met most of these characteristics, most of the time.

When you were planning in the early days at Wollongong did you engage broadly with your stakeholders? You spoke about a regional presence which is one of Wollongong's strengths. Obviously the staff and students are stakeholders, but can you remember how important the stakeholder perspective was at the time?

I would say it was significantly important. Wollongong at the time was an 'off-shoot' cut free from the University of New South Wales (UNSW) and trying to find its way. The story goes that there wasn't much left after the removalist vans left for Sydney. Although I wasn't there to see that; it set the tone. When I arrived at Wollongong it was just three or four maybe five buildings, a few coal wash car parks and staff and students who were coming out from under UNSW. Ken McKinnon[30] was a magician. He turned the University of Wollongong into a completely different sort of campus for a start, and he also transformed the culture so that it was much more confident and outgoing. The thinking at Wollongong was to ensure the university community was recognised for what it was good at. We didn't stop other people doing what they wanted but we focused our energies behind five or six sizeable groups, and then, as that built confidence, we had something of value to offer to the external stakeholders. We had to build the foundations. Not completely from scratch but we were starting from a different base from other institutions I worked at.

That is an interesting perspective. I would have thought stakeholder engagement emerged later in the evolutionary strategic planning scale, but of course, you are right, it is not a timing issue, it is a context issue. Wollongong had to grow critical mass. Whereas the ANU in the early 2000s was a powerhouse itself and it didn't necessarily need to think along these lines.

Yes, ANU was very successful whereas Wollongong was at a

---

30 Emeritus Professor Ken McKinnon was Vice-Chancellor of the University of Wollongong 1981-1994.

much earlier stage. But ANU also needed to change to adapt to the contemporary world. We knew the 'old world' was never going to be replicated and there was a risk it might not even continue. So, we implemented very substantial internal change at ANU. It was the same at Wollongong, but at ANU we were able to achieve this much more quickly, even if it will take a generation to work through.

In 1995 I read the Hoare Report and came across the following statement. "Over recent years our universities have made progress toward more contemporary management practices, largely through the development of strategic planning and a focus on improving quality. However, this progress has not been even". When I read that as a professional member of staff working in the sector at the time, I would have contested that. I looked at the Hoare Report with great interest and wondered if you agreed with this statement at the time?

I agree with the statement and it is probably not 'even' yet. At that time I was Chair of the Higher Education Council and would have said that the institutions that were the most advanced in terms of strategic planning were the former institutes like the Queensland University of Technology (QUT), The Royal Melbourne Institute of Technology (RMIT) etc. It was patchy in the sector because it depended enormously on the personality and capacity of the person at the top as well as the origins of the institution.

It was leadership dependent?

Absolutely. I mean you would go to some places and wonder how they managed to open their doors each morning. You would also go to other places and ask them what was happening, and they would know. They could tell you what they planned to do and why. This was a good lesson for me, too, because I think that in my early years at ANU I made sure that I knew a bit about everything that was happening of any significance – well once it got above a certain threshold I wanted to know about it. I didn't interfere with it necessarily, but I would have been seen as very hands on by some people. A 'feudal war lord' according to a Chancellor who came along much later and wasn't part of the change – with 'too many direct reports' – as if that were a sin when you were introducing significant change. I did know how universities actually worked. The Chair of the Higher Education Council was very much part of the whole process of change at that time. We visited many institutions each year, some of them several times, and I got a feel for how things were evolving and changing in a relatively short period. When David Hoare went to talk to people in the institutions he would surely see examples of planning and also examples that were the antithesis of strategic planning. So, yes I agree with his statement, and I was not surprised. We all take different approaches.

The last ANU Strategic Plan that I led was in 2005-2010. We made a firm resolution to put a Strategic Plan in place that was really an umbrella statement about values and what we stood for – with few numbers. That reflected our view of the particular context of the time – a scepticism about universities and their value (and values). We then let the various units of the university develop their own plans aligned with the values and objectives set out in the plan. They put the numbers in. I didn't think there was any point in me saying that ANU should have for example X% PhD students and divide them up amongst the academic units. But if we were going to say that each part of the ANU will develop its PhD programs beyond what they are now then I could say to each, "how many PhD students are you going to take"? And we would engage in a discussion, but I would leave it to them to come back to say, "this is what we think we can do". Part of my role, as I saw it, was to challenge the assumptions that underpinned their operational plans. Were the targets stretch or aspirational enough? Were they trying hard enough? Anybody can develop an objective that they know is achievable, but what we did was to set ourselves fairly sizeable, aspirational objectives within a value set that would drive the whole university.

This represents is a different approach to Strategic Planning to the one you described earlier. Was this because you were more experienced?

Yes, partly, but also because I think at the time somebody had to stand up for the value of universities. And I took a very serious view of that because I thought we were being unreasonably criticised by some politicians and some in the business community. And I didn't think that as a sector we were standing up for ourselves.

You were making a political statement, using the Strategic Plan?

Yes. We were saying that this is the ANU and this is what it stands for. We will do this for the people who work at ANU, we will do this for the students who will spend their money to be part of ANU, and we will do this for the community. This began the long, long effort to shift the culture of the ANU through an emphasis on our values and a declaration that we stood for something of value to our community.

Did you involve the government in the development of that strategic plan?

No, not at all.

As one of the primarily stakeholders it is interesting that you didn't involve the government. Perhaps, in those days, the government was a bit hostile?

Yes, they were. I spoke frequently to elected politicians as this is an important part of the role, and they were in a sense representing our stakeholders – the Australian community. It is interesting that I was often labelled by some journalists as 'being close to the Labor Party', whether that was right or wrong didn't matter but it coloured their stories. It did not matter what I was discussing, the idea that

I was close to the Labor Party seemed often to be mentioned. I had to work with both sides of government and had some amicable personal relationships with Ministers in the Howard Government as well as his opponents. Howard himself I didn't see much, but we spoke when we needed to, and never with any hostility. The Howard Government was actually the first recent government to acknowledge ANU's responsibility as the Federal Government's university which was a hard case to make. I didn't expect to be able to achieve it. I didn't expect it to be easy, but it had to be done, because we are. And John Howard came to the party.

Did that come from ANU or was it a government initiative?

No, it was our initiative, but it took a commitment from both sides. When I refused to lie down on an industrial relations issue and signed a union agreement on the national day of action, I became a hero for a day. I thought the Government might be angry, but if they were I didn't know about it. I didn't do it for political reasons, although it was obviously political. I thought I knew better than Minister Andrews[31] how to employ staff and what the right conditions for their employment at the ANU were, and I told him so.

AUQA was established by MYCHEECA in 2000 and the first audits were completed in 2001 and 2002. Were you involved in the development of that model? What did you think when AUQA was established? The sector seemed to be divided – there are those who suggested that the fitness for purpose was the only model that would work but there are others who thought that regulators should stay out of university business.

My answer to this is complicated. I began an interest in this area in the early 1990s when Peter Baldwin went to the government of the day and secured about $70 million for 'quality'. We then needed a

---

31 The Hon Kevin Andrews MP was Minister for Employment and Workplace Relations in the Howard Government who introduced the changes to industrial relations law, now known as 'WorkChoices'.

mechanism by which we could demonstrate to the government that we were not just spreading this funding thinly across the sector but were focusing on issues that mattered. The immediate argument that broke out was 'the money should go to the under performers so that they can improve'. The other side was 'reward the high performers so that they could be even better.' This was a constant refrain. We opted for 'fitness for purpose'. But what ruined it was that nobody was prepared to make a judgement about the 'purpose' of each institution. Possibly because if you took out identifying marks, you would be hard pressed to tell the differences in any case. So, it became very complicated and I guess it was partly this aspect that coloured my reaction to the issue over the next 20 years. I still maintain that Australia gets nothing by levelling its universities to some easily achievable average. Supporting quality and supporting differences should be our driving principle.

With respect to AUQA I was not a fan in its early days; it gave me ample reasons to take the view that I did. I think they measured what they could measure and then drew inferences from that. For example, the number and proportion of students who graduated. Ok, that is important but what does it actually mean in a system where each university sets its own standards and is self-accrediting? The real issue is how good the graduates were. But how do you measure that? It is hard otherwise we would all be able to do it. ANU graduates a lots of young stars and then people say "well so you should because they are all good when they come in. We take people with lower school grades and graduate them, so we add more value". The issue then is whether the output is the same. Is their degree equal to an ANU degree? AUQA didn't bother about that they just concentrated on the process: did this work, did you do that? Good, tick. Have you got this policy or that one and do staff and students know about it? Good, tick. It might not be a good policy, but just having one received a tick. I told them to leave us alone basically. I admit was a bit tetchy. I said all you should be interested in is how good we are and how do we know. How we achieve this is none of your business. And I still maintain that, but of course, I lost the argument. And I think they got better from what I saw.

I am interested in AUQA because the institutions' own strategy documents were used to measure performance. And as you mentioned earlier, some universities had stretch aspirational targets and others were more achievable. It seemed unfair from a professional point of view to measure an institutions performance against its own strategy document when many universities were not very experienced at strategic planning at the time.

Yes. You can stretch yourself and aim high or you can take an easier path. Also, I had been around a long time and I did not welcome a process driven analysis. At that level, I didn't need them to tell me what needed to be done or what should be done. I held the view that if I didn't know these important things then I should be sacked. I was paid a large amount of money to lead the university. I did believe in expert reviews – deep and meaningful ones. We had previously done a large review of the whole university, so I gave AUQA that material and eventually reached a sort of compromise.

The Reviews of ANU were very good.
Well, yes, and I believe they should have been. They sent a good team and I insisted on the inclusion of a couple of international representatives. It was a fairly tough group, but the review was good. They pointed out that we didn't know well enough, for example where our PhD graduates were going and a handful of other matters. Maybe we should have known those things. We certainly got around to it, so it was a timing issue as much as anything. I felt sorry for the AUQA group that came to the ANU and met me on the first day as I am not sure they knew what to

expect. But they were very decent, committed people who did a good job and my argument wasn't with them, it was the principle of avoiding an answer to the question – how good are you and how do you know? That is what we need to ask – not how often does your Academic Board meet and what is its membership? If you get ticks in all these boxes then there is some assumption that the quality is high and then you have this inevitable value-added argument.

The irony is that when we had the Teaching & Learning (T&L) review the then Minister introduced, the expectation was that those institutions that did not do a lot of research would do well in the T&L evaluation. It was probably designed for that purpose. But the irony was that the ANU came out on top or close to the top. And we were there on our own I think, one year, maybe two. We certainly were there one year and with a couple of others the other times. Some of the others were large institutions with high student entry criteria and large research bases - Sydney also did well in the first year with us, for example. But, when the data first came out and ANU and Sydney were 1st and 2nd they took the raw data and massaged it so that we came out 7th or 8th and it cost us around $1m. It was hard to accept. We were a big research institution and the sector has argued for ever about a teaching/research nexus and then to everybody's surprise the big research institutions came out the best in education as well.

There are some very prestigious American institutions that do very little research. But then again the US has a differentiated system.

Which is what we should have here, but we don't. Our universities have different strengths. And I have always thought we should play to the differences more than we do. And co-operate better in a policy framework that encouraged it. I still maintain that.

What role do you think culture plays – I am looking at strategic leadership and planning – how important is culture to that process?

It is very important. This was very well illustrated in the early days after Dawkins. As a general rule you could say that Colleges of Advanced Education and Institutes of Technology had people who were called directors and their role in those days was very much to direct. This was quite different from the leadership of a Vice-Chancellor of the pre-Dawkins universities which had a very different culture. Some of the strategic plans that were developed at some of those Institutes and CAEs were qualitatively quite different from the plans that were coming out of the universities in those early days, because the cultures were so different. This led to some of the patchiness that David Hoare was referring to. But there were significant differences. Some of the original universities had fairly dynamic, tough leadership and they realised that in an era when you are always going to have to choose between options and prioritise you need a sensible planning model. The factor that encouraged a much more comprehensive approach to planning is that none of us would ever get enough money to do everything we could do. We had to make choices all the time. How do you handle all that without planning?

The competitive market forces you to do more with less.

Yes, you always are. We were partially funded for everything – partially funded for teaching, partially funded for research. The more successful you were at research, for example, the more it cost you because no research grants were fully funded which meant you needed to find money from somewhere else to cover the salaries or provide the infrastructure or the services. The Group of Eight (Go8) used to say that we were the only country that put such a high price on success. We were in fact millions of dollars short.

The government has increasingly become an entrepreneurial research agent directing Australian research towards national priorities which you may or may not agree with.

That is the conflict with local strategic planning. If you make it too rigid you can easily get out of step with plans being developed in agencies that influence your activities. It would have been wonderful if the ANU could deliver 100% on its strategic plan because it had total control over everything, but it didn't. I mean if the ARC chose not to fund Atomic Physics and we had decided that Atomic Physics was a priority for the ANU who wins? There is conflict between the processes – but it is usually managed. With respect to national priorities I am a supporter. There are issues that are important to this country that we could not expect researchers in other countries to do for us. We have to make sure that we do what we need to do to look after ourselves. But I do not believe that the whole research framework should be based on priorities. There should always be adequate room for the individuals or groups who work in areas and who are functioning well in their field. Researchers like that also warrant our support.

But this is going to continue to shape universities in ways that universities might not want to be shaped?

Yes, I do think this had an influence on us and it was significant. This is one of the reasons why a real Strategic Plan for a university is one that understands the impact of the external environment. Anyone can divide one number by another and say that is our target; but if you think you have got total control achieving that target you are … unwise.

Some people would like to see increased funding in health areas, such as mental health, which has been underfunded for decades. So, it depends on who is making the funding decisions ...

That is true but that is the role of the government. They set priorities. And the best do so on advice, and after careful consideration. There are others who do it for political reasons, or to be popular. Sadly. There is always going to be a tricky balance between priorities. And cases have to be made. Once the funding priorities are determined, I believe in accountability with minimal intrusion. I believe in accountability because I think taxpayers have a right to know that we don't waste their money. They might not understand what we do; they might not even care. But they have a right to know that we are not wasting their money, and this should be achieved through government processes.

This brings us back again to the issue of leadership.

Yes, but on both sides. As I've said, I believe a leader needs to stand for something. You need to have convictions, and once you have convictions you need to have the courage to stand up for these convictions. If they are bizarre and idiosyncratic you will soon be found out. But if they are serious issues of principle your message will always be consistent and will change very little over time.

That actually leads me to the last question which is that there is a generational handover of sector leadership underway, what advice would you give to the next generation of leaders who will be tasked to lead the sector?

Stand for something. Be courageous. Be consistent. Learn. And stand up for what's important for the sector or your own part of it. It's important for Australia that they do. I think that one of the disappointing aspects of my career is that as a sector we did not always stand up for important issues firmly enough. The problem is we often didn't stay together longer than it took to leave the room. And the consequences of that were that the government could always divide us and rule us. It was very convenient for them to have the Australian Vice Chancellor's Committee (AVCC) say one thing on Tuesday and 37 things on Wednesday. I don't think this was a deliberate political strategy, but it was a definite outcome of a chronically under-funded sector. I mean this is potentially catastrophic. So, how do you get actual, real, quantitative, improvement in the sector? It is not by bringing the best down to some modest average level. What you need is a policy framework that encourages every university to aim to be better – and to be fit for its purpose. Some will be genuine international players on a big scale. Others have and should have a more regional focus. All have value and all have a role to make Australia and its place in the world better. Somehow we have got to work out a system that enables that to happen. It does mean a political process where there can be consultation, but the strategy has to be more than a rhetorical commitment to quality and excellence – and difference. It's got to be real.

And do you think TEQSA will help to achieve that?

I am sure it won't. I'm not even sure it's their role. The issue is about whether we are any good and how we know. I can't sit here and tell you that there is a single answer to that question. We need to think about how we can improve and then begin the process of achieving that systematically. I suspect that the reality is that we don't want to do that because it will show that there are large discrepancies between the levels of achievements of graduates across the sector.

And institutions?

Yes. There are real differences that are presently glossed over. At ANU we had very good links with, for example, UniSA and Charles Darwin. This was partly designed to let people study locally something for which they could get full credit if they came to ANU to complete an ANU degree. We offered things those institutions couldn't; but they did things that we didn't, so the plan offered a good two-way flow. And the system should support that.

These institutions didn't see this arrangement as 'cherry picking' their best students?

Well, not the ones we had arrangements with because they benefited as well. We sent them students in areas we didn't cover. There should be support for all of us - but that would mean pursuing a rational national approach. But, you know, the statistics don't let us share students easily.

It all comes back to the funding model?

Yes, and leadership; and these two little things keep getting in the way.

CHAPTER SIX

Professor Jim Ife

Professor of Social Work, Western Sydney University

Professor Jim Ife is a well-known and internationally respected author, teacher and conference presenter on social work, community development and human rights.

He has been active in social work education since the 1970s holding positions at the Tasmania College of Advanced Education (now part of The University of Tasmania), Curtin University, The University of Western Australia.

Jim has been involved in social work education and community activism around human rights and social justice since the 1970's and is currently Professor of Social Work at Western Sydney University.

Prior to joining Western Sydney University, Jim was Professor of Social Work and Social Policy at The University of Western Australia, and Curtin University, prior to his appointment in 2003 as the inaugural Handa Professor of Human Rights education and Head of the Centre for Human Rights Education at Curtin University.

He 'retired' in 2006 but remained active in writing and in sessional teaching at several universities, before coming out of 'retirement' to take up his current position in 2017.

Tess Howes: Professor Ife, thank you very much for agreeing to participate in this study. Could you please start this interview with a brief summary of your career as a researching and teaching academic focusing on the leadership positions you have held?

Jim Ife: I have worked in academia since the mid-1970s. I started in Hobart at the former Tasmanian College of Advanced Education and in 1980 I moved to what was then the Western Australian Institute of Technology (WAIT), now Curtin University. I was Head of the Social Work School at WAIT from 1981 to 1986 then I moved to the University of Western Australia (UWA) initially as a senior lecturer, then as Professor of Social Work from the mid-1990s. In 2001, I accepted the position of Professor of Social Work at Curtin University, and then in 2003 became Head of the Centre for Human Rights Education at Curtin, a position I held until my retirement in 2006. I then did some sessional teaching at the Australian College of Applied Psychology (ACAP), Victoria University and RMIT University. I came out of retirement in 2017 to accept the position of Professor of Social Work at Western Sydney University.

Can you remember the first time you were involved in a strategic planning process that produced a formal Strategic Plan?

No, I can't really. I have not been involved, or wanted to be involved, in strategic planning processes in universities, other than school or faculty-based planning days which were more or less compulsory and were operational rather than strategic.

Was this intentional?

Yes, more or less intentional. I recall planning retreats at WAIT in the 1980s which were very much like the operational planning retreat I attended last week at Western Sydney University; however, I would not call it strategic planning. During those early retreats at WAIT we were given a business model to work within, and I remember a CEO from a mining company being brought in to emphasise the importance of operating as an effective business. The message from Senior Management was loud and clear – we had to operate more like a business than a traditional university. This was part of the ethos of WAIT, which was very business oriented perhaps because the Director, Professor Don Watts[32], who was a very good academic, there is no question of that, but he was also an entrepreneurial person and very business focused. When I moved to UWA in 1986 I did so partly because I wanted to get away from that business orientation. I left WAIT as Head of Department accepting a position of senior lecturer at UWA. This was a conscious decision to step down in terms of seniority as I found being Head of Department quite draining. I can remember writing to Don Watts to tell him that one of the reasons I was leaving was because I was not comfortable with the corporate emphasis at WAIT and wanted to research and teach at a more traditional university.

Do you think there was any concept at that time that the entire university sector would gradually move towards the corporate model?

People were certainly talking about it in the 1980s which was well before the Dawkins Reforms. We were not naïve enough to think it would not happen; there was considerable pressure on universities to become more business-like, to become more entrepreneurial. However, UWA in 1986 was much more collegial in structure and still had a Professorial Board that made many of the important decisions.

Was it like stepping back in time to another world?

Yes, it was totally different from WAIT and from the way universities are organised today. As an example, I was not interviewed for the position, there was no selection panel. The professor's word was

---

32 Macintyre et al. describe Don Watts as 'buccaneering'. He defied the Commonwealth Tertiary Education Commission to transform the Western Australian Institute of Technology (WAIT) into Australia's first university of technology Curtin University of Technology in 1987 (2017, p.62).

law. He said, 'this is the man I want' and that was it. It was more like a community of scholars in the old traditional sense.

Were you happy to be working in a traditional, collegial university?

Not entirely as it was also very patriarchal and an 'old boys club' environment. There were a few pompous professors who liked the sound of their own voices and used to engage in quasi-scholarly debates quoting Latin at each other. Decisions were also made by way of 'gentlemen's' agreements. However, I was not employed at a senior level at UWA at the time, so I was not really part of it. I was an academic at UWA from 1986 to 2001 and, during this time, I saw the decline of the importance of the old Professorial Board. Decisions were increasingly taken by management and the Professorial Board was left to debate less important things such as whether we should have terms or semesters, or whether staff should be fined for not returning library books. They no longer had authority to make any of the key decisions. It was rebranded as an Academic Board and spent a great deal of time debating who should be on the Academic Board. Why would you want to be part of an Academic Board that spent so much of its time arguing about its own membership? This was all part of the move towards the managerial model that was occurring at the time. I was appointed as a professor at UWA in 1996 just when people were saying the days of the 'God professor' were over. But, even so, the decision-making at UWA was still quite informal and if you needed to bend the rules a bit all you needed to do was phone someone who would have a word with 'Bob', and it should be alright. This was useful at times but also indicates that UWA still operated as an old boys' network. The policies were not always formalised or even written down. I can remember wanting to know how to deal with a particular issue, so I enquired about the policy and the reply was 'well there is no policy, but the usual thing is to do is …'. Whereas if you wanted to bend the rules at Curtin you would need to write submissions to a number of committees to progress it through the various levels of management.

So, UWA it was a trust employment environment? And respectful?

Yes, it was. There was this idea that Jim knows what he is doing in Social Work so we should let him get on with it.

After you were promoted to professor at UWA were you part of any strategic planning processes?

No, I was not. I know UWA was planning but it wasn't something I had a lot to do with. Of course, the university had a Strategic Plan – but I was quite cynical about strategic planning in universities, so I did not want to be involved. I was also cynical about the prevailing neoliberal context. Shortly after I arrived at Curtin University of Technology in 2001, I had to write a submission about some course changes I wanted to make and demonstrate how these changes were aligned with the Strategic Plan. Now, I had no intention of reading the Strategic Plan, but I thought I had a very good idea of what it said. So, I wrote the submission focusing on excellence in research, internationalisation and quality teaching which were the issues all universities were focused on at the time. Interestingly, I did not experience any problems with the submission. I am also cynical about Strategic Plans as they tended to be 'motherhood statements' that everybody has to agree with.

So, you think that Australian universities would have become more commercial, more entrepreneurial, as part of a process of adaptation within a neoliberal environment? Regardless of the Dawkins Reforms?

Yes. Some institutions were already assuming this model before the Dawkins Reforms were implemented. I think that Dawkins was more of an enabler of the change and if it hadn't been Dawkins it would have been something or someone else that would have transformed the sector. Perhaps a series of policies that would have implemented the change in a more incremental way.

Business Schools were already moving in this direction.

Not only Business Schools, WAIT was organised in this way in the early to mid-1980s well before it became Curtin University. Professor Don Watts saw this as the future. And he was right – it was the future. I don't see the Dawkins Reforms themselves as being that important. They were more symptomatic of the times and similar things were happening in university systems in other countries.

The Profile meetings were underway in 2001 and strategy was supposed to be driving all the university activities.

Yes, it was. This was also when the role of the Vice-Chancellor started to change. The Vice-Chancellor became more of a manager than a researching scholar as in times past. This was slower to arrive at UWA because the Vice-Chancellor in the later 1990s, Professor Deryck Schreuder, and Deputy Vice-Chancellor, Professor Alan Robson, ran the university in a more traditional way. Deryck Schreuder was wonderful at maintaining links with industry and strengthening external engagement and Alan Robson ran the academic side of the university exceptionally well; he subsequently became Vice-Chancellor after Deryck left. Both Deryck Schreuder and Alan Robson were what you might call 'old style' Vice-Chancellors and academics were able to relate to them on those terms. Alan Robson in particular was very popular and highly regarded by the people working in the university. When I went to Curtin, Professor Lance Twomey was Vice-Chancellor. He had a long institutional history with Curtin, was also more of an old-style Vice-Chancellor and well-regarded. Alan and Lance were almost a throwback at the time, as VCs became increasingly CEOs of businesses rather than leaders of universities.

Although you elected not to participate in the planning processes – could you have been involved if you wanted to?

I am sure I could have been involved if I had wanted to, but I did not choose to get involved.

If these men were old style Vice-Chancellors can we assume that they were more collegial?

Yes, they were. But, at the same time, the structures were changing and becoming more managerial. Executive Deans were appointed, rather than elected Deans, which changed things considerably. At UWA this happened in the early-1990s and although there were still elected Faculty Deans they were no longer significant positions and made decisions about changes to courses and curriculum changes rather than key strategic initiatives. However, not all the Executive Deans were more aligned with the senior management than the faculty staff. At UWA the Executive Dean of Arts, Professor John Jory, was an 'old school' professor of Latin and as far as he was concerned, he did not know anything about Social Work and did not pretend to, so he trusted me to get on with what I was doing. He respected the old traditions and although he took on that managerial role, he tried to do it in a collegial way, in a way that respected people's expertise and autonomy. We were very lucky to have an Executive Dean like that.

Did this ease the transition for the academic community?

Yes, it did. John understood the norms of academic culture and respected these traditions. My move back to Curtin in 2001 was quite a cultural shock as Curtin and its predecessor WAIT were more commercially managed institutions with entrepreneurial leadership.

Yet, you left the collegial leadership environment at UWA to move to Curtin?

I left because I had been at UWA for 15 years. I was ready for new challenges and new horizons when Curtin made me an offer I could not refuse. The person at Curtin who persuaded me to leave UWA and accept the position of Professor of Social Work at Curtin, Tom Stannage, had been at UWA as Professor of History and was also more of a traditional academic. So, although it was a very different managerial environment, it did not really impact on me. After 18 months as Professor of Social Work I was appointed Professor of Human Rights Education leading the Centre for Human Rights Education, which was externally funded by a Japanese philanthropist. This provided an opportunity for me to establish a program in Human Rights and attract some excellent postgraduate students. I was very well supported by Tom Stannage as Executive Dean of Humanities and sheltered from the commercial cut and thrust of Curtin at the time, so I stayed in this role until I retired in 2006.

Do you think you intentionally made career decisions that kept you out of the commercial planning environment?

Yes, to some extent. This was the reason I moved from WAIT to UWA in 1986 to a less senior position as I did not want to be arguing about budgets and doing all the things that a Head of School had to do. I was frustrated in the Head of School role; it was not what I went to university to do. So, yes, most of my career was spent trying to avoid managerial responsibilities. At Curtin in the small Centre for Human Rights that was externally funded we did not have to worry about these types of responsibilities. We had some wonderful students – it was a real privilege researching and teaching in this environment. I continue to avoid managerial responsibilities where I can. For example, in my current position at Western Sydney there are two Professors of Social Work and I have not put my hand up to be Director of Academic Programs or anything like that. This is not what I want to do. I think I have been very lucky to have enjoyed the type of academic career that people used to have. It is totally different for people doing their PhDs now as there is an expectation that you have to prove yourself all the time, and that you can bring in lots of money, which has never been my strength. The imperative for funded research has devalued the importance of scholarship, which is unfortunate. I am also sceptical about some of the research that is funded and published in reports as it has very little impact. We are still working on the assumption that if we do good research then people will take notice of the report and implement the recommendations, but of course this does not happen in my field, where policy is often implemented that contradicts the research evidence, for purely political or ideological reasons.

Yes, the short-term funding horizons makes it very difficult to lead significant change. Has watching the university sector change, culturally, structurally and ideologically over the last 40 years, had any impact on your ideas of leadership?

Yes, absolutely. I am much more aware of issues of gender than I used to be. I am also much more aware of issues of culture and race than I used to be. When I think back to the beginning of my career I did not have the level of understanding I have now about these leadership dimensions. Universities have had to deal with a number of challenges as they became less elite and enrolled large numbers of students which increased the size of the institutions rapidly. Although the student body is now more representative of the overall population than it was when I was a student, this rapid growth has raised the issue of standards. Also, as students are paying fees there are high expectations that they will pass their subjects. And I am also aware that the academic standards are very white, and still reflect our colonial heritage.

Yes, our colonial 'elite' universities had multiple entry and participation barriers that made it difficult if not impossible for First Nations students, women, people with disabilities and people from different social, cultural and language backgrounds to enrol and successfully complete their programs of study. So, in a sense there are positive outcomes from the Dawkins Reforms from an access perspective.

Yes, that is true and at Western Sydney we are still educating students who are first generation university students in their families. This is a tremendous opportunity that I think the university does not quite know what to do with. I do also worry about seeing so many white academics from the inner West, North Shore or Eastern Suburbs coming out here to teach students from a range of cultural backgrounds. This results in a level of discomfort for me and has resulted in a deliberate focus on promoting diversity in the staff team.

Interesting, there is not much diversity in the executive leadership structures in universities.

No, there is not - executive leadership university structures are still largely male and largely white. Whereas, in my view, executive leadership university structures and practices should be more inclusive, and the tradition of white, male leadership needs to take a back seat.

What do you think would happen if the executive leadership in universities started to change to reflect the diversity of the university community?

It would start to validate other knowledge forms, other forms of research and forms of teaching. It would enable us to be more creative and innovative in our teaching and research. Just look at climate change, the white men who have conducted the research demonstrating the impact of climate research have not been able to drive this change. If we were able to move to a place where we were living much more in harmony with the natural world and listen to Indigenous people and people from other cultural backgrounds with a range of epistemologies, it would make a difference. We are firmly located in white, western ideas of modernity and parliaments and leadership structures around the Western world reflect this.

Despite this leadership uniformity, do you think university cultures have changed? Obviously, we can't discuss culture in terms of a single organisational cultural identity and need to acknowledge that university cultures are multi-cultural and dynamic.

Yes, I have seen significant changes in the 'traditional' university culture. We discussed changes to leadership earlier in this conversation, however the changes are also manifested in the lack of common rooms and the loss of collegial space where people can connect and converse. I also think the tolerance of the eccentric has been lost. Eccentrics were often found in universities and made important contributions to academic conversations and to the culture of the university. Today eccentrics would not be appointed to academic positions. The staffing profile of Australian universities has become much more uniform and shaped to fit a particular model which does not tolerate the eccentric, and this is a real loss to the university. Having an appropriate 'public persona' is a criterion for academic appointments today and if an individual does not fit this mould then they will not be given the job. They would not even be interviewed.

I would now like to bring the conversation back to the Dawkins Reforms and the commercialisation of the Australian university sector. You suggested earlier in this conversation that the process of commercialisation was underway before the Dawkins Reforms were implemented.

Yes, it was already underway because it was part of the broad narrative of the time.

Do you think this was primarily a funding issue? We know that resources were tight because of the fiscal circumstances in the 1980s.

Yes, but this was also a time when managerialism became the dominant narrative and was positioned as the way to get things done, to produce change. This, together with the obsession of measuring things, such as using indicators to measure performance. It was the neoliberal era more than the Dawkins Reforms that changed things – the introduction of student fees also made a significant difference. Student fees had the advantage of reducing the number of frivolous enrolments, but it changed the role of the student to that of a paying customer. As students are now paying for their university education they expect to pass which had an impact on standards. Anywhere else, if you work hard you get paid for it, but at university you have to pay for the privilege of working hard. Today, you see more of this customer focus in students, and staff are compelled to respond to it.

Yes, this can sometimes place staff in a difficult position.

The implementation of student fees, both local and international, has been a transformative influence in terms of teaching. The other thing that has changed from the pre-Dawkins era, is time. We were not as busy in the 1980s and when I used to give my social policy lectures to the social work students at UWA we would go to the cafe afterwards, have coffee and continue talking about the information in the lecture and what was going on in the discipline and in the wider world. The connections built during these informal campus conversations spilt over into campus life. No one has time to do this anymore. The classes are programmed back-to-back, I often have to attend a meeting about something, and the students have to go to work. This type of interaction doesn't happen anymore, and I think this is a big loss. When I think back to my days as a student at Sydney University I learned more from the extracurricular activities that were going on than I did from the lectures. University campuses had a vibrant culture in the 1960s - it was a wonderful time to be a university student. We held protests that tried to stop the Vietnam War, students went on the 'Freedom Ride' and, at lunchtime, you could choose between going to a meeting of a religious society, or a political group or an activist group or an academic seminar, or a debate about whether God existed or not. It was a rich campus life in the 1960s and 1970s but is very different now which is sad – campus life has become so much more commercialised and segmented. But, then again, this is also a part of the move away from elitism – because when I was a student it was only people from well-off or middle class families who could afford to attend university and we didn't need to work, or if we did, it was very part-time.

You mentioned earlier that the world environment was influenced by neoliberalism in the 1980s so it stands to reason that universities would not remain immune from these types of changes. What does this mean for people seeking a leadership pathway? Can people still enjoy a research and teaching role without assuming leadership responsibilities? If you wanted to become a vice-chancellor, how would you go about it?

Well, if you want to become vice-chancellor you need to join every committee you possibly can and participate in that side of the life of the university as much as you can.

The political side?

Yes, but I can't think of anything worse than being vice-chancellor!

One of the other contributors wondered if universities actually needed vice-chancellors, explaining that she had seen some hopeless vice-chancellors leading institutions that were actually doing quite well which made her think critically about the role itself.

Well, they are not always loved. And the other thing people hate about vice-chancellors is that they are always restructuring.

Whenever anybody wants to make their mark on a university they restructure and change the corporate image and the corporate language.

Carolyn Noble also commented on this in her chapter, suggesting that the constant restructures generated a great deal of anger and resentment among academic staff (p.239, 252).

The other thing that impacts on academic work is the move towards open-plan offices – not at this campus – but the Liverpool campus is all open plan. This is increasingly being seen as the norm and I think it is a pity because it means that people work from home a lot more. Although it is meant to increase collegiality as people are working in the same room, it actually decreases it. I understand the rationale behind this as the offices are often empty, but it makes it difficult to have conversations with colleagues and meetings with students. At the Liverpool campus you basically have to go to a coffee shop to have a meeting with a student which is not ideal. So, there is a feeling that a lot of academic rights have been constantly eroded but having said that I think this university is better to work at than many others. In our School, we still have access to good conference funding, we have teaching loads that are less than some other universities – they are manageable here which makes it possible to do the other things academics do.

Yes, these changes have transformed the working environment considerably for academics – I am a sessional academic and not always happy with the lack of certainty although flexibility has its advantages. So, in thinking more broadly across the sector – what do you think the key challenges of the sector are?

International students. I am really concerned about the money flow from international students. Can it continue? I don't know that it will. If we have a government like this one that is hostile to some parts of the world this may cause students to select another educational destination. In Social Work we have lots and lots of students enrolling to complete a qualifying masters all over Australia, but the government only has to decide that we don't have a shortage of Social Workers in Australia and turn off that tap which would have a significant impact on the discipline.

Yes, we must not forget that the government also controls the issue of the student visas – so any policy changes in that regard will also have an impact.

Yes, but I also think that depending on the international student market for resources is fraught with danger.

Yes, it is a high-risk strategy. However, the level of public funding for universities is inadequate, so universities have to attract resources from available markets. The only other option would be to increase the level of funding to our public universities which is not likely to happen given current government priorities.

Yes, this is a problem. We also can't increase student fees much more than current levels as they are already high. The lack of commitment to public education as a public good is not likely to change.

So, where to from here?

I think it is going to be a struggle for universities to survive. As long as we have governments like the one we have now that insists on a user-pay approach and continues to drive the research agenda to support what they see is in the national interest, it is going to be very hard for universities to maintain a critical, independent position. I think they are already compromised in terms of the kinds of things they do and don't do. However, there are other options for people who want to educate themselves. For example, if I wanted to become an expert in medieval history I would not have to go to university, I could learn through books and open education sources. The way universities have embraced technology has also devalued interpersonal communication in education in my view. I am sufficiently old fashioned to think that the personal interaction component, face-to-face communication in teaching, is important. I am concerned that, because of the ever-increasing budget restrictions, teaching will become more and more instrumental. It won't be long before questions are asked about why we have so many teachers in Australia teaching, for example, Introduction to Sociology. What I fear may happen is that universities will employ the best people to do this and then sell the unit of study to other institutions.

The ultimate rationalisation.

Yes, it would be a natural thing to do if funding is further restricted. This would mean you would have a small number of top academics designing courses that large numbers of low-paid tutors would deliver across the country. We are already seeing this in some institutions - we have a large reliance on sessional teachers at this institution as a result of funding cutbacks and resource pressure. This is happening all over the world; however, I think this devalues the quality of the education students will have access to. My role as a professor has largely become one of managing the sessional staff who do the teaching in the courses we have designed. My fear for research is that it will be driven more and more by market pressures and conservative government ideas of what is in the national interest, or the global interest. Continuing to de-fund fundamental research would be tragic and produce more and more instrumental research. I am also surprised at how conformist academic staff are and how they just accept what comes from management. I suppose this is because they probably fear for their jobs. I am fortunate that I can say what I want, and I do, as I am senior and have the power to speak my own mind.

You are a Social Worker – you are supposed to be radical and an advocate for others!

I wish this was the case. However, I have been to meetings where I have jumped up and down and said a few contradictory things and people have come up to me after the meetings and said, "I'm so glad you said that, I could not have said it'. Whether this perception is real or not I really can't say.

As a 'God professor' in a mass of sessional staff of course you can say what you like! Which makes me think, when all the God professors have retired, who will speak up for traditional university values?

I think that many people are only saying or doing things that will advance their careers which is disappointing, although there is still an element in the university that values dissent. Our Vice-Chancellor has, at times, indicated that he quite likes me saying controversial things and stirring the pot. There are people who know that we need robust debate and to be a bit heretical at times as this can help us to come up with new ideas.

So, losing its radical voice is another challenge for the sector?

Yes, it is a huge challenge. It is still present in some university areas, particularly in the disciplines of Humanities and Social Work. For example, when I was at Curtin, the student association held a demonstration protesting against the Minister of Education at the time – they shouted, yelled and roughed up his car, nothing terrible but the media got hold of it and made it into something much more than it was. As a result, the head of the student guild had to attend all the Faculty board meetings to explain and apologise for what happened. But when he came to the Humanities we all said, "great, good on you" and cheered him on, a response he did not get from other Faculties.

There are very few protests on university campus today – that strong radical voice of protest seems to have shifted to other communication mediums. It was school children who inspired and led the recent Climate Changes protests, not university students.

There were a lot of other people at Climate Change protests – but yes it was initiated by school children. I was at Sydney University in the 1960s and we were protesting almost every day. Being in that environment forces you to think about issues, to analyse, to share ideas with others, to learn and to think critically. It is a really important aspect of university education.

CHAPTER SEVEN

Professor V Lynn Meek, Professorial Fellow
LH Martin Institute of HE Leadership and Management

Professor V Lynn Meek was Foundation Director and is now Professorial Fellow at the LH Martin Institute of Higher Education Leadership and Management at the University of Melbourne. Having completed a PhD in the sociology of higher education at the University of Cambridge, he has more than three decades' experience researching higher education policy issues in Australia and elsewhere.

Specific research interests include governance and management, research management, diversification of higher education institutions and systems, institutional amalgamations, organisational change, and comparative study of higher education systems. He has attracted numerous competitive research grants (including the Australian Research Council), is regularly invited to address international conferences, and is frequently invited to be a guest editor of international journals with respect to special issues on particular aspects of higher education policy.

Professor Meek has published over 30 books and monographs and numerous, book chapters and scholarly articles. He has been on the editorial board of several international journals and book series and has worked with such international agencies as UNESCO and OECD. In 2012, he was appointed Editor-in-Chief of the prestigious international journal *Studies in Higher Education and* chaired several university quality reviews including the Irish Universities Quality Board's audit of Trinity College Dublin.

Tess Howes: Professor Meek, thank you very much for agreeing to participate in this study. Could you please start this interview with a brief summary of your career focusing on the various leadership positions you have held in the Australian university sector?

Lynn Meek: I grew up in Colorado, completed my degree at Drew University in New Jersey and my PhD at Cambridge in the United Kingdom. However, since 1975 I have lived and worked in Australia. One of the things which helped to shape my career over the years is that I have a range of experience of different systems of higher education. The focus of my academic work is also on comparative higher education systems, so my personal experience helped to shape my research.

I commenced my academic career in Australia in 1975 at Macquarie University and then accepted a position at the University of Melbourne Centre for the Study of Higher Education (CSHE) where I stayed for 5 years.

I was then employed as an academic at the University of New England (UNE) for 23 years before returning to the University of Melbourne as the Director of the LH Martin Institute at the beginning of 2008. In 2012 I became a Professorial fellow at the Institute and assumed the role of Editor-in-Chief of the leading international journal *Studies in Higher Education*. Most of my experience in leadership and strategic planning in Australian universities was at the UNE. My role as Director of the LH Martin Institute had a different leadership emphasis. It was not a line academic role, and although it was aligned with a Faculty it is a national institute. Therefore, the strategic leadership responsibilities were quite different. I went to the UNE as a lecturer and left as a Professor. I was promoted to Associate Professor in the 1990s and full Professor at the end of the 1990s. I was also Deputy Chair of Academic Board and Head of School on a number of occasions. In terms of my experience of strategic planning in Australian universities it would be mainly through my position with the Academic Board and working with the senior executive of the UNE as part of this role.

Can you recall the first time you were involved in a strategic planning process? When you first worked with a group that put together a formal Strategic Plan?

This is an interesting question as, in my view, universities are at very different stages of strategic planning. It is not that they all started at different points and have come up to a certain level – many of them remain very disparate in terms of their sophistication in their approach to strategic planning today. One of the things I found when I came to the University of Melbourne, although I am also not directly involved in strategic planning at Melbourne, is that the overall sophistication of management, including strategic planning and its approach to it, was light years ahead here in Melbourne than at some other Australian universities. I think the University of Melbourne is one of the best organised universities in Australia in that respect. I don't say that to position Melbourne in a positive light, however, I think it is helpful to reflect on this to think about how the different processes develop in terms of sophistication in strategic planning. When I moved to the UNE in 1985 there would have been virtually no strategic planning as we know it today. It is something that has gradually developed over the years. I completed a national study for Department of Employment, Education, Training and Youth Affairs (DEETYA) with the Evaluations and Investigations Program (EIP) with Fiona Wood[33]. Some of the questions and information in that study involved the discussion of strategic planning at the Executive Dean and Head of School level. While strategic planning increased in terms of both importance and methodological sophistication throughout this period of time, different Vice-Chancellors gave different emphases to it.

---

33 V Lynn Meek and Fiona Q. Wood, *Governance and Management in Australian Universities*, EIP, DEETYA, Canberra, 1997.

At the UNE, our Vice-Chancellor came from a teaching, learning and management background. She progressed strategic planning slowly during the 1980s however when I left in 2007 it still lacked an overall unified approach to develop a university strategic plan and sub-plans. There were some attempts to do that, but it also depended upon the approach of the Deputy Vice-Chancellors in the Research, Academic and International portfolios. In my experience, as the approaches were different, the outcomes were varied.

Can you recall when the first UNE Strategic Plan was published?

There would have been a Strategic Plan published by the Vice-Chancellor's office by the end of the 1990s if not earlier. Most of my practical involvement in strategic planning would have been in the teaching and learning theme working with the Deputy Vice-Chancellors at different times, particularly the Deputy Vice-Chancellor Academic.

The strategic plan was themed?

Yes, there would have been three plans incorporated in the overall Strategic Plan covering the areas of Teaching & Learning, International and Research.

Thinking about these early planning processes, would you describe it as authoritarian, collaborative or consultative?

I think the intention would have been to be consultative and collaborative, but the result was more authoritarian. It was a process, even when I left, that was very much top-down rather than bottom-up. There were opportunities for people to make submissions, I can recall several meetings were people were invited to express their ideas. However, in my view, the process lacked involvement and a commitment to the strategic planning process from the academic community. This might have been something peculiar to UNE as

UNE experienced a few management problems and a clash between the Vice-Chancellor and the Chancellor which impacted on all the management processes during this period of time. And, strategic planning is one of the key management processes at the university. I also felt that there was a real sort of 'us' and 'them' development between the Executive, or at least parts of the Executive, and the academic community. There was also a tendency for the executive, both in terms of strategic planning and setting performance indicators and the measurement of achieving the strategic goals, taking a much more a compliance, risk avoidance approach to the whole process, rather than trying to get everyone to pull together and work collaboratively as an academic community. I don't think that UNE was unique in this respect – these types of leadership tensions were fairly widespread throughout the sector then and now.

In relation to the tension between the academic community and the executive, where were you positioned?

In the middle! Particularly in relation to my role on the Academic Board, as I had the Executive on one hand and the academic community on the other hand pulling in different directions. The Academic Board was supposed to promote academic wellbeing and academic values, particularly in the teaching, learning and research areas of the university. However, it often found itself in a difficult position between the dictates of management and the angst of the academic community. Some of the Academic Board meetings could be a bit fiery and at times I felt manipulated by the Executive and/or at least by some of the people who occupied senior positions within the Executive, to be honest.

This says a great deal about leadership which is critical to the strategic planning process. Do you recall if the first strategic plan was high level or detailed and operational?

I don't really recall. However, the last plan at UNE that I was involved in which would have been published in 2007 before I left in 2008 was framed on a theme of 'think global, act local' which I felt was a bit convoluted. It had also been written by consultants. This was another thing that divorced the strategic plan from the rank and file academic staff - employing consultants to write the strategic plan.

If you were to lead a strategic planning process now, how would you approach it?

I would do it very differently. I would try to put mechanisms in place to develop ideas much more from the bottom up. The Executive has to take leadership responsibility for it, but part of that leadership is to get the troops truly on side and engaged in the process. You are always going to have contradictory advice and decisions to make but if you ignore the rank and file academic staff, or don't take their opinions seriously, those pockets of dissent are more likely to coalesce and become much more important than if you try to build a cohesive process. It is harder to do it that way, but I think you will produce a more enduring outcome.

I was at the UNE for 23 years. There were a lot of changes at UNE during that time including the schism between the 'coast' and the 'country' and an amalgamation and dis-amalgamation. It was quite a difficult time. I can't remember if there was a Strategic Plan to 'bed down' the amalgamation, as I wasn't in a management position at the time, so I don't recall. Grant Harman who was Pro Vice-Chancellor (Research) at the time was involved in the process and published a book on amalgamations in higher education[34]. This publication offers a very interesting perspective on the topic and would provide information on the strategic planning process at the time.

Do you think the strategic plan was well received by the stakeholders? Were the stakeholders considered?

Internally, I don't think it made much difference. In terms of external stakeholders, not much at all as far as I can remember. There would have been some nominal attempts to seek opinions from people in the local community, particularly representatives of the big industries, but I don't think there was a real, systematic attempt to involve and gather information from a broad range of stakeholders.

The students – as your primary stakeholder?

I don't think there were students on the committee. Certainly, the Strategic Plan would have taken account of student matters, such as student recruitment, looking at student load in terms of the financial basis and the recruitment of international students. But in terms of looking at students as a stakeholder? Perhaps, but I don't think it would have been a major part of the process. There were student representatives on the sub-committees, such as the Teaching and Learning Committee and Academic Board, but the quality of the input varied greatly depending on who was involved. By and large I don't think their input was very valuable, unfortunately.

The Hoare committee stated that by 1995 universities had all made progress towards more contemporary management practices, largely

---

34 Grant Harman and Rob Robertson-Cuninghame (eds). *The Network UNE Experience: reflections on the amalgamated university of New England.* Department of Administrative and Higher Education Studies University of New England, 1995.

through the development of strategic planning, with a focus on improving quality however this progress was uneven throughout the sector. Do you agree with this statement?

Yes, I think this statement is probably true. There was much more emphasis on strategic planning throughout the 1990s, for various reasons. The government was promoting it and there was an emphasis on strengthening all the management processes within higher education institutions as this was one of the primary objectives of the Dawkins White Paper. There was also a focus on entrepreneurialism. The government was trying to encourage institutions to take a more market driven approach to their operations. The institutions had to be more responsive to market conditions as at the same time, particularly from 1996 when the Howard Government was elected there was a reduction in the public financing of higher education in real terms, so we had to find new markets. Institutions had to become more entrepreneurial. There was also an emphasis on reducing the size of the governing Bodies to reflect more of a Board of Trustees. This corporate board type of approach became a growing theme in the post-Dawkins years. One of the milestones in this process was with the introduction of Executive Deans. These Deans were appointed rather than being elected from the academic community and regarded as much more a part of the Executive than elected representatives of the rank and file academic staff.

Did you also think that the leadership power shift was moving towards the centre?

Yes, definitely. One of the examples is Executive Deans and another is the diminishing power of Academic Boards, both politically and directly. From what I can remember in terms of UNE in the 1980s and early 1990s the Budget would be considered at Academic Board before it went to Council. However, during the late 1990s this step in the Budget approval process was removed completely. It was a conscious divorce from what was seen as executive responsibilities and academic responsibilities. The Executive became responsible for the Budget and the academics for teaching and research, and never the twain shall meet! But of course, what you do in teaching and research has budget and planning implications. In the decades since Dawkins the significance and certainly the power and responsibility of the Academic Board at UNE diminished. This also happened at most Australian universities.

John Dawkins, I suppose, predicted this in many ways. You could see it in the changes outlined in the changing of governance structures and size, separation of powers and strengthening of the Vice-Chancellor as CEO of the university.

Yes, I would agree that this happened by design. It began with Dawkins and the Hoare Report and there were also a number of State Reports that were pursuing the same sort of argument. Certainly, from Dawkins onwards, you saw a strengthening of management practices, including strategic planning, coming to the fore.

Do you think that strategic planning was both a driver and an enabler of that process?

Yes. However, I hope that as we become more sophisticated about this, we will realise that one of the crucial aspects of management and leadership is actually to bring the troops with you. Also, that having conflict and a type of alienation between management and the academic community is counter-productive for the institution. In our study on the nature of the academic profession[35] we asked participants if there was a collegial approach to management at

---

35 L. Goedegebuure, H. Coates, J. van der Lee & V. Meek (2009). International dimensions of the Australian academic profession. *RIHE International Seminar Reports*, No.13, 2009. See also Bentley, P., Coates, H., Dobson, I., Goedegebuure, L. & Meek, V. (2012). *Job Satisfaction Around the World.* Springer Science and Business Media, Dordrecht https://link.springer.com/book/10.1007%2F978-94-007-5434-8

your University and the answer was "No!" Is there strong top-down management? Is there friction between management and staff? And the answers were "Yes" and "Yes". This is not only in Australia although we do stand out in comparison to most of the other countries. It was similar in the United Kingdom which is not surprising because we both had to deal with similar set of policies within a few years. Actually, I think it was even worse in the UK.

The value of the United States higher education system, although it is also troubled in different ways, is that it maintained institutional differentiation and they still have strong community colleges, and various tiered institutions that are able to meet the needs of different markets.

Yes, lack of diversity is a problem for the Australian tertiary education. And we need to look at that as we now have a mass universal system in terms of participation.

I would now like to discuss the establishment of the Australian Universities Quality Agency (AUQA). I know that you were involved in the process - are you able to recall your thinking at the time?

Actually, Grant Harman and I were instrumental in setting up AUQA. We were approached by Mike Gallagher, who at that time was Head of the Higher Education division in the Department of Education Employment Training and Youth Affairs (DEETYA). He invited us to prepare a report outlining the structure of a quality assurance system. So, we prepared a report for the government and organised a symposium to consult with the higher education sector. The Minister attended the symposium and announced that AUQA was going to be established using the 9 principles we identified in the report as a framework. In our view, the 'fitness for purpose' approach was both the right approach but also the only approach that was going to be politically acceptable to the sector at the time. Quality assurance actually came to Australia later than most OECD countries.

There was an earlier exercise in the mid-1990s under Brian Wilson, Chair of the Australian Government's Committee for Quality Assurance in Higher Education and Vice-Chancellor of the University of Queensland at the time. Then it lost momentum. The Australian Vice-Chancellors Committee (AVCC) had the opportunity between 1995 and 2000 to set up their own national Quality Assurance Agency, but it didn't happen. By the end of the 1990s there was an obvious need for some form of national quality assurance agency within Australia, and the Norfolk University setting up a campus spurred things along as there was a feeling that we might have a few of these 'fly-by-night' institutions being established.

It was regulatory?

Well, we were certainly conscious that we needed to regulate nationally and catch up with what the rest of the world was doing. By adopting a 'fitness for purpose' approach we could assess the quality of the institution against what it was trying to achieve, in terms of its own stated goals. And so, it wasn't directly regulatory in that sense, because the institutions were evaluated against their own strategic priorities. The Tertiary Education Quality and Standards Agency (TEQSA) is taking an entirely different approach, based upon minimal standards across the sector. As part of this there has been a great deal of criticism of AUQA, saying that it ignored standards and overemphasised the 'fitness for purpose' approach. I think these criticisms are unfair in the sense that AUQA was set up for various political reasons that were supported by the sector at the time. So, to turn this around now is a bit unfair to AUQA.

My interest in AUQA stems from the fact that the institutions strategy documents were used to measure their 'fitness for purpose' and universities were not very good at planning strategically at that time. Do you think that is a fair criticism?

Yes, probably in the beginning, but institutions over time became more sophisticated in terms of their self-studies. In actual fact, I think that the self-study became as valuable, if not more valuable, than the actual AUQA reviews. The Reviewers also became more sophisticated in terms of asking the right questions. While AUQA didn't have any direct regulatory responsibilities certainly the publication of the reports did have a regulatory impact on the institutions. For example, AUQA helped clean up some of the offshore provisions of a few higher education institutions. So, there were areas where AUQA had an impact. I chaired a Review of a university that was doing a terrific job in teaching and in terms of the pastoral care it offered its students particularly in areas such as nursing. To then ask this institution to establish a research profile so as to be considered a university diverted effort and money away from teaching, from what they did very well. This raised questions for us all at the time, however, the university had no choice. This was something it had to do.

Perhaps, as its disciplinary strengths were in areas where the research output wasn't treated the same as other disciplines, the impact was magnified?

There is nothing wrong with that. However, there are very strong, even elite, higher education institutions in the US system that don't do any research. I find the research/teaching nexus here, particularly the way it is legislated, is a nonsense. This is an example where imposing one particular standard can actually divert institutions away from areas where what you are doing is valued as an institution. Even within a very research-intensive university, like the University of Melbourne, using a very generous criteria about what constitutes a 'research active' member of staff, such as a publication in the last 5 years, only about 50% of the staff would meet that criteria. There are pockets of active researchers and you need to make sure you protect those areas but ... and I think this is true across the board, and probably is as true of Harvard and Stanford as it is for Melbourne and even UNE ... approximately 20% of your staff produce 80% of your research results and the rest of the people are teaching. And in my opinion, they should be supported and encouraged and rewarded for being good teachers because they are never going to be good researchers. They should certainly be good scholars, read the journals and stay up to date with what is happening. But to have them actually applying for research grants and doing the research, no. It is interesting to note that the recent review of higher education provider category standards retained research has one of the defining characteristics of an Australian university.[36] In my opinion, the report missed an opportunity to promote more diversity within the Australian higher education sector.

What did you think of the AUQA Reviews? For example, when you read the UNE review did you think it was too critical, or did you think it was fair?

Most of the Reviews produced by AUQA were fair, in my opinion. There were, of course, opportunities for institutions to correct any factual errors that might be in the Report before it was published. But, by and large, I think the AUQA Reviews generated a reasonably accurate profile of the institutions at the time. And I think the AUQA Recommendations helped to marginally improve the self-study aspects of it. This was even more important than the actual review, in my opinion, but you wouldn't have the seriousness of the self-study without the external review.

---

36 Peter Coaldrake (2019). *What's in a Name: Review of the Higher Education Provider Category Standards*, Final Report. Commonwealth of Australia.

I thought the Macquarie Review in 2003 was a bit harsh and that some of the Group of Eight (Go8) institutions might have been given preferential treatment in being able to delay the audit process.

I am not too sure about that, because Ian Chubb tried it but didn't get away with it. And if Ian Chubb couldn't get away with it, then no one would! I also think that it was the right approach to keep AUQA as a small agency and to use outside experts and trained auditors to form the Review teams with AUQA providing the secretariat. I think that worked well.

I agree that the most important benefit AUQA brought to the sector was to teach institutions how to cast a critical eye on their activities and the strategic priorities they were pursuing.

Yes, but this has taken time. We had to educate the institutions on how to go about it which is another thing that feeds back into self-review and strategic planning as there is a strong connection between the two processes. I would argue that AUQA probably did an almost unrecognised job in furthering those goals.

Some of the institutions had ambitious targets that would have been difficult to achieve during the reporting period, others didn't finalise their targets until they had achieved them so that they looked good from a performance perspective. However, that did not seem to influence the Review teams as they were quite generous with institutions that had aspirational targets.

Yes. One of the other positive aspects of it was that it taught institutions that they couldn't just have motherhood statements – they had to back these claims with evidence to prove they were doing something. I also think it was helpful to get institutions to admit their failings and accept that failure isn't always a negative thing. What is important is thinking about the plans they were putting in place, if it is a significant part of their operation, to correct it. AUQA, by and large, was rigorous but sympathetic in that respect.

Yes, AUQA made sure some universities looked carefully at their risks and were taking steps to manage these risks.

This lesson still hasn't been learned by all institutions, but it played an important part in teaching institutions that there is a big difference between risk management and risk avoidance.

Do you think your experience of leading strategic planning influenced your understanding of leadership?

Well, yes, I think it has. But whether I could articulate exactly what impact it has had, is another matter. But certainly, being involved in those processes, being involved in the debates, observing them, being a key actor either from leading an AUQA Review and looking at what other universities were doing in terms of their strategic positioning, it certainly helped to shape my opinion and attitude towards leadership. The more you are directly involved in these sorts of things, the more access you have to inside information as to how things work and the impact this has had.

It is not easy for leaders to plan strategically across the university, as they are complex organisations with a range of different sub-cultures. Strategic planning puts pressure and a spotlight on university leadership – which is why I am interested in the process.

Yes, and there are very few institutions that do it well.

New leaders are appointed and assume responsibility for the next strategic planning process. They may attempt to lead it differently and be more collaborative and/or consultative or more directive and/or authoritative but the new leadership has an impact on the organisational culture and various sub-cultures so the various factions will make the process difficult.

The other thing to keep in mind is that universities may have problems in this area, but they are not unique. Many organisations also have to deal with this problem. People often make invidious comparisons between management in universities and management in the corporate sector, but if you take a good look at what has happened in the corporate sector, they haven't managed this very well either.

Universities are a unique in many ways which makes them different from the corporate sector.

More than a little bit different! They are the most complex organisation you can imagine. There is also the pure quantum. The University of Melbourne has an annual budget of more than $2 billion and is the second biggest employer in Melbourne.

As strategic planning is led from the centre, has this had any impact on the organisational dynamics in the universities you worked in?

Yes, certainly. But it depends on how it is led. Once again you have to go back to the quality of the leadership and management. Strategic planning has to be almost by definition, led or initiated by the centre. But if it goes no further than that, it is probably not going to adequately serve the institution. In my experience here at Melbourne, although I was not directly involved in the planning process I am a member of the academic community, the implementation of the Melbourne Model in a highly conservative institution had to be both initiated and led from the Centre. Because certainly individual departments and individual faculties were never going to make those changes.

It also needed very skilful leadership at the top, supported by people who knew what they were doing, knew how to structure an argument and convince the troops. Or at least, the majority of the troops, as you are never going to have complete consensus on anything, particularly within a university. But to bring something like that about is a good example of the leadership skills of

Glyn Davis.[37] As a statesman in the higher education arena, he was instrumental in implementing the model. He has strong interpersonal skills and a very powerful intellect but also had a very strong team around him too. You need to have change champions and other people who are ready to go out and work with others to help bring these things about. So, it is strong leadership, but that strong leadership has to recognise that you have got to get people to follow you, if you are going to achieve your goals.

I would say there are two criteria of success: one is the acceptance, grudgingly or otherwise from the academic community, and of course there need to be modifications to the plan over time. The other is acceptance within the wider stakeholders and your primary stakeholders are the students.

So, it is leadership dependent?

Yes, it is leadership dependent until the change becomes institutionalised. After that it does not matter as much.

Before we conclude, I would like to discuss some contemporary challenges in the Australian higher education sector. Which approach to you think will enable Australia to deliver and sustain a viable, quality, higher education system?

The Bradley report attempted to charter a new future for Australian higher education, the so-called demand driven system being only one element. The other key element was the recommendation for a national "tertiary" education sector that incorporated universities and vocational education. At the time of the release of the Bradley report, there was great optimism and enthusiasm for change across the academic sector, led by the then Commonwealth Education Minister, Julia Gillard. But that enthusiasm was soon to be

---

37 Professor Glyn Davis was Vice-Chancellor of The University of Melbourne from 2005-2018.

extinguished by national and international political events.

The Global Financial Crises that hit in late 2008 changed fundamentally the political landscape. For over a decade now at the federal level there has been a lack of any meaningful, coordinated and future oriented higher education policy. What policy that has been developed has been ad hoc and driven primarily by cost savings. The increase in subsidies to private providers proved to be a disaster. The introduction of performance-based funding has not worked elsewhere and there is no evidence that it will work in Australia. The government has done little if anything to extend the contribution that higher education can make to social and economic innovation. In order for Australia to deliver and sustain a viable, quality, higher education system, policy must be evidenced based and informed by the best higher education experts available. In my opinion, for this to happen Australia needs an independent high-level policy structure that sits between the institutions and government. What it does not need is another review of higher education.

Denise Bradley agrees with you arguing that it is now time for action (p.62). Which funding model do you think will enable us to fund a quality, comprehensive higher education system for all Australians? And if so, what would it look like (politics aside) ...

The demand driven system was probably not going to be sustainable over time. Nonetheless, it did achieve its major goals of increasing access and the proportion of Australian holding a degree while maintaining quality. The present national higher education funding environment is a shambles. Many institutions have been able to maintain their financial viability despite declining government funding, mainly through international student fees. I think the first step is to establish a quality, comprehensive, diversified "tertiary" education system (higher and vocational education) and simultaneously developed evidenced-based policy on how best to sustain such a system. This should be part and parcel of broader structural reform of Australian higher/tertiary education to establish a national, comprehensive higher education/VET sector. At the moment, being State based, the quality and effectiveness of the VET sector differs dramatically from State to State and lacks coordination and funding continuity. The series of reforms over the past decade has done little to change this. Clearly, there is strong evidence that higher education contributes significantly to the nation's economic, social and cultural welfare. Its contribution to the betterment of the individual is also considerable. Of course, more can be done, particularly in promoting an innovative environment.

So, then, in closing, what advice would you give to the next generation of individuals who will be tasked to lead the sector? There is a generation of leaders in their 40s and 50s who did not experience the Dawkins Reforms personally. They do not know what it was like to be an academic in the 70s and 80s with the freedom to teach and research independently as long as you were looking after your students.

My advice to future leaders is that they need to appreciate what makes a university different from other types of organisations which means developing an understanding of the culture and the organisational dynamics of the university. Effective leadership requires an appreciation of the culture and values of the organisation you are leading and if you do not or are not able to do this you are doomed for failure. It does not mean that if you do, you always going to be successful, either. But I think that it is almost pretty certain that if you don't do this, you won't be successful.

CHAPTER EIGHT

Emeritus Professor Peter Coaldrake AO

Emeritus Professor Peter Coaldrake AO, completed his almost fifteen-year term as Vice-Chancellor and CEO of Queensland University of Technology (QUT) in December 2017, and is a former Chair of both the peak body for Australia's Universities, Universities Australia (UA) and the governing board of the OECD higher education group (IMHE).

Professor Coaldrake is currently the Chair of both the Board of the Queensland Performing Arts Trust and Jobs Queensland. He is also an external Council member of the University of Newcastle, and Board member of the Queensland Community Foundation.

In October 2018 he was appointed by the Federal Education Minister, the Honourable Dan Tehan, to conduct a review into the Higher Education Provider Category Standards. In 2018 he also undertook two separate Reviews for the Queensland government: one dealing with the present and future Queensland public sector workforce, and the other of the future of vocational education, training and skilling in central-western Queensland, focusing on the performance of the Agricultural Colleges.

A dual Fulbright scholar, Professor Coaldrake has authored or edited a number of books and monographs including, most recently, *Raising the Stakes: Gambling with the Future of Universities* (co-authored with Dr Lawrence Stedman, UQP, 2013; 2nd ed. 2016).

He is a recipient of a 'Queensland Great' Award (2017) and the Asia Pacific Leadership Award by the Council for Advancement and Support of Education (2016).

Tess Howes: Professor Coaldrake, thank you very much for agreeing to participate in this study. Could you please start this interview with a brief summary of your career focusing on the various leadership positions you held on your pathway to Vice-Chancellor[38].

Peter Coaldrake: Before we start discussing this topic, I would like to make an initial comment. I am one of a few Vice-Chancellors who spent time outside the university system during their career. I happen to think this is one of the best things I ever did, because working with Wayne Goss leading the public sector reform initiatives after the change of government in the post Bjelke-Petersen years, gave me a great opportunity to apply my expertise in management, political science and public administration outside of the sector.

Taking time out of the university environment was very useful in terms of being able to look reflectively on it. Over subsequent years I wrote two books with Lawrence Stedman: *On the Brink: Australia's Universities Confronting Their Future (1998)* and then *Raising the Stakes: Gambling with the Future of Universities* (2013, updated in 2016). So my perspective on the higher education sector is quite well known.

In terms of my leadership pathway to the role of Vice-Chancellor, I had a university background in the city of Brisbane before I chaired the Queensland Public Sector Management Commission, established by the Goss government to review Queensland's public sector. I was then appointed Deputy Vice-Chancellor at the Queensland University of Technology (QUT) and in 2003 commenced my term as Vice-Chancellor, a role I held until I retired in 2017.

I also chaired Universities Australia between 2009 and 2011, an enlightening experience. My colleagues at Universities Australia described me as a 'diplomat', whereas anyone who knows me

---

38 This interview was conducted before Professor Coaldrake was appointed to lead the Higher Education Provider Category Standards (PCS) Review.

probably would not describe me quite that way. My task as I saw it was to get people to understand that we had much in common to deal with, for example, the establishment of a national regulator, and if we were divided, and therefore not working cohesively, the government would be able to do whatever it wanted.

Can you recall the first time you were involved in the development of a strategic plan?

I will start with our last strategic plan. The QUT Blueprint is a concise document as we thought it was important to summarise our key priorities. Strategic plans are important, for example in a place like QUT which is very ambitious but relatively young, the strategic plan sends messages as a living, breathing document. We developed the first QUT Blueprint in 2004 after I was appointed Vice-Chancellor in 2003.

Why do we keep releasing new versions? Because we met most of the targets outlined in the earlier plans, so they are continually being recalibrated. I like simple notions and our corporate colour is blue, so we called it the 'Blueprint'. At the end of the document we list the key performance indicators and report to the governing body against these key performance indicators on a regular basis. Behind all that there are a lot of statistics, but we only include the descriptors in the published document.

We gave a lot of thought to what we want to do and decided that we didn't want to become unmanageably big, so we limited our international student enrolments. This was reflected in the Blueprint. I tried to avoid exposing QUT to the risk of having too many international students as this can distort our community and raise issues around quality. We also maintained very high cut-offs both domestically and internationally and tried to limit our exposure to some markets, particularly China. We had learned that lesson earlier when we were overexposed in Singapore. We were more interested in building our research higher degrees and attracting quality international and domestic undergraduate students.

Strategic planning was a very serious process at QUT. My predecessor was incredibly strategic and clever but never had a printed plan. I am not critical of this, because he was very smart and strategic; however, I thought we needed to give the plan an articulated form. We also integrated our plan with all our activities, for example, if one were to talk to the fifty or sixty people who applied for promotion each year, they would all be able to speak about the Blueprint. Whereas in some of the older universities - and I mean old as in grand, not old as in withering - which are often highly decentralised, the first debate would be whether there was a need for a plan! We would not have that debate at QUT.

I prefer to use non-formal communication channels rather than formal ones. For example, when we started to build the first Blueprint we had more than seven hundred staff attend the planning forums to discuss ideas. My strategy has always been to throw some ideas up on the board – if people want to use them as target practice that is fine - because it meant that we had to work through these issues. For example, when we did reiterations of each Blueprint many hundreds of staff turned up to the meetings, which meant that people were engaged. My view is, if they don't participate, they can't complain later. So, if one builds the body of support the formal mechanisms look after themselves.

Would you describe the QUT Blueprint as a bottom-up plan, where many of the ideas were generated by the community? Or did you give them ideas to think about and finesse them?

When we started strategic planning it was much more top-down because people were not as familiar with the process. Whereas with Blueprint 3, six years later, the process was more organic: it may have been initiated top-down, but from the outset a great deal of discussion came percolating up from the community. People like to test the ideas and technology helps nowadays because anything one does and says is electronically available. We had a dedicated site where people could make comments and contribute to the process.

Was the site moderated?

Not in a formal, external sense. We did not need to do too much process overlaying because everyone knew what was going on. My view is that anything that is said is public information; we had held a related exercise the previous year which also helped. I also wrote to all staff in November each year because staff tend to become stressed by all the work pressures toward the end of the year. If there are problems with systems, or people have frustrations with the place, these will come to a head at the end of the year when people are tired.

So, I wrote to all staff asking them what makes them go "nutty" at the end of the year? All the replies came to my email inbox. We had four hundred and forty responses one year and I personally replied to each one. I also copied the managers who were responsible for these areas with details of the issues raised. The biggest frustrations which emerged were with the higher degree student processes and travel approvals. And you know what – it was good to hear and seek to respond to that frustration.

These are issues that are quite easy to address.

Well, relatively. So, I would say that the planning process started off as top-down, but people will not engage with it unless they think they can influence it. I had one other rule: the Strategic Plan of this university does not have my face, or my name, or the face or name of the Chancellor on it. Because as soon as one puts a message from the Vice-Chancellor on such a document, or my photo on it, or a photo of the Chancellor, it becomes my plan or his or her plan, and I wanted it to be OUR plan.

People can say that I pushed it along, but it never had my name or the name of the Chancellor on it. And a lot of Vice-Chancellors frankly do not get this. It belongs to all of us. A governing body might like to think it is theirs, but they don't write it. I have a strong view about the things one does and the things one doesn't do if one wants to engage the community and if one wants the process to work.

Do you think your approach to strategic planning now is different to the way universities were planning in the early to mid-1990s in the immediate Dawkins years?

Yes ... well, I was Vice-Chancellor from 2003 to 2017 and before that I was Deputy Vice-Chancellor. QUT completed a fairly complex amalgamation under my predecessor, Dennis Gibson[39]. He did a masterful job in that regard. QUT commenced as an institution that was focused on Brisbane and South East Queensland and its reputation was based on graduate employment outcomes. We did not forget that legacy, but now have moved a long way beyond.

We know that in order to compete with the Group of Eight (Go8) universities we must differentiate our educational product and make distinctive strategic choices. We may be able to compete strongly in a limited number of areas. If we do this we can build depth equivalent to a Go8, but we may not be as comprehensive. Still, in my view, some Go8s should not be as comprehensive as they claim to be. We also have had very significant philanthropic investment. Chuck Fenney, for example, has been a very generous supporter and helped us to fund a new science complex in partnership with the Commonwealth and State Governments.

---

39 Emeritus Professor R Dennis Gibson AO was Director then Vice-Chancellor of the Queensland University of Technology from 1982 to 2003.

You have described a very different form of strategic planning in the early post-Dawkins years to some of the other contributors in this edited collection and my earlier research which is interesting.

The Hoare committee stated that by 1995 universities had all made progress towards more contemporary management practices, largely through the development of strategic planning, with a focus on improving quality however this progress was uneven throughout the sector. Do you agree with this statement?

In the 1990s budgeting and financial management started to modernise. Quality assurance units also emerged; whether or not they had an impact is more contestable. However, universities were moving away from being parochial collegial institutions to understanding that they were complex organisations and needed to be relevant.

I think the Hoare statement may have been gentle and generous, but it recognised that things had happened since the 1960s and 1970s, and progress might have been uneven across the sector. As far as I can recall no university in the country much liked the Hoare report. I could hardly get our own governing body to take it seriously and I was the Deputy Vice-Chancellor. The Vice-Chancellor was very supportive but himself probably not entirely convinced. The notion of modern management was heavily resisted by many in the university sector. It was not until Simon Crean[40] became Minister that some acid was put into the equation. This was done by attaching some conditions to indexation.

I actually welcomed these changes as I did not think that it was a problem for universities to be required to demonstrate modern management practices and be expected to achieve their Key Performance Indicators (KPIs) in order to receive public money. Some people thought this was an intrusion into our independence,

---

40 Simon Crean was Minister for Education, Employment and Workplace Relations in the Gillard Labor Government in 2010. The ALP Government led by Prime Minster Julia Gillard AC held office from June 2010 to June 2013.

but that was a rubbish proposition. Rather, the change was an intrusion into our convenience. There is a world of difference between academic convenience and academic independence.

Universities have never been independent in a real sense.
Well, independence of thought is one thing but having to attach conditions to your money is not an outrageous proposition.

I also wanted to talk about AUQA and its establishment. Were you involved in its establishment?
Not really. I was more involved in TEQSA, which replaced AUQA. I did not take much notice of the mechanics of AUQA. It came in a blaze of glory and did a round of institutional visits and audits. It then became, in most people's minds, a bit so-so in the second round. And the interest shifted towards thematic review, for example, how each university was performing in, say, its international strategies or how they were achieving in particular areas. After a while the institutional-specific reviews had become a bit 'same old, same old'.

We were AUQA'ed again in 2012. We had a mock audit early that year and prepared a portfolio for it. It was fairly rough and ready, compared to the finished document prepared for the actual audit that October, and we had a good story to tell.

I took the view that QUT would receive a strong AUQA result because we were performing well. But would I say for a moment that we were performing well in every area? Of course I wouldn't. But, we were relaxed about that. If the overall story is good, then in my view, such audits are about listening to what the auditors had to say and think about what we could learn from the exercise. Some Vice-Chancellors took the view that the way one should prepare for an AUQA audit was to close the shop down for eighteen months, man the barricades in readiness, and when the auditors arrive, don't let them in, keep the infidels at the gates.

My view was that you prepare properly and professionally, but you also need to continue business as usual. A small number of people will be responsible for writing the portfolio and they will consult with a large number of people about the accuracy and adequacy of it.

One should obviously think about the line of questioning but don't over-rehearse; bring some spontaneity to the process because otherwise the panel members will pick it. You know when something is a charade, or when something rings true, so my view was to ensure that there is spontaneity around the process of audit. This requires some maturity on the part of the organisation.

I was actually very relaxed about criticism. Every three years we surveyed all our staff and I was very involved in this activity as Vice-Chancellor. People become very cynical about these things, but over the years we sought to develop our capacity for self-criticism. We operated a Climate Change survey instrument with the process run by an external organisation; that is, it was moderated externally. The university could not edit it or do anything to tangle itself up with it. In one of the last surveys we did when I was Vice-Chancellor, more than eighty per cent of the staff who responded indicated they were very proud to work at QUT. The fact that they would give management a belting over a particular issue is fine.

There are two measures that are important from my perspective: the first is the response rate, because if people are not prepared to engage – well, that is a serious problem. And if they are prepared to engage, but give the place a belting, well it may not be as nice as telling you they like everything, but at least they are engaged and there is a chance of getting through to them.

I think that conducting the survey suggests to staff that you are interested in them; you want to know what they think and are keen to have a personal conversation with them.

In the early years of my vice-chancellorship we used a homegrown survey instrument. But as climate surveys became the norm across the university sector we transitioned to one which was being used by many other institutions. This had to be the case if we were going to be able to benchmark our performance nationally.

It was pleasing to see that, over the years, our level of staff active engagement in these surveys increased to above eighty per cent, very high by national standards, and stayed at that level. I would like to think that this level of engagement occurred because staff did come to believe that we would listen to their criticisms and try to respond. The sessional academic staff were the fiercest group of critics, but they had every reason to have their say: much of the undergraduate teaching in the place fell to them, their workloads were heavy and the support available to them, especially in the earlier years, was meagre. We really did try to respond.

Who do you see as your major stakeholders? The students, staff, industry, the professions or the government? Are the stakeholder priorities reflected in the Blueprint?

Yes, all the stakeholder priorities are reflected in the Blueprint. It was deliberately formatted to achieve this objective. For the internal staff and the student union the key component was the key priorities on the first two pages. For example, in the earlier versions of the Blueprint, the context was described in one page; Blueprint key priorities two pages placed together; two pages were devoted to research and innovation; two pages to culture and sustainability and two pages on student learning and teaching. Meanwhile, the vision, values, and the Key Performance Indicators (KPIs) were set out on the final page. And for those who only wanted a quick dip, we provided a separate snapshot of the key elements: student numbers and completions, budget, and major achievements.

All our staff know about the Blueprint and it reflects some interesting things about QUT that have a lot to do with the culture. A place like University of Sydney has had huge endowments almost from the start, but at QUT we developed a philosophy 'don't brag until you are sure'. For example, in 2011 we attracted $28m in philanthropic donations; the previous year it had been $19m. Most Go8s didn't attract anything like that at the time. But we didn't boast about it. Over the last five years of my time at QUT we probably attracted close to $100m in philanthropic donations.

Of particular interest, we had a very large number of staff contributing by voluntary payroll deductions every fortnight to fund student scholarships. We had 500 staff givers by 2015, and that figure reached 700 by 2017. For me, a lot of this was about building a citizen community, and that was of course linked to issues of pride and ownership. It was almost a spiritual matter, a little corny I know, one involving the capturing of the hearts and minds.

This involves thinking about the difference between leadership and management. Leadership is often seen to be about the guy or girl at the front with a vision of a new horizon and so on, whereas management is often seen as the tawdry, operational, boring dimension. But I actually see the position very differently. Leadership is important to set and clarify the direction, but it is management that gets us to the destination. A lot of people in universities are accomplished talkers, but only some of them prove capable of managing people or systems.

I really believe, and you can quote me on this - leadership is not just about fancy talking. It is about getting to the destination, and the job done.

I agree with your take on leadership and management and think that separating these two concepts is sometimes counterproductive. The most effective leaders I have worked with are excellent managers. Leadership and management merge, come together, and separate. They have distinct and common purposes but if they are in synergy with each other, then the leadership is very effective, and the organisation is doubly strong.

The other thing that is very important is collaboration; this is critical in a competitive environment. In Brisbane we had a number of strategic collaborations with the University of Queensland (UQ) and Griffith University. For example, we had a collaborative teaching program with UQ in which UQ taught QUT students in Japanese and French on QUT campuses in the QUT semester. This meant that our students could study these languages and it made the UQ language departments more viable.

We were also in partnership with UQ on a $340 million building. This is a deliberate strategy … I mean we fight like crazy for the best undergraduate students, but we collaborate significantly as well. And I think this brings a meta-dimension to strategic planning. People tend to think of it in terms of our isolated institutions – whereas people should think about the positioning of Brisbane, Queensland and Sydney in terms of international reputation. The only way we can beat Sydney and Melbourne, for anything nationally, is to collaborate.

I am often surprised that, for example, the University of Sydney and the University of New South Wales did not collaborate more – a collaboration like that would be very powerful. Obviously, I believe that strategic collaborations are a very important part of strategic planning.

This is a very interesting point and something to think about. Some of the best Strategic Plans demonstrate productive internal collaboration. For example, a well-crafted plan reflects strategic input from the Deputy Vice-Chancellors or Pro-Vice-Chancellors who have worked very well with their teams to bring together a collaborative plan.

Yes, strategic planning can take many forms. For example, I think the Melbourne Model was a very courageous model and I admire its innovative qualities. But, whether it would work was a very different matter. And obviously it was nuanced as it was rolled out. A plan needs to be tested by the realities of its context. Did the Professors at the Parkville campus support the plan? Could they be persuaded to support it? What would the implications be? This implies that any plan must be developed and executed in its own context.

One can write a fancy plan for Sydney or for QUT or Melbourne, but it would be totally meaningless if it did not understand its own context. For example, in some older universities the Faculties more resembled medieval fiefdoms and seemed almost antagonistic towards the institution which paid their wages. There is very little pull, it is all push, push, against the centre. So, the first thing one would need to do in this type of context when seeking to lead strategically would be to persuade one's own colleagues to come along on the journey.

We mobilised our first Strategic Plan when we were leading a major invigoration of our ranks. There were a lot of people at QUT, and the Queensland Institute of Technology (QIT) before it, who had been there for many years. We didn't want to push these people out, but a lot of those folk had been in place for 30 years plus and were ready to go. We were trying to prepare the institution for the new challenges, so we thanked those people sincerely for their contributions and allowed them to leave with dignity and with a smile on their faces financially. Then, we started working on reinvigorating the ranks. In 2011 for example, we hired seventy-five early career academics and ran this program for some years.

That is a significant investment. Do you think these ECRs will stay at QUT?

We didn't want our new early career academics to stay forever, but they do tend to stay. If we are a good employer, and we are a dynamic place to work, and if there is a good sense of community then people won't leave prematurely. QUT, historically, has not lost staff. In fact, we wanted to increase movement. However, we brought in a lot of good people and lost very few of them. Our objective was to bring in a total of 500 Early Career Researchers (ECRs) by 2015. This was a significant investment in people.

We were the first university in Australia to invest this much in a centralised ECR-type program. The difficulty was for this not to be seen as pushing out the existing academic staff, so it had to be managed carefully. This is what had to happen to reinvigorate the place and achieve demographic change. And, most people want to think about leaving when they are about 65. If someone is a fantastic professor they might stay on longer and that is fine, but most people are ready to go by the time they are in their mid-60s. So, in terms of the persuasion process, one needs to understand who needs to be persuaded to leave.

This relies on knowing your community and being engaged with them.

Yes, one needs to know one's community. QUT is a very different organisation from some of the Go8s. For example, everyone at QUT in my years as Vice-Chancellor called me by my first name. I could also just pick up the phone and call anyone. Yes, it is important you know your constituency, and more importantly, the dynamics of the constituency, particularly if the ranks are being replenished.

This significant investment in ECRs should help you to excel in your Australian Research Council Discovery results – do you track this against the ECR performance?

Yes, we looked carefully at the funding results and also tracked performance in Excellence in Research Australia (ERA). Although there were lots of problems with ERA, as with any such methodology, we performed well. We primarily focused on the number of disciplines, or sub-disciplines in which we were in the top four or five. For example, we invested a quarter of a billion dollars in science, technology and engineering facilities. We were in the 'top five' Australian universities in applied maths and statistics and very good in physical chemistry.

You need to know where you are strong, so that you can build on those areas. The rest can rise later but you must have those anchors. We took a bit of a risk that a lot of our research was so called crossdisciplinary or interdisciplinary. This meant going through a phase where traditionalists might not think such endeavour was serious or valuable. So it had to be deeply rooted research linking into deeply rooted disciplines, not shallow activity. I was confident the strategy would pay off. But we needed a team approach from the relevant disciplines.

One last question, what advice would you have for the next generation of individuals who will be tasked to lead this sector?

Two bits of advice. A period outside university, outside the university sector, is very good for the head, for widening perspective, so collect a bit of lateral experience, as it were; and second, understand that none of these things is achieved by the guy or girl at the top without a big team effort. Team is everything. And don't personalise or 'egotise' one's leadership. That is one of our core messages in the Blueprint – people might see a strong leader or whatever but never make the mistake of believing your own excreta!

CHAPTER NINE

Professor Simon Marginson

Professor of Higher Education, University of Oxford

Simon Marginson is Professor of Higher Education at the University of Oxford. He formerly worked at Monash and Melbourne universities in Australia and at UCL in London.

He is also Director of the ESRC Centre for Global Higher Education, and Editor-in-Chief of *Higher Education*. CGHE is a research partnership of five UK and eight international universities with £6.5 million in funding for 16 projects on global, national and local aspects of higher education.

Simon focuses on global and international aspects of higher education, higher education systems, and higher education and social inequality. He was the Clark Kerr Lecturer on Higher Education at the University of California in 2014. He is a Fellow of the Academy of Social Sciences in the UK, Fellow of the Society for Research into Higher Education, and a member of Academia Europaea.

His most recent books are *High Participation Systems of Higher Education* (edited with Brendan Cantwell and Anna Smolentseva, Oxford University Press, October 2018), and *Changing Higher Education for a Changing World* (edited with Claire Callender and William Locke, Bloomsbury 2020).

Tess Howes: Professor Marginson, thank you very much for agreeing to participate in this study. Could you please start this interview with a brief summary of your career focusing on the various leadership positions you held before you were appointed Professor of Higher Education at the University of Oxford?

Simon Marginson: I commenced my career in a series of professional research and advocacy positions. In 1991 I was seconded to the Centre of Study of Higher Education (CSHE) at the University of Melbourne initially on a one-year contract as an expert on Industrial Relations. My contract was renewed annually throughout the 1990s, we used to call it extendable tenure. Although I was promoted from Senior Lecturer to Associate Professor and Reader in 1998, I was still on these one-year employment contracts. My focus was on research and consultancy, research in particular. I had also attracted Australian Research Council (ARC) funding as well as government project funding and was doing a lot of academic writing. I then graduated with a PhD that won two awards, published three books from the thesis and was offered Chairs at three institutions including Monash which I accepted, as it gave me a 5-year contract. So, in 1998 I commenced a conventional teaching and research position in the Faculty of Education at Monash University.

A year later I was made Director of the Monash Centre for Research and International Education, and a year after that I was appointed Professor in a Personal Chair after being nominated by the Vice-Chancellor. I stayed at Monash until 2006 as a Professor of Education and Director of the Monash Centre for Research and International Education and was also Editor of the *Australian Journal of Education* (AJE) until 2005. In 2006 I was appointed Chair, Higher Education, at the University of Melbourne then in 2013 I moved to the UK as Professor of International Higher Education at the University College London Institute of Education. In 2018 I was appointed to my current role, Professor of Higher Education in the Department of Education and Linacre College at the University of Oxford. So, I have really been a research professor since 2006 on the understanding that I publish frequently, which I do. I was Associate Dean, Research, at Monash for two years which is the only time I held an academic leadership position. It was not a high-level position, but it did involve leadership responsibilities and it was time consuming as I had to attend a lot of meetings. I actually avoided academic leadership positions at every turn so that I can continue to be a research professor.

As a result, I have not contributed much to the collegial side of academic governance. But then again, I don't think universities are run on a collegial basis, they are run by managers who work to budgets. I work to my managers and my budgets and am very careful about those relationships because they are important. So, my experience of collegiality comes from my research and teaching, not from being actively involved in university governance.

Have you been actively involved in any strategic planning processes?
No, not really, but I know about strategic planning because I have studied universities and understand how they work. University governance and management is one of my sub-fields although, interestingly, I have never actually been involved in a strategic planning process. I was involved in some planning processes at the faculty level when I was a member of the University Research Committee, but I don't think we ever dignified it by calling it a Strategic Plan or a Research Plan of the university. So, no, I have never been involved in anything that developed that kind of iconic plan, a plan that becomes an icon as I did not look for responsibilities like that although I am very active in a public sense. I put my energies into public intervention rather than interventions in internal university governance which in my experience don't achieve much. Basically, if you want to implement change in universities, then being in a leadership position is indispensable. You can't achieve change by being a participant on a committee,

or agitating from below, or being a unionist, which I was before I became an academic – I used to work for the tertiary education union. Change is driven by key individuals, in key positions, using consensual processes that bring people along with them. You can't lead a university change process by riding over the top of people, unless it is the kind of situation where the resource position is so dire or some other major change is taking place, like a merger, which allows things to be pushed through more easily. Most of the time, you just need consent, active consent, and participant energy to implement change.

Because I never made management my priority, I haven't been involved, seriously, in university administration. My energies have been focused on studying universities, analysing the exercise of managerial responsibilities, publishing widely and initiating public debates to stimulate social change or awareness at that level. Leading change is a matter of timing as change is possible sometimes but not at other times, so you really need to be able to 'read the play' to know when the time is right so that you do not miss an opportunity. This is something Glyn Davis[41] taught me. When I was at the University of Melbourne, we frequently discussed various issues relating to leadership and strategy. Of course, he did not consult me directly on what he was doing, but we talked things over and discussed what was going on at the time.

You would be an excellent sounding board.

Glyn Davis was an excellent sounding board for my work. He read most of it but let me say that it was not an equal relationship because he was far more important than I was! He worked quite closely with a number of people and is certainly the best university Vice-Chancellor I have ever worked with or known. I have met a lot of good Vice-Chancellors and some very good Vice-Chancellors, but

---

41 Professor Glyn Davis, AC, was Vice-Chancellor of the University of Melbourne from 2005-2018.

he is the best. He knows how to take the initiative at a time when it is most likely to be successful and has a knack for reading 'the play' well enough to know when to intervene as timing is critical. Timing is everything. Especially when you are dealing with the government. So, when an opportunity becomes available you must take it as soon as you can, partly because it is a very competitive environment and also because the opportunity can disappear quickly. These windows of opportunity are often very short term. This is part of the nature of life; the ebb and flow of events that make certain things possible at certain times only as a lot of change is not directed. It is just the spontaneous endogenous interactions of different forces and different people which produces results that no one has necessarily forecast or planned. That is the nature of life too; a lot of what happens just accumulates and then has knock on effects and you don't always know what they are going to be. Some of these things are orchestrated but many are not. It is a bit of a mix; it is neither in total flux, nor is it all predestined or controlled.

So, some significant change could be an accident of timing?
Yes, but it can also be engineered. Universities are complex environments that can be manipulated but also have their own endogenous logic and things happen despite the wishes of all the participants, for good or bad. For example, Glyn Davis' job was to transform the curriculum structure and the degree framework at the University of Melbourne, and he achieved that. He knew that this type of change takes 10 to 15 years to institutionalise and in my view the Melbourne Model was implemented successfully because Glyn Davis stayed at the University of Melbourne to push it through until the end.

The Melbourne Model was one of the biggest changes in the sector at the time.
Yes, it was a substantial shift in the nature of universities. This

should not be understated; it was a significant mission shift. Basically, it was the adoption of a North American model. The great American research universities offer a liberal first degree, broadly speaking, with some exceptions, followed by the graduate professional schools and graduate discipline schools. This is what Glyn Davis established at Melbourne. It was not a typical Australian model at the time although the University of Western Australia (UWA) has since adopted some elements with variations as part of its curriculum restructure.

Yes, Alan Robson, former Vice-Chancellor of the UWA mentioned this (p.80). The University of Melbourne is now accustomed to the Melbourne Model – it has been institutionalised?

The community has always regarded the University of Melbourne degree as the most desirable degree in the State of Victoria. The status of the Melbourne degree is well ahead of Monash, which is the next best, in my view. Whatever form the degree takes is less important than its status, particularly when you consider market demand. There are always people who are going to be inconvenienced by the fact that they can no longer do a first degree at Melbourne, for example, in law, engineering or medicine. Some of these students will study elsewhere, but there isn't enough of them to have an impact on Melbourne's power of attraction for the top students in the State or to lower the entry scores for these degrees significantly.

As you have not personally been involved in strategic planning, could you discuss what you think about strategic planning in Australian universities?

There was a high point of strategic planning which has passed, and most of this work is now being done through more notional or nominal Key Performance Indicators (KPIs) or targets followed by a Quality Assurance (QA) evaluation, the *post hoc* end of things.

It has been more of a 'nudge, nudge' steering going on with key managers using evaluations and follow up processes as a control system to pull everyone into line and look at where things went wrong so they can do it differently next time. This is not the same as strategic planning which should be more explicit and detailed about what it wants to achieve. One variable lies in the degree to which it alters as it goes, and the other variable is the degree to which it is consultative initially and also consultative as it progresses – these are the key variables. In my experience, there has been a wide range of approaches to strategic planning in Australian universities, with different levels of density in terms of detail and different kinds and rhythms of consultation. Some planning has a period of consultation at the start, some is entirely consultation driven, some planning involves continuing consultation as the plan is being implemented, and some doesn't have any consultation – there is a great deal of variation. One of the things that characterises Strategic Planning, in a sense of a capital S and capital P, is that the process of *post hoc* evaluation is not well developed. Perhaps this reflects a weakness in the concept of strategic planning.

Should it be authoritarian, collaborative, or consultative? Well, there is a great deal of variation on this. The odd thing about management and leadership, especially leadership, is that different approaches can be successful. You can have a charismatic leader, a visionary, the first among equals, the extensive consulter, but also the person who goes off on their own and then comes up with a great idea and brings everyone along with them. Some people see their job as getting everyone on side, keeping them all motivated, protecting them and making them feel included and valued. Richard Larkins[42] at Monash was that kind of Vice-Chancellor and he was very good. Some of his predecessors were focused more on leading strategic change and were very good at that approach. Successful leadership can take many different forms. Successful strategic planning can

---

42 Professor Richard Larkins AC was Vice-Chancellor and President of Monash University 2003-2009.

vary a lot in terms of the degree of expertise required to develop a brilliant set of ideas which can then be sold successfully, because they are eminently good, so that people buy in despite the fact they weren't consulted. I don't think there is a hard and fast rule about the best way to lead strategic planning.

I agree in terms of strategic planning, so, what might a successful Strategic Plan look like?

Why do some of them work? Well, partly it is a question of timing as I said before, when the time is right for a certain kind of thing then it can happen. And if the time is not right, it is hard to make it work, even if the plan is very good. It is also a question of … and this is most important … of the plan reflecting a good reading of the trends as the planning has to reflect an understanding of the context. A SWOT (strengths, weaknesses, opportunities and threats) analysis approach is almost a caricature of the kind of detail and depth you need in terms of being able to really understand the context. Not only the 'what is' and 'where is it going' but also an understanding of what is possible at that particular time. The other variable is flexibility. The capacity to respond to changing events and the willingness to feed this information back into the plan to monitor unintended consequences, either positive or negative. You need to be willing to shift a bit, read the context and shift again quickly and effectively. You also need to know what those shifts mean to the various stakeholders, so you have to read the politics as well as the environment and manage the way the politics reads the environment. These are the two main things. A good strategic plan is more than a plan; it needs a good leader and manager of the plan. It also needs someone who sits in between the constituencies affected by the plan and the larger environment who controls to a degree how the environment is understood, picks up signals from the constituents and feeds that information back into the strategic planning process.

I agree, strategic planning is a very complex task. I have worked with people who view the finance team as the strategists and frame the strategy primarily around the budget. In my view, and I seem to hold a minority view on this, if you plan within the available resources framework you run the risk of locking yourself into continuing to do what you are doing today with, perhaps, a few minor exceptions. If you use this approach then the planning can become primarily operational and is no longer strategic.

Some of the planning has to be driven by the budget and the virtue of that is that you are able to lock in the plan and make it almost as if it is a political economy at an institutional level. Money is a sign of status and power as well as a direct resource driver. The budget process is the core process in the institution however if you base your planning on that, it rigidifies the plan and creates inflexibility. It can also limit the ability to imagine things that are really different. But on the other hand, it implements the plan strongly and makes it unstoppable to a certain degree. The conjunction of planning and budget results in a very powerful instrument. Strategic Plans will always need a financial aspect, a budget that is part of the plan and connected and consistent with it. But if you ground the whole thing in the budget process, including the consultation over the plan it locks everyone in, but it won't be as flexible, or as visionary or as interesting as it could be. And maybe people will not buy in with the same level of enthusiasm as it can be very restricting. I also think that although we are primarily political economy driven, we also do things through an older symbolic universe of values and commitments to which we attach emotionally in a way that we don't to parcels of money.

Yes, and at times it is hard to reconcile these two things.

Sydney University is perhaps the place where these two things are most obviously separated in my view. There is a kind of romantic culture in the sector. I am not saying this as a criticism, because there are a lot of fine, talented, people working in universities and this attachment keeps them in the sector. For the majority of general staff as well as the academic staff this raises questions around the mission and values that are even more important than the prestige of the institution and are really strong motivators. Most people working in universities are bright, but a lot of them are really bright, and most of those could earn more money outside the university system but they continue to be connected to universities as they have a grounding in a much larger set of human values and this holds it all together in lots of ways. The planning process needs to tap into these human values to be most effective at an affective level.

The Hoare Report argued in 1995 that universities were all planning fairly well and reforming their management practices, which I originally contested. What did you think of the Hoare Report?

I think that Hoare came in on the mainstream trends, reflected those trends, spoke to those trends and pushed them along. It wasn't a process from left field; it was not a departure from what was actually happening. One of the shifts that occurred was towards more reliance on quality assurance, as I said previously on post hoc evaluation rather than detailed planning, but there was certainly no less utilisation of comprehensive management. There is an even greater emphasis on comprehensive management now than there was in the mid-1990s together with an increasing emphasis on sophisticated quality assurance initially through the Australian self-evaluation regimes. There has been a shift towards standards and external evaluation with a stronger focus on the measurement of activity than there was previously because of the limitations of self-evaluation. In the mid-1990s when Hoare said there was a focus on the "development of strategic planning and focus on improving quality" whereas now you would say that quality is more important.

I am also looking at the establishment of the Australian Universities Quality Agency (AUQA) in 2000 as the methodology was to assess quality against the institution's strategic plans, when many institutions were not experienced in strategic planning at the time.

I think that the two things: evaluating quality against institutions plans and allowing institutions to essentially run their own self-evaluation process are both flawed. As parts of a larger process they could be fine but by themselves as a gold standard for determining quality assurance in the sector they don't work. Both have the capacity for local variability and for self-marketing to take over from serious evaluation and a warts and all type of assessment.

Some of the plans had stretch targets that the university would not have been able to achieve for a long time, they had a long-term strategic horizon, which is actually what strategically planning should be about ...

A lot of quality assurance seems to be about demonstrating that you are doing a great job, and that contaminated the objectivity of the process. Once you make it an internal process that makes it worse, because there is no opportunity to conduct a stand-alone, arms-length, evaluation. It can be really limited. The five-year reviews were essentially reviewing the self-assessments, they were not reviewing standards, or quality, in an objective, external sense. So AUQA I think was stymied from the start by its adaptation to the self-regulation model. Unfortunately, people soon learned that modern management tasks could be fulfilled by good marketing, both internal and external, as much by actual processes which were both modernising and improving. AUQA fitted in with that because of its focus on self-evaluation as the main mode of quality assessment and assurance. It did have nuisance value which meant that everyone had to manage it, but basically what they were asked to say and do was limited and, in my view, it lost its edge.

Everyone knows that universities should have to work towards their mission and the mission should be institution and stakeholder specific. But I think that 'fitness for purpose' can be abused. You can explain any poor performance in terms of fitness for purpose and set the bar as low as you like if you are doing badly in an area and that is pretty pointless. Universities have some of the best minds who write spectacular grant applications and know exactly how to tweak the words and shape the text to satisfy a range of audiences. When I read some of the self-assessment reports, I thought ... well ... at times it seemed like creative writing!

So how useful was AUQA?

I don't think it was useful, in the end, because it didn't create dynamic ongoing improvement across the sector. That is not to say that improvement does not happen, it does happen despite rather than because of these processes some of the time, but not all of the time. However self-assessment quality assurance creates a reflective culture, a reflexive culture. And, of course, that is good, that is its virtue. Whether that is translated into continuous improvement over a period of time is a much arguable proposition. You can only assess it in terms of particular cases, but at least the questions being asked about how we are doing and what we are doing and whether we are doing things according to what our intentions are useful. But I don't think that self-evaluation drives institutional improvement.

The market?

The market in an economic sense creates competition. In essence, competition drives improvement in those domains which are open to competition-driven improvement; reliance on competition in organising people can shut down some domains altogether or greatly reduce them. The competition for prestige in a hierarchical system which the Australian higher education system is results in universities trying to emulate their peers and move up the status ladder. Although we know how hard it is to change an institution's status, everyone is trying to do it. This is how institutions are judged, such as research outputs for example. Global university rankings were also introduced which made the market even more of a driver and generated new competitive pressures. These pressures have been material and become a struggle for esteem and a struggle for resources, both at the same time. Avoiding major problems and scandals is also part of this for example the disaster at the Royal Melbourne Institute of Technology (RMIT) when they invested $42 million in the wrong IT system. Those mistakes can be very costly if they surface. They don't always surface, of course, but if they do and your international student numbers collapse, these things matter. And if your research performance dives, compared to the rest of the Group of Eight (Go8), that matters. Look at what happened to Adelaide University in Excellence in Research Australia 2010 (ERA10).

Sydney University didn't do as well as expected in ERA10 – perhaps the process was flawed?
Sydney is huge and has too many units which are not first-class academic units. Melbourne had that too, to a lesser degree, but then again Melbourne did not amalgamate as broadly as Sydney did after the Dawkins Reforms. But I think that Sydney has more raw talent that Melbourne does. If you look at the ARC Discovery results, in most years Sydney gets more ARC Discovery grants than Melbourne, and this is a good measure of raw talent.

Sydney and Melbourne are large, complex organisations. Do you think organisational complexity makes it more difficult to plan strategically from a cultural perspective?
I think the complication lies in the dual loyalties that academics have to the institution and to their discipline or field. General staff, by and large, are more committed to the institution but of course they also loyal to the faculty or their work unit. But on the whole my research suggests about 90% of university staff feel connected

to the institution. Of course, it varies across the sector, but I would say this is true of Melbourne University. This is one of the reasons why Melbourne is different from Sydney because Melbourne has been able to integrate people more fully into the institution.

How did Melbourne achieve this?

There are a lot of ways in which this happens, but the Vice-Chancellors at Melbourne have been much stronger in my view. Although the faculties are strong, they are managed most of the time, except Medicine which mostly runs its own race. I have interviewed people at Sydney, so I know this to be true. Monash is almost the same and the Australian National University (ANU) was like that to a degree but the research schools have since changed things. However, in the disciplines, there are many academics whose real loyalties are not to the institution, but to their field. They are connected to their academic unit within the university of course but also to the larger disciplinary field outside. This tension is always there in universities as this is the nature of academic work. If this tension was not present it would mean that the dynamic of academic identity itself was weak. You may be able to find some institutions in Australia where the disciplinary pull is weaker, perhaps for people on teaching only contracts this could be true, as it is the research mission that shapes strong disciplinary identities. This means you need to think about whether people are following a discipline plan or a university plan. Sometimes there is no overt discipline plan, but they have one in mind that is guiding the things they are trying to do, the things that are important to them.

A good example of this is the double game many of us find ourselves playing in relation to research indicators. For example, when I was working in Australia, the journals I regularly published in are the ones where the interdisciplinary conversations are taking place in my fields. One of those journals is an A ranked journal, it is not an A* journal because it publishes 10 times a year and covers the whole field and is not as exclusive as some of the American journals which are ranked A* (which are impossible to get into unless you are from the US anyway). The other journal I principally write to is a B ranked journal because practitioners write to it and it is the best journal to have a conversation about international education. The difference between an A ranked journal and a B ranked journal is very important in ERA, the way it works, the way it is structured. A to A* does not matter as much, but A to B does. However, it is important we sustain some kind of disciplinary presence, so we need to encourage people to publish in non-ranked publications, for example, consultancy reports and policy reports for the government. Other people write for professional journals, newspapers and magazines and so on and we need to continue to do that although we also have to work to the ERA journal quality indicators.

It is like you have two sets of indicators. The ERA indicators are the ARC's preferred list of publications[43], but we also have our own indicators for the applied work. This makes our discipline of education more complicated than say physics, for example. I will continue to maintain a double set of indicators to guide my work and to a lesser extent other faculties are keeping their own modus operandi but they will pay a price for it in ERA. Faculties that had long tails of non-A and non-A* publications and books will not be ranked highly in ERA. But we need to maintain this work as much of our impact lies in that broader group of publications so perhaps the question is whether we should include them in our publication counts. We know we shouldn't include them for ERA and DEST but perhaps we could maintain our own lists of what we do and reward people internally who are working towards that larger discipline base. It is tricky because there is overlap and the two lists can appear to contradict each other and make quality assurance complicated. It is a bit different now, in the sense that the emphasis in official

---

43 https://www.arc.gov.au/excellence-research-australia/era-2018-journal-list

data collection has moved from quantity to quality as indicated by the status of the journal, but the principles are the same – we still have a conflict between official, codified measures of knowledge, and a comprehensive accounting of all knowledge related products we produce. Of course, the fitness for purpose and self-evaluation formulas allow a good deal of diversity which is precisely why they are useful. This can help managers implement a quality assurance regime much easier when there is variability at the coal face. These notions allow for variability, they almost iconize it and make it central. But you pay a price in terms of external consistency, internal validity and external standards as well.

Could ERA be improved if some of the objections raised were taken on board and modifications made.

For a comprehensive census of research activity like ERA you need systems that are category neutral and have category standards across the whole system of activity which is very difficult to do. They clearly haven't got it right yet. I think that the indicators for Arts for example, are disastrous and do nothing to promote excellence in the arts, film or media in Australia. The process needs to allow for corrections, and we have been going through a process of correction since ERA10, but you know ... it is also a political process.

Over the years I have reviewed the AUQA Reports trying to categorise the Commendations and Recommendations to identify leadership strengths and weaknesses and shadings of organisational activities. This was difficult as for every Commendation, there was a parallel Recommendation which means they cancelled each other out in the data set. It did not seem to matter how good you were, there was always a Recommendation for improved practice.

Oh yes, standards.

I was also trying to examine if the publication of the AUQA Reports started to change the way universities were planning strategically.

I don't think it did, it just became another process to manage. There is a lot of thinking and planning going on regardless of whether you had an AUQA or TEQSA[44] audit coming up or not. One of the things that we never really got on top of, is that if we were very good at something, there must be opportunities lost because we are not doing something else. It is not an unambiguous virtue to be performing very well in an area and may make us think about putting less resources in it if we are doing very well and consider resourcing something else. We may also consider that an adequate level of performance is appropriate for this – these are the things we don't often think about.

The AUQA process was inflexible in that way, it was very path dependent and focused on what you did but not about what you could be doing. Whereas strategic planning has the virtue that it allows you to imagine a new future. It allows you to start again, if you like, open a clean sheet. It is a bit of an illusion because path dependency still plays a huge role in the process. But it is useful to be able to reset the settings and, in that sense, there should be more strategic planning, because it can create scope for transformation which the post hoc assessments do not.

What impact then do you think strategic planning has had on the Australian university sector?

I have been looking at universities systematically for decades and I think that strategic planning as part of the larger package of management changes has had a considerable impact in the last thirty years. My father, Ray Marginson, was one of the first

---

[44] The Tertiary Education Quality Standards Agency (TEQSA) replaced the Australian Universities Quality Agency (AUQA) as Australia's independent national quality assurance and regulatory agency for higher education in 2011: https://www.teqsa.gov.au/

strategic planners at the University of Melbourne as Vice-Principal for twenty-two years. He developed strategic plans, called Master Plans in those days, in the 1970s. I think the first one was in 1971.

Was the focus mostly buildings and campus infrastructure?

Certainly, site planning was a significant component, but it was much broader than that. In fact, these plans did more about site facilities and capital planning, compared to planning of human resource management and performance objectives, than institutions do now. I think that the planning process has become shaped by resource flows and activities and achieving institutional objectives has been a driver of most resource decisions especially over the last few decades. The process has just got tighter in the sense that more control was being exercised on the basis of planning objectives, even though the plans were perhaps are not always as detailed as they once were years ago. Objectives are certainly central and perhaps a larger, broader set of objectives with tighter Key Performance Indicators (KPIs) is a more common approach now. The process has been more and more instrumental in directing resource flows, personnel decisions and priorities to different areas with potential for development. Not only plans in general, but plans in particular areas, like International education. Research is another area where they need to go into a lot of depth about what they want to do and how they are going to achieve it. So, whether you call it strategic planning or not, it is a form of planning. It is certainly forward thinking; it is an attempt to try to align resources with objectives prospectively which is probably a reasonable definition of planning. But you can't divorce that from the rise of the strategic executive or the kitchen cabinet around the Vice-Chancellor, the Deputy Vice-Chancellors (DVCs) and Pro-Vice-Chancellors (PVCs) and the transformation of the Faculty Dean into an Executive Dean who manages down primarily rather than managing up. Executive Deans are aligned more with the centre than the academic staff which shifted discipline leadership down to the department or school level.

All that is part of the mix, as is the control exercised through the Budget process. So that regardless of what selection committees might want to do, or what a discipline might want to do in terms of growth or its own reproduction, it all comes down to a question of whether a job will be created from a budget perspective. Decisions are made as part of the budget process and the budget determines academic priorities whereas I have always argued that they should be separate. If, for example, you put your students first and built something around the best possible outcomes for your students, the plan would look quite different and then perhaps the outcomes might be better. Successful students, engaged students, will stimulate a positive learning, teaching and research culture which would be successful financially - rather than doing it the other way around. And when I say things like this in my meetings ... well! But how do you frame this? What signals do you use? The lack of engaged students is a problem for the sector. It is all unravelling at that level, higher education, and we don't have an answer. The strategic plans we are developing are not helping us engage our students, even though we know we need to do more with social media than we do. Many of our students are working and often off campus. If we can't engage them, they will not become effective internal agents in this transformation process. I think this is a real problem as I was a very active student leader. We thought a lot about what was going on in the university and how we would run the university if we had the opportunity. But there was only a handful of active student leaders in our year and there are even less now. I don't think students are prepared to put in the time and effort involved in educational reflexivity and continual improvement. They are just trying to survive, to get through. This disconnect is happening, but I am not sure that universities are aware of it or even taking it into account.

The other disconnect is that public funding is eroding year by year and we don't seem to be able to change that trend from inside the universities. We don't know how to shift the thinking of the government or the public, but clearly the current approach is not working. Maybe these two problems are related, the disengagement of students and fact that we are losing the basis of public funding. However, I am not sure as one is internal and the other external. When I went through university in the 1970s there was an understanding that the students who went to university, although it wasn't very hard to get in, were worthy of social support. Society was happy to see students educated as this was in everyone's interest and this was the basis of the underpinning of public funding. Yes, graduates gained personal benefits, but this was incidental to the educational process. There was also an unspoken assumption that the students would work hard but when they started protesting and marching in the streets there was a sense that they betrayed their mission, their part of the deal. All of that has unravelled now; those assumptions are gone. Whether we are talking about conformity with the course requirements or an activist life, these things are no longer on the agenda. Maybe if the students were more engaged, that would help with public funding too. I don't have the answer to this disconnect but I know that strategic plans are not connecting with these issues. One of the more positive things the strategic plans have done is engage in more activities with local government, industry and the professions. There is also more facility building in cities and locations where universities are viewed as central players. If you visit a place like Rockhampton in Central Queensland, for example, you can see how important the university is to these communities – it is a civil institution.

Yes, and Bathurst, Armidale and Lismore for example.
It is also true of the big cities too. Melbourne prides itself on being the education city and the universities are a central part of this

positioning. But this does not improve the commitment to public funding or increase student engagement. It is part of the plan and in a lot of ways it is a significant growth in the mission, but the odd thing is that it does not seem to be connected back to resourcing. I am not sure how strategic plans can get at those core issues, but maybe the answer is that you can't drive everything from the inside and planning is basically an internal activity. There is no such thing as an external plan. No one wants the government to run universities. I mean what a ghastly idea that would be!

They do, in some respects. They run the research agenda and exercise control over student load.

Yes, they have control in some areas and research is the area they exercise this control the most. They also are involved in the enrolment of low-SES students and equity but that is not as effective because it is engineered. But most of the time, the government does not run universities - internal managers do. Maybe if there was more external involvement it might help to ground the university mission better.

I initially thought that AUQA was a quality 'watershed' moment, but the contributors to this study made it clear that quality audits started well before AUQA was established.

When I started at the University of Melbourne, Professor David Penington[45] was Vice-Chancellor. He organised a seminar on quality in conjunction with the CSHE as there was a great deal of support for quality at the University of Melbourne at the time. Ian Chubb was also involved as he was beginning to shape the

---

45 Professor David Penington AC was Professor of Medicine 1970-1987, Dean of the Faculty of Medicine 1978-1985 and Vice-Chancellor of the University of Melbourne 1988-1995.

Commonwealth work in this area.[46] Clearly, it was an emerging agenda, but it was Melbourne that moved early to wave the quality flag, perhaps because the internal operations were tighter in Melbourne. Professor Penington actually used quality as one of his reform devices. He reviewed all the departments and faculties of the university and made them more cost effective, cleared the dead wood in some places, thinned it out in others and made a number of programs operate with a smaller number of units and larger classes etc. He also employed experienced managers and created incentives for them, guided them. He did not reform the entire university, but he made a difference to Law and also Medicine as he had been Dean of the Faculty of Medicine.

Denise Bradley also acknowledges David Penington's reform capabilities (p.47) and suggests that is one of the reasons why Melbourne is now performing so well. Alan Robson also describes David Penington and Glyn Davis' leadership capabilities as excellent (p.75).

Yes, Melbourne had strong central reformers in the 1970s and the 1990s who adopted a strong political economy approach. These decades of reform made a huge difference to Melbourne, including my father, Ray Marginson, who was Vice-Principal for two decades prior to this time as I explained earlier. Professor Brian Wilson[47] was Vice-Chancellor of the University of Queensland (UQ) for sixteen years and during this time he transformed UQ from a country campus to a research powerhouse that will continue to improve and may be ranked number 1 in the ARWU in the future. In 1993 Professor Wilson was appointed Chair of the Australian

---

46 Professor Ian Chubb AC FAA was Deputy Chair and Chair of the Higher Education Council 1990-1993. He was also Deputy Vice-Chancellor, University of Wollongong 1986-1990, Senior Deputy Vice-Chancellor, Monash University 1993-1995, Vice-Chancellor of Flinders University 1995-2000, Vice-Chancellor of the Australian National University 2001-2011 and Chief Scientist of Australia 2011-2016.

47 Emeritus Professor Brian Wilson AO (1930-2019) was Vice-Chancellor of the University of Queensland from 1979-1995.

Government's Higher Education Quality Review Program and commenced a process of quality reviews of Australian universities. So quality assurance was part of the mix in the 1990s well before AUQA was established.

Yes, several participants in this publication have discussed aspects of the Wilson quality reviews in their chapters. This suggests the need for another study to look at these higher education reformers in more detail and an attempt to link individual leadership approaches with organisational outcomes.

The important thing with all these studies is that you have to get all the different parts of this puzzle and fit them together. You need to fit strategic planning and quality assurance into the larger map of management and organisational change as well as the political economy of the sector.

Yet, quality is still an issue as Australia's completion, progression and retention rates are not as good as they should be. Do you think this a quality issue or a social issue?

It is both, but of course it depends on what you mean by quality. Fitness for purpose? If you mean quality as the underpinning resource conditions that enable teaching, learning and research to occur, then it is easy to point to material trends and the student/staff ratio is a primary one. Despite that, it is a broad-brush measure and there are problems with it however the large shifts that have occurred over time are meaningful and they tell us something. For example, it is much harder to maintain the same level of interaction between teachers and students than it was before, because there are twice as many students per staff member as there were in 1984-1985.

This is something that Jim Ife raised (p.160) that I also know to be true as I teach management students in two Business Schools. My students are all working, hardly ever on campus and seem to be more demanding than I was. I think the increasing tuition fees for domestic students and outrageous fees International students are required to pay has also contributed to this as many of them experience financial hardship and are constantly under pressure. So, in closing, what would be your advice to the next generation of university leaders?

I think there should be more planning that produces flexible plans. The plans have to be adaptive and forward looking. The problem with strategic planning has always been its rigid nature and the fact that it becomes a kind of ideology that managers require everyone to adhere to, whether it is still working or not, whether the plan was well based or not and if it incorporated sufficient feedback. Many plans do not have enough potential for evolution and limited flexibility. We now have much more sophisticated IT instruments and software that allow us to communicate more effectively and gather data more efficiently, so we should be able to evaluate as we go much better than we do. There are data systems that allow us to modify plans as you progress and although I think that the best managers do that instinctively in the way they work, but this does not always happen. The best managers plan as if they are driving a car according to the traffic they can see not according to some rigid notion of where the car is going regardless of the obstacles that are in the way.

CHAPTER TEN

Professor Carolyn Noble

Professor Emerita, Victoria University

Professor Carolyn Noble is the Foundation Professor of Social Work and Head of the Discipline of Social Work, Australian College of Applied Psychology (retired) as well as Professor Emerita at Victoria University, Melbourne.

She has been an academic since 1984, and mental health and child protection practitioner before that, in Sydney and London. She has taught and developed undergraduate and postgraduate programs in social work, counselling and psychotherapy, social science, mental health and professional supervision. She is active in Australian, Asia Pacific and International Schools of Social Work Associations and has held executive positions in each of these organisations.

Her research interests include social work critical pedagogies, work-based learning and professional supervision and theory and practice development in social work. Further areas of research include right-wing populism, gender democracy and equal employment opportunity for women in higher education and human services. She has published widely in her areas of research and continues to present her work nationally and internationally. She is editor-in-chief of IASSW's social issue online magazine https://socialdialogue.online/.

Tess Howes: Professor Noble, thank you very much for agreeing to participate in this study. Could you please start this interview with a brief summary of your career focusing on the various leadership positions you held?

Carolyn Noble: I graduated as a social worker in 1972 working in mental health and child protection both in Sydney and London. I then started my family while living abroad. I undertook my Master of Social Work (MSW) in 1986 and with this qualification decided that academia would give me a better work-life balance, having recently separated from my husband with three children to support. My academic career was fairly typical of women's careers: I commenced as a casual teacher in the social welfare school at the Macarthur Institute of Higher Education (MIHE) in early 1980s. In 1986 I was appointed as a part-time lecturer, in fact, I was the first job share appointment in the higher education sector which I thought would help me balance my family life and work aspirations. In 1989 I became full time lecturer just as MIHE amalgamated with other Institutes in Western Sydney to form the first university located in Sydney's west, the University of Western Sydney (UWS), now Western Sydney University. I was promoted to Senior Lecturer when the university was establishing a social work program in the early 1990s so, the first leadership role I held was developing a professionally accredited Social Work degree at UWS. I then assumed the role as Director of the Field Education Program for the newly accredited Bachelor of Social Work and the Welfare Studies degree, another program offered by the department. I knew if I wanted to succeed as an academic, I needed to undertake a PhD and begin researching and publishing in earnest. I did this while seeing my children through school and their various trials and tribulations! Undertaking research and a higher degree was an absolute pleasure.

After completing my PhD in 1997 I immersed myself in research and writing and found absolute pleasure in the collegial sharing of ideas and exploration of new ones. I loved the scholarship and the challenge of creating new knowledge. I spent many additional hours in the library and at the computer expanding on current social work knowledge, applying this to my teaching and as basis for further research projects and scholarship activities. I also wrote and developed many new social work units informed by my scholarship and that of my fellow research active colleagues. I developed new programs at both the undergraduate and postgraduate level and managed to teach for a semester in Canada to expand my work in the international arena. This was a time when Australian social work academics were entering the international arena leading important research projects and publishing critical texts for students to use. After I was promoted to Associate Professor at UWS, I continued to develop the social work program, the field education component, strengthen relationships with other courses across the university, as well as developing networks to expand the program's community engagement within the human services sector. In 2005 I successfully applied for the position of Head of Program and Professor of Social Work at Victoria University (VU), Melbourne. Uprooting from Sydney was both an exciting and stressful time for me and my family. My new role as Professor of Social Work was to grow and develop the small social work program which was located in the outer western suburbs of Melbourne. Under my leadership, the program became a strong, vibrant, undergraduate program, as staff were encouraged and supported to undertake higher degrees and begin to research and publish. It wasn't long before we were able to enrol postgraduate students and when I left VU in 2010 there were ten-twelve PhD students enrolled which increased the program's profile as a serious academic discipline. During my career as a social work academic I also accepted leadership positions on committees such as the Promotions, Ethics and Equal Employment Opportunities (EEO) Committees. At UWS I was responsible for establishing the EEO Program and a suite of Affirmative Action (AA) policies which were key to the development of a number of gender equity initiatives at the time. VU is a dual sector university so, as part of my role in expanding the Social Work program, I developed pathways for TAFE courses in the human services sector into the VU Social Work program which was a valuable contribution to the university and the discipline. We also moved the Social Work program from a satellite campus to one of the city campuses, co-locating it with TAFE establishing what was the very first dual-sector higher education department at VU. I led the team on this initiative, and, as far as I am aware, the social work and community welfare teams at VU are still having productive interdisciplinary conversations. I took leave from VU in 2010 to return to Sydney and quickly found a temporary position as Head of a private higher education provider offering counselling and psychotherapy courses.

My work as mental health social worker provided a solid footing to undertake this role as well as heading a successful social work department at VU. It wasn't long before I accepted a permanent position and began to lead the College in its planned growth initiatives. Additional courses were developed, and accreditation and reaccreditation of new and existing programs was undertaken. It was an exciting and productive time for the College expanding its programs and growing student numbers. However, equity players soon came into the sector and luckily for me I was head hunted to another private HEP to develop its social work offerings before the cost cutting and asset stripping had its impact on the viability of the College I was leaving. So, in 2013 I embarked on establishing the first social work suite of programs in the private sector. While this might seem like a contradictory move, I saw it as a challenge to create social justice programs in a reputable private provider intent on developing high quality human service degrees. Under my leadership the social work department was established and currently there are four hundred students enrolled in a range of undergraduate and postgraduate programs. I recently retired from this position and still regard my work there as one of the more supportive, productive and rewarding career choices. The structure was flatter, and the autonomy of the course leadership was left to the academic appointed to lead the programs. During this busy time, I continued to publish widely in national and international journals, wrote many book chapters and edited several books. I also continued to travel and represent my discipline in international arenas and help develop social work programs in developing countries as part of my involvement with International and regional social work associations.

And, outside the sector?

I took on several leadership roles both nationally and internationally, including President of the Australian Association for Social Work Educators (AASWE) and founding member of the Women in Welfare Education group, a national group promoting women's scholarship in social work. I edited several peer-reviewed journals and chaired many successful national and international conferences. I was also one of the founding members of the Australian Council of Heads of Schools of Social Work which established itself as a national body to lobby the government for better funding for Social Work education, and was Vice-President of the Asia Pacific Association of Schools of Social Work for a number of years. I have also held several leadership roles in the International Association of Social Work as well and currently edit a well-received social dialogue online social issue magazine (socialdialogue.online). Throughout my career I have pursued every major leadership role in my discipline that was available to me. I enjoyed the collegial interaction and networking and knowledge sharing from these experiences and opportunities.

UWS was one of the new post-Dawkins amalgamated universities. Did the implementation of the Dawkins Reforms have an impact on your academic work?

There seemed to be constant restructuring going on at UWS and VU in the post-Dawkins period, so I made sure I was on ALL the restructuring committees. A friend of mine said to me some time ago "your whole career has been marred by the almost biannual university-based restructuring". I am still resentful of this, even though I reached the top of my profession, as I believe that these constant restructures stifled my career and that of a number of my colleagues. It took away from our academic strengths and our minds away from our teaching and research. I spent too much time in cycles of endless meetings designing and redesigning things that were working. I viewed this as university executives shuffling people around as part of their reason d'être in ways that cost the university a great deal of money because everything; university logos, letterheads, business cards and promotional material had to be changed. New discipline structures were introduced that moved colleagues into work groups with little consultation and no apparent rationale. Our offices and even the size of our offices were also changed resulting in cultural and physical dislocation and major disruption to collegial relations as colleagues were separated by campuses and building locations. Redundancies were introduced and career moves stifled as an increase in administrative load followed the restructures. Every restructure meant that all the university governance and administrative arrangements, faculties and discipline areas and supporting committees and staffing had to be reformed and new position descriptions developed. While, at the same time, academic staff had to satisfy the requirements of their substantive position which was to teach and research and contribute to their profession. When UWS undertook another round of restructures, in the mid-1990s, our faculty briefed the National Tertiary Education Union (NTEU) and we took the university to the Industrial Relations Court!! We had to try and stop this madness! We thought rather naively if we could stop this latest restructure it would save much angst for the future as we thought that restructuring was possibly going to be an ongoing and endless process.

What was the basis of your objection?

We were resentful that the university was changing the disciplinary groupings we thought were cognate with our service user needs, that is the students and community service sector. In this particular new restructure, which was significant, staff were going to be grouped with areas that were historically hostile, which we argued would thwart scholarship in our discipline and lead to territorial fights. There was also an industrial basis to this action as the planning process was not consultative; it was top-down and developed without any recognition or acknowledgement of our substantive contributions to the university. We had two or three hearings in the Industrial Court and the Industrial Commissioner directed UWS to consult staff (at all levels) about these changes

What was the outcome at the end of the consultation process?

We saved the current discipline arrangement for a couple of years. But, while the consultation process improved as a result of our industrial action, a conservative Federal government was elected, university funds began to dry up and the National Tertiary Education Union (NTEU) and the Student Union started to lose power. So, our department and faculty became part of the quicksand of change, like every other higher education institution. Campus-based courses were closed, indeed entire campuses were closed, reopened and then closed again. Community action groups tried to save campuses located in their area earmarked for closure with little success. As far as I can recall, every restructure that UWS attempted in the 1990s and the ones VU undertook in the 2000s were opposed by staff, students and constituent consumers. The social work department at both institutions developed a reputation of being very 'bolshie', and we were, because we were actually really, really angry about the lack of consultation and ill-conceived groupings of disciplines along lines that didn't have any integrity with staff synergies.

So, you did not agree with the rationale at the heart of the change?

No, no, no, no. I think the strong tide of opposition at UWS more specifically could be traced back to the time when the university was a number of independent Institutes of Higher Education with very stable and committed workforces of 20 to 25 years duration, specialising in teacher education and offering key employment pathways for residents in the catchment areas. Many of these teachers were committed to delivering quality teaching and achieving high levels of student satisfaction and saw these restructures as diminishing the very purpose of teaching and student engagement in the learning process. When UWS became a university, everyone was upgraded to university level appointments, but a lot of people resented the changing conditions and the emphasis on publications and research. They felt continually thwarted by new groupings, the establishment of new research centers, the introduction of new ways of counting your academic output, new strategic priorities, new mission statements, new research objectives, the new Key Performance Indicators (KPIs) that had to be met with every new restructure. Many staff were also tired of the university continually reinventing their substantive positions, rearranging working conditions and lines of accountability etc. And, from my experience, bad feelings existed between management and the academics most of the time. However, in some ways these restructures turned out to be a good move in terms of women's leadership opportunities as several women were promoted when new administrative structures opened up and new leadership positions were created. But many of these roles e.g. Vice-Chancellor and Deputy Vice-

Chancellor became a poisoned chalice. These executive positions were caught up in neoliberalism of Federal politics of successive conservative governments and, rather than lead an educational institution towards academic excellence, they began implementing new managerialist practices and policies and initiating more restructures, with the specific aim of reducing funding and cutting jobs and resources and changing university cultures permanently.

So, would it be difficult for you to recall the first time you were involved in a strategic planning process in an Australian university?

Yes, it would be difficult because there were so many. When I left UWS, there must have been six or seven Strategic Plans in the bin and each one would take a couple of years to complete. There were layers and layers of Strategic Plans at the university, at the faculty and school level – the University Research Centres also had their own Strategic Plans. Indeed, my whole career in academe has been marred by successive strategic planning and academic realignment.

Were the academics involved in the development of these plans?

No, these plans came from the Vice-Chancellor's Office and then the Dean would be tapped on his or her shoulder and told that the strategies for the next five years would be … and then it would be something else for the next three years … and then change again for the next few years. There was, of course, some consultation but mostly it was tokenistic, as each new Vice Chancellor and Deputy Vice Chancellor undertook a restructure to establish their position in the university and to make a mark for themselves in the university culture. It was almost a pre-requisite for all new senior appointments to restructure their portfolios without any consideration of previous attempts. Dean and Heads of Schools were often blackmailed with threats of cuts to funding, courses and resources if they didn't get their staff to co-operate.

All these plans were top-down? You can't recall a time when the academics got together to develop a new strategic plan?

That's right. All these strategic plans were instigated top-down. Academic leaders were asked to comment but not design or develop these plans and strategies. When I was in leadership positions at UWS and VU, I was involved in the early consultation phase, but mostly we saw this as a futile activity. Every time a new Strategic Plan was released, we knew that money would be squeezed out of teaching and allocated to some other scheme or short-term consultant appointment. On the ground, at the teaching interface, all that changed was less money for teaching and more bureaucracy and decreasing student satisfaction. I really don't think much has changed. Colleagues across the sector report frequently of funding squeezes, changes in course delivery (e.g. online) and entry requirements to attract students but fail to support them and the staff with the necessary resources, including administrative support. Staff were expected to increase their research productivity as well as manage the cumbersome administrative systems put in place to streamline administration and save money by replacing support staff in the process. Open plan offices and vertical campuses also became part of new strategic plans to save money and cut costs, resulting in staff and student dissatisfaction and increased academic and administrative workloads.

You mentioned that the strategic planning process that you took to the Industrial Court was top-down and not consultative. Did the approach to strategic planning change during this later period? Were they more collaborative or consultative?

No, although they started out as top-down they had to be consultative because they needed to involve the NTEU and senior staff. The Deans also had to be involved as they were responsible for making sure their staff were on side; but I would not call it collaborative. I can remember meetings when the Dean would call us all together and say "OK, it is on again. We are going to have to reorganize ourselves because I have been told to do it. So, you can either come with me or we will all be in trouble". Although we would moan and groan and hope that things would be different this time, it never was. I know a lot of people were burnt out at the Dean and Pro-Vice-Chancellor level, by the number of restructurings and amount of strategic planning and budget planning and accountability for everything that was forced on the staff mainly ... even the amount of paper used in the photocopier! The NTEU established roadblocks whenever they could, to protect jobs, to protect courses, to protect campuses, and protect students with varying degrees of success.

You felt you needed to protect the students?

I never saw a Strategic Plan that benefited the classroom experience. There were pockets of success, I am not saying that there weren't as buildings were constructed, new staff were hired, and new facilities built. But, in my view some of these resources could have been spent on things that improved the student experience and opened our students' minds to new ideas and new ways of thinking.

Were these plans published and circulated? And did staff refer to them?

Yes, they were published on the website and yes, yes, they did. Every research grant applied for, every course and every unit of study that was developed had to be aligned with the Strategic Plan. This process increased and became even more micro in the 2000s when everything, even new staff positions, had to be linked to the strategic vision, or the mission statement or a strategic goal, such as community engagement, or quality research, or applied education. We used to say to each other "we can't distinguish our mission statement from, for example, La Trobe University". Across the sector university executives were spending vast sums of money on management consultants and branding exercises so we all ended up with graduate attributes, mission statements and strategic goals that were essentially the same. There was a brief period when forms of differentiation started to occur as universities made a concerted effort to find something distinctive. At one point it was 'community engagement' but then every university was a community engaged university; another one was 'excellence in teaching' but then all universities were pursuing teaching excellence. So, it was a very fluid discourse that linked everyone together around the planning process, in my view, homogenising the sector in the process.

Did any positive initiatives emerge from the strategic planning process?
No, I can't think of any.

There are many university stakeholders, including staff, students, the professions, alumni, industry and the government. Were these Strategic Plans well received by the relevant stakeholders? In your view, did these plans miss the target audience across the board, or was it just some of the academics that did not necessarily relate to it?
The students would always resist changes when they saw the resources shrinking, teachers being overloaded and unavailable to support them. Students were always very perceptive but I'm not sure about the other stakeholders. What the public wanted was to have access to courses that suited them, good quality teachers and employment opportunities at the end of their course – but I can't for the life of me think of what a Strategic Plan would have to look like to get students excited! The professional associations also had their own issues with restructures and planning that mirrored what was going on in academe.

Were these early strategic plans very detailed, did they have specific KPIs?
Yes, we were constantly having to demonstrate performance; this is the period when performance-based education became the norm. There were online performance evaluations that measured us not only against the Strategic Plan and our associated KPIs but

also against a range of corporate behaviours. Our job descriptions were linked to outputs in the Strategic Plan and promotion and study leave were based on both performance and compliance with the cultural change that was part of the shift to a more strategic perspective. The other thing that happened during this period is that the number of senior administrative staff rapidly increased, while discipline based administrative support decreased. A colleague said to me before I left VU, "watch out when the administrative staff car park is double the size of the academic car park, because then we will be all in trouble". We knew we were being squeezed out, both metaphorically and physically. The move towards strategic rather than academic planning, the large scale organisational restructuring, increasing government regulations, compliance, surveillance, risk management, performance-management, even our research had to be linked to strategic outcomes, all of this changed the ideology and ontological underpinning of academia.

I am being very critical and cynical; however, there were also some high points in my career. When I started at the Macarthur Institute of Higher Education in the early-1980s it was a fantastic place to work. There was a hiatus for five to six years and we could spend money on workshops that had personal development outcomes, invite guest speakers to engage with the students and had classrooms alive with applied education. It was fun, exciting and rewarding. We dealt with issues like diversity and gender and the politics of the curriculum was thriving, but bit by bit this was quashed. And what you have today in higher education, in my view, are numbers of disaffected students because they are not getting the right teaching experience, they don't get time for reflection and they don't get the hours of instruction needed to train them adequately for their careers.

One day I realised that I had enough and needed to reactivate a form of resistance. I was acting Head of School when we were called to a meeting and informed that a large number of academic staff would be made redundant on Christmas Eve – pink slips issued on Christmas Eve! This was in 2010. The presentation outlined a dire financial situation to justify the large-scale redundancy scheme. However, we all knew that we were in the middle of a construction boom and that the executives were on very high salaries so there was obviously money for some areas of the university, but not for us. When we came out of the meeting, we said to each other "if you can get out …. get out". Then the university developed a new strategic plan to implement this strategy and for some people who had been in academia for fifteen to twenty or even thirty years, this was the last straw. But our faculty refused to cooperate. We called in the NTEU and mounted what was now viewed as the last rearguard resistance at VU and at the end of the year the Vice-Chancellor left. However, that reprieve was only temporary as further restructures and realignments continue today. I consequently moved back to Sydney soon afterwards and started a new phase of my career.

I am interested in when universities started to think strategically and of course the shift of power to the centre is an important part of that process. However, although the universities complained and protested about these changes, they complied with the process and the Dawkins Reforms were enacted in various ways throughout the sector. This brings me to my next question, if you led a strategic planning process recently would you approach it the same way, or, would you do it differently? Would you do it at all, if you had the choice?

Restructuring, as part of strategic planning, began in earnest after the Dawkins era in the 1990s and hasn't really stopped. Initially I think we thought participating in strategic planning that was going to benefit staff and students and model sustainable growth that would facilitate productivity, career betterment and improve the student experience. However, in reality the process was more tedious and at times destructive, undermining the very purpose of higher education. More recently I have been involved in the development of a number of Strategic Plans for my private provider employers. As a senior member of staff, I was expected to lead my team in implementing these initiatives. The initial strategic conversations were framed around delivering rewards for teaching, rewarding the students and looking for a niche in the market. Senior management assured us that the income generated from restructure in teaching and resources allocation would be spent on salaries, on campus improvements and teaching facilities which will benefit the student experience. We are yet to see this happen!!

Were you more receptive to this strategic ambition?
I know that you need frameworks for growth and development, linkages with people's jobs and to a common vision supported by a budget as the institution needs to be profitable whatever way you define it. But, in my view, the planning process should be done in smaller work groups as I really resent senior people coming in on large salaries squeezing everybody below them, telling them to start thinking about different ways to do the academic work they have been doing for years. I never heard someone say "you are a wonderful work force. Tell me what you are doing that is so successful and we will resource you?" It was a challenge and not surprisingly there were always hidden agendas, more resource shrinkage, more management and less academic control, more micro-management, more (unproductive) accountability measures, more division between the academics and managers, more harassment, bullying, marginalisation and increasing student dissatisfaction. I think the people who run universities aren't necessarily managers, or if they are managers, they are not necessarily educationalists. It is very hard getting the right mix. The people running the private educational institutions should know how to run a good university (with all its complexities), and they also know how important it is to keep their staff happy, well paid and well-resourced, so they can deliver a quality educational product. Universities used to be like

that in the early years of my career when the NTEU had the power to negotiate fair salaries and the university itself was pursuing quality education. But these important educational elements were restructured out of the picture when money became scarce and the movement against academic autonomy gained traction. I also felt that some senior managers resented the conditions that academics had become used to and thought we were fiddling the system and not working to our full capacity. When management consultants were engaged to lead the strategic planning process and corporate players had positions on academic boards any semblance of educational philosophy went out the door. Millions of dollars were spent on marketing, rebranding and other strategic projects – a skerrick of that money would create a classroom with up to date technology that would enable teachers to engage students in the learning process.

What did you think when the Australian Universities Quality Agency (AUQA) was established? Did you greet this initiative with the same degree of skepticism?

I was involved in the AUQA Reviews because I was the Head of Department. There was no way to avoid it. Pages and pages of data were compiled for each audit. We had to produce minutes of meetings as evidence of community consultation, collect data to demonstrate student satisfaction, update all the staff profiles, outline our research focus and make sure the handbooks were up to date with all the different policies and practices required to comply with the new standards of education. The audit culture that AUQA introduced required all staff from the top down to document their performance against abstract indices and evaluate every program offered. The result was compilation of documentation to fill a several rooms full of filing cabinets! In my view, preparing for and post AUQA were always an opportunity to enact much of the ideological change that was occurring in the sector: primarily the implementation of managerialism, and the anti-academic attitude held by management. This was a sentiment shared by almost all senior staff who regarded AUQA reviews as just another opportunity for the University and its layers of bureaucracy to further homogenise the culture of the university, weed out any innovation, and direct research into areas that were 'profitable' and of economic value. Interestingly enough, during this time two significant changes occurred. The NTEU continued to lose power and staff were badgered to produce quantitative outcomes from educational products, and, as a result, the value of social capital was lost from the discourse. And some of the humanity disciplines also started to disappear from the curriculum, disciplines such as art and art history disappeared, but it was the philosophers who were the first to go, then ethics departments. Research funding was directed towards the physical sciences; the human sciences never attracted the same resources. And so, it is a complex picture to paint because the fabric of influences was conflating.

Did you look at the AUQA web site and read the Review Reports? What did you think of them?
We thought they were fair. Especially when our report was good and other universities, such as Macquarie, did not do as well! But we would also have a chuckle about it as it could well have been us. We were very aware that it was mainly a political process but we survived without too much public and private embarrassment or any internal pushback.

Did you ever object to the findings or lodge an objection with AUQA about the results of the audit?
We didn't have to, because the reports for the institutions I worked for were always passable, even commendable – we never got into any trouble. We were good citizens when the external auditors came in to assess the university and its courses. We were

disillusioned and fed up in many ways, but we did everything we needed to do to get a good report for the institution as our futures depended on it. I led the self-review for AUQA and its replacement, the Tertiary Education Standards and Quality Agency (TESQA) at the private colleges after I arrived, with help from my colleagues of course, and the Final Review Reports were very good. However, these reviews took time away from the classroom, teacher support and resource allocation and of course research and scholarship activities. A large amount of information is produced for the audits and filed away somewhere until next time. Any benefits were left in abeyance.

What role do you think organisational culture plays in the strategic planning process?

There are lots of cultures in universities, across the campuses, in the disciplines, departments and faculties, yet strategic planners seem to treat university staff as a homogenous group and talk about organisational change as if the university is mono cultural. They just don't get it. I am aware that organisations must change, be responsive to changing trends and receptive to new ideas and developments but ... As a quality education provider, you need to find ways to keep the best and get rid of the worst, but at some point, we should be allowed to consolidate and build on what we had before it was restructured again. I think there are some universities and private providers still trying to establish a good cultural fit. They are attempting to build a bonded culture; by investing in education, building libraries, and establishing professional development opportunities. For many these changes have come too late. The sector is under resourced and staff and students are disillusioned and skeptical that they are getting the best opportunities available.

Do you think that your experience leading, developing or avoiding strategic planning processes has had an impact on your understanding of leadership?

My colleagues and staff have told me that the leadership roles I assumed were significantly important in minimising the impact of these changes on my department and my staff. I seem to be able to interpret what is needed and satisfy this in ways that created less angst for the members of my team. I also think that my training in Social Work and good facilitation skills helped with this. I knew I had to involve my team in the process while calming their fears and allaying their anxieties. My aim was to help them move from a constant state of flux and, instead of going to the union, take on a leadership role and say … "look we have done this before…. we can do this again". In situations of poor leadership, staff burnout increased, and the educational results suffered. This negative impact would also cascade down for years, if not forever. In therapeutic terms, the workplace was constantly being retraumatized.

So, you think that the shift to centralised strategic planning had an impact on the internal organisational dynamics of your employer institutions and the sector in general.

Yes, very much so. When I first moved from the public to the private sector I was pleasantly surprised by the experience. The structure, as I have said, was flatter and more autonomy was given to academic staff. For example, we used to be responsible for timetabling and subject allocation but when centralisation was implemented, errors started to happen. It is difficult to administer a timetable system across 7 or 8 different work groups and several campuses on a systemised basis. However, management will never stop trying because as they seem to be addicted to an ideology that claims restructures save money and increases productivity. This is despite the experiences across the sector that indicate an increasing level of staff and student dissatisfaction with current management approaches and university cultures. The student experience seems to be lost in new strategic planning processes as executives look for more cost cutting ventures in an environment intent on decreasing funding for higher education. In terms of the impact on the sector, there has been a lot of growth in research and scholarship in the hard sciences that has been politically determined by strategic plans across the sector. There are pockets of people who have done really well since the Dawkins Reforms were implemented and they would be very positive about the growth and opportunities that came their way. But it has divided the sector and academia, I think. The social and human sciences have done very badly.

Finally, what advice would you give to the next generation of individuals who will be tasked to lead the development of new Strategic Plans in Australian universities.

Centralisation is not the right way to go. Smaller work groups that identify more directly with what the academics are doing, and the educational outcome being pursued, are more effective. However, these new leaders are Generation Y and Generation X; they are a different cultural group. I moved out of the public sector, for my own sanity, as I thought it was cannibalising people and I wanted a better work-life balance. I wanted to enjoy going to work and interacting positively with my colleagues. However, I can see the private institutions becoming more like universities over the next ten years. It was fun initially helping these new players in the higher education sector to outline a new commitment to education, a cultural commitment to the students and staff, and involving people in the strategic planning process. But they have also been hit hard by reduced funding for student educational support and funding. One of the key issues is structure: a flat structure is important. Hierarchical structures based on accountabilities, establishes a whole lot of values of ownership and power particularly if the Vice-Chancellor and senior managers are able to retreat to their ivory towers.

I think we all know that unless the executives are in touch with their staff and find ways to resource them, inspire them, value them, reward them, train them and respect them, it will not work. Resources should also be allocated directly to the academic units where staff are delivering the educational product. The more you move away from that, the more disenfranchised the academic community will become. There also needs to be a balance of power – power sharing with the academics and also a redistribution of resources. Resource the teaching areas 80:20 instead of 20:80. If we don't achieve this then it will all break down eventually. Can you imagine, allocating twenty per cent of the institutional resources towards teaching – in a teaching institution! The current resource and power imbalance is not sustainable and needs to change if we want to maintain a healthy, vibrant, quality higher education sector.

CONCLUDING COMMENTS

Observations drawn from the preceding chapters demonstrates that strategic planning was introduced to the Australian university sector by five primary parallel change forces. Firstly, managerial innovations developed by a few entrepreneurial academic leaders to improve institutional performance and increase efficiency; secondly, strategic positioning initiatives developed by the competitive business schools; thirdly, the publication of strategic planning literature by the North American business schools; fourthly, the prevailing neoliberal operating environment; and finally, the enactment of the Dawkins Reforms. All these change forces contributed to the 'managerialisation' of the Australian higher education sector.

There was widespread sector support for the growth and equity initiatives outlined in Dawkins' 'Green' and 'White' Papers, however, concerns were expressed by the Australian Vice-Chancellor's Committee (AVCC), the Vice-Chancellors, tertiary education advocacy groups and individual academics about the preservation of academic values and institutional autonomy in the new managerial operating environment (see for example, AVCC Press Release 9 December 1987). Nevertheless, strategic planning, supported by performance management and review, was positioned as the most appropriate mechanism to deliver efficiencies across the sector and increase institutional performance in areas of national importance ('White' Paper, 1988).

Although many academic staff were critical of the Dawkins Reforms, the findings of an immediate national post-Dawkins study indicate that other institutional leaders were supportive of the new managerial focus. Participants in the Meek and Goedegebuure (1989) study include the Chair of Council, the Executive Officer, the Registrar/Secretary of universities and CAEs, as well the Chairman or Executive Director of higher education agencies. An overwhelming eighty-four per cent of respondents replied in the affirmative to the survey question asking if institutional management should be strengthened? Forty-eight per cent replied that it was "highly desirable" and forty-six per cent indicated that it was "desirable" (p.67). The study participants agreed unanimously with the statement that "in the next ten years strategic planning will be an integral part of management". Sixty per cent of the participants "strongly agreed" and thirty per cent "agreed" with this statement, only one participant had "no opinion"' (p.69). These findings suggest that a number of institutional leaders in the Unified National System (UNS) who participated in this survey (149 participants from 203 targeted potential participants, providing a response rate of 73%), were philosophically in agreement with the managerial agenda outlined in the Dawkins Reforms. And, as the Academic Board's leadership role steadily declined over the following decade, the managerial reforms were progressively enacted without a strong coordinated counter academic leadership challenge. "I was an academic at UWA from 1986 to 2001 and, during this time, I saw the decline of the importance of the old Professorial Board. Decisions were increasingly taken by management and the Professorial Board was left to debate less important things ..." (Jim Ife, p.155).

Rowlands confirms that contemporary Academic Boards in Australian universities were effectively 'disempowered', and their role increasingly focused on curriculum developments and quality assurance in the post-Dawkins era (2012, p.2; see also Bradshaw, 2002). Peter Coaldrake agrees confirming that in "the 1990s budgeting and financial management started to modernise

... universities were moving away from being parochial collegial institutions to understanding they were complex organisations and needed to be relevant" (p.198). Marginson and Considine also found that the participants in their large-scale study viewed the collegial decision-making pathway "as an obstacle to managerial rationalities" (2000, p.11). This was all part of the movement "towards the managerial model that was occurring at the time" (Jim Ife, p.155). Denise Bradley explains that this was necessary as difficult internal resourcing decisions had to be made that would have been contested in a collegial academic forum (p.57). And, although this tension is less obvious in 2020, it has still not been resolved.

> What is also interesting about this period of time, is that many of us were working in the old academic culture, which we thought was the pursuit of knowledge, teaching and research in its best aspects. But the new breed of people who were becoming Vice-Chancellor, or Deputy Vice-Chancellors, tended to think, that is all very well, but we have to achieve the corporate mission so that we can do all this academic work (Geoffrey Sherington, p.113).

The implementation timeline varied from university to university, Vice-Chancellor to Vice-Chancellor. Denise Bradley, Ed Davis, Ian Chubb, Jim Ife and Simon Marginson describe instances of strategic planning and the implementation of modern management practices in institutions in the mid-1980s, well before the Dawkins Reforms. For example, Denise Bradley and her colleague Professor David Lee led the development of a research plan for the University of South Australia (UniSA) a year before it was established, to provide the research foundations for the amalgamation of the South Australian College of Advanced Education (SACAE) and the South Australian Institute of Technology (SAIT) that formed UniSA. This was unusual in some respects as Denise Bradley explains "[v]ery few people in those days took planning seriously" (p.43). Alan Robson, Geoffrey Sherington and Carolyn Noble recall the release of the first Strategic Plans in the 1990s after the Dawkins Reforms were implemented. Lynn Meek and Peter Coaldrake discuss the release of the first formal institutional strategic plans in their employer universities in the 2000s. The first Strategic Plan was not released at Peter Coaldrake's university until 2004, a year after he assumed the role of Vice-Chancellor, explaining that his "predecessor was very strategic but did not think it was necessary to have a formal printed plan" (p. 195).

Lynn Meek moved from a regional university to a Group of Eight (Go8) university in 2008 and was therefore able to compare the strategic planning capabilities at two different universities at the same moment in time. He found that his Go8 employer university was "light years ahead" (p.174) of some other Australian universities commenting that the regional university "still lacked an overall unified approach to develop a university strategic plan and sub-plans" at the time (p.175). Geoffrey Sherington recalls "I don't think that Gavin Brown believed in strategic planning; he was not that sort of person" (p.122). These statements lend weight to a contention of this study, that the Vice-Chancellor's leadership was a crucial component of the implementation process.

The 'White' Paper stated, "it is from an institution's strategic plan that its educational profile should be developed" ('White' Paper, 1988, p.104) and "triennial funding based on agreed priorities for institutional activities and performance against those priorities" (p.27). Strategic Plans were used as points of reference to develop institutional funding 'profiles' or 'compacts' with the government and provide the framework for the institutional audits conducted by the Australian Universities Quality Agency (AUQA) from 2001 as well as its replacement, the Tertiary Education Quality Standards Agency (TEQSA) in 2011. Compliance was mandatory; it was not optional. Yet, the findings of the West Committee ten years later (1998) suggested that traditional academic governance arrangements were still in place in many Australian universities in the late 1990s and that this was hampering the introduction of modern management practices (pp.89-90; see also Marginson and Considine, 2000, pp.60-61).

A distinction should be made at this point between the *introduction* and the *implementation* of strategic planning in Australian universities. For although the Dawkins Reforms introduced strategic planning to Australian universities, the reforms were implemented by Vice-Chancellors, their Executives and the professional staff recruited specifically for this purpose. The appointment of Vice-Chancellors, Deputy Vice-Chancellors, Pro-Vice-Chancellors and other senior members of the Executive with management, finance or tertiary education expertise, discussed by Geoffrey Sherington and Simon Marginson, provided Vice-Chancellors with a professional advisory group that was not initially part of the collegial governance framework. Geoffrey Sherington explains that when professional staff started to attend the strategy sessions the concept of who was a "'significant person' at the university" started to change (p.116). The planners produced performance data and the status of the 'God professor' started to erode because "the sorts of knowledge you now needed in order to make the corporation work was different" (p.117). According to Jim Ife, this was not unexpected. "We were not naïve enough to think it would not happen; there was considerable pressure on universities to become more business-like, to become more entrepreneurial" (p.154). Geoffrey Sherington also concedes this point explaining that "we could see there were problems in the sector … if the government was going to restructure the economy as the Hawke-Keating government did, why would they leave aside a big publicly funded sector like tertiary education which was so important to economic growth?" (p.115).

The accumulation of professional knowledge and expertise in the Office of the Vice-Chancellor, and the administrative 'centre' of the university, exacerbated a growing divide between the Vice-Chancellor, Academic Board and the academic community. Marginson and Considine (2000) found that "in most Australian universities the new style of executive management had its first impact right at the top and centre, and then spread downwards and outwards to the academic units" (p.64). Not only did the Vice-Chancellor and Executive hold positional power over the university community, they also accumulated the 'new' knowledge required to manage the non-academic activities of the university. This commercial knowledge quickly became the intellectual capital of the executive and was used to assess academic performance and distribute funds within the university. This internal power shift is described from a professorial perspective by Jim Ife and Geoffrey Sherington. "This was a time when managerialism became the dominant narrative and was positioned as the way to get things done, to produce change" (Jim Ife, p.163). "I could see that the power was shifting away from the Academic Board towards strategic planning in terms of resource distribution, ideas of market competition and how we needed to position ourselves to attract the best students" (Geoffrey Sherington, p.112).

New executive structures termed for example, the Vice-Chancellor's Advisory Committee, the Vice-Chancellor's Executive, the Senior Management Group, or Senior Executive, assumed responsibility for making strategic resourcing decisions that impacted all aspects of academic work, as Lynn Meek explains. "The Executive became responsible for the Budget and the academics for teaching and research, and never the twain shall meet! But of course, what you do in teaching and research has budget and planning implications" (p.180). This led to protests from academic staff concerning a lack of leadership transparency, collegiality and consultation, together with accusations that decisions impacting on the academic community were being made by the Vice-Chancellor and Senior Executive 'behind closed doors' (Connell, 2013). Although Ed

Davis recalls when he was appointed Dean and advised his Heads of Department that they were going to meet frequently and share information in a transparent and open way, something that had not been done before in the faculty, his direct reports "all looked at me suspiciously" (p.95). Planning was also constrained for Faculty Deans, as Geoffrey Sherington admitted that the "main planning was taking place at the 'Centre' in the Strategic Planning Office and we had to work within those parameters" (p.121-122). Carolyn Noble describes the impact of this lack of collaboration and lack of consideration for the consequences on the academic community had on her academic career. "I believe that these constant restructures stifled my career and that of a number of my colleagues. It took away from our academic strengths and our minds away from our teaching and research. I spent too much time in cycles of endless meetings designing and redesigning things that were working" (p.239).

These findings suggest there were two related, complementary leadership forces that drove the implementation of strategic planning strongly and effectively in Australian universities. Firstly, strong authoritative macro level leadership from successive Ministers of Education and the Australian Commonwealth Government in enacting and adjusting elements of the Dawkins Reforms over the subsequent decades. Secondly, the rise of the 'strategic Vice-Chancellor' supported by the Executive and senior professional staff, which established a micro power cohort at the 'centre' of each Australian university outside the traditional collegial governance structure. The centralisation of power in the Office of the Vice-Chancellor was further strengthened by the appointment of Executive Deans, which Ed Davis, Lynn Meek and Simon Marginson position as another key change driver. These appointments were made by the Vice-Chancellor, whereas under the more traditional academic appointment process staff would be inclined to elect "known friends" who "would defend the faculty from the university's Executive" (Ed Davis, p.94). As Executive Deans were part of the Executive they were expected to support the decisions made by the Vice-Chancellor, even if these decisions were not necessarily beneficial for the Faculty. This contributed to what Lynn Meek describes as an "'us and them' development between the Executive, or at least parts of the Executive, and the academic community" (p.176) which senior academic staff felt was "counter-productive for the institution" (p.180). Carolyn Noble recalls that from her experience "bad feelings existed between management and the academics most of the time" (p.241).

These internal leadership forces combined to provide receptive organisational conditions for the Vice-Chancellor and Executive to progressively and effectively implement strategic planning in all Australian universities. Several contributors describe the rise of the 'strategic' Vice-Chancellor supported by cohorts of Deputy Vice-Chancellors, Pro-Vice-Chancellors and professional members of staff with management and planning skills. As Simon Marginson suggests, these leadership changes are all implicated in this internal shift of power: "… whether you call it strategic planning or not, it is a form of planning … you can't divorce that from the rise of the strategic executive or the kitchen cabinet around the Vice-Chancellor, the Deputy Vice-Chancellors (DVCs) and Pro-Vice-Chancellors (PVCs) and the transformation of the Faculty Dean into an Executive Dean who manages down primarily rather than managing up" (p.225).

The position of Vice-Chancellor has always been a very powerful role in Australian universities. However, a supportive collegial decision-making pathway contains checks and balances to ensure major initiatives are subject to debate and scrutiny by representatives of the academic community before decisions are made. When the Vice-Chancellor assumed control for setting the strategic direction of the university, she/he then had the positional authority to lead change in ways they thought would be most effective, with or without input from their academic colleagues. This can represent a significant leadership risk for the university if the Vice-Chancellor has been poorly briefed or develops a mindset that may not be in the best interests of the university. For example, some of the private colleges and overseas campuses established by various Vice-Chancellors were not uniformly successful, Melbourne University Private, for example. If a collaborative decision-making pathway was in place, the risk that one individual, or a small group of individuals, could make a poor decision for and on behalf of the university could be mitigated. Alan Robson agrees that this is important, stressing that he valued the "checks and balances and a separation of powers and robust discussions about contentious issues between Academic Senate and the Executive" (p.86). He also recommends that you need to work closely with people who will challenge your ideas and bring some creative tension to the planning process. "Do not select friends who will just reinforce your thinking and support your decisions. You need people who will challenge you and tell you when they think you are making a mistake" (Alan Robson, p.76).

The contributors all concede that universities needed Strategic Plans to outline the strategic direction of the university, consolidate institutional mergers and amalgamations, direct resources to areas of strategic priority and accommodate growth in student numbers. Some of the new post-Dawkins universities were more receptive to the Dawkins Reforms, as they had businesslike internal operational processes which some of the more traditional universities did not have at the time. Denise Bradley, for example, states that "it is not by chance that most of the Australian Technology Network (ATN) universities are strongly planned institutions. All of these institutions commenced with a notion that they are businesslike, and it is easier to plan strategically in an institution that sees itself as a business. Whereas it is much harder to do in an institution that thinks it is doing something grand and vague" (p.55). Ian Chubb expressed a similar point of view, stating that the former institutes such as the Queensland University of Technology (QUT) and the Royal Melbourne Institute of Technology (RMIT) were "most advanced in terms of strategic planning" (p.138). It could therefore be argued that this represented a strong compliance incentive for the former CAEs and Institutes, which helped to drive the structural and organisational reforms through the sector.

And so the implementation process continued to gain momentum. Australian universities were compelled to develop strategic planning capability in readiness for the academic audits that were conducted by the Australian Universities Quality Agency (AUQA) established in 2001. The first cycle of AUQA audits commenced with the University of New South Wales (October, 2001), Charles Darwin University (November, 2001), the University of Ballarat and the University of Southern Queensland (July, 2002), Curtin University of Technology (August, 2002), The Australian Catholic University, Newcastle University and Swinburne University of Technology (September 2002), Macquarie University and the University of Adelaide (October, 2002), and concluded with the Australian National University (July, 2007) after which the second cycle of AUQA audits were commenced.

AUQA concedes that the timing of the audits caused concern for some universities as there had been "a substantial organisational restructure in the previous two years and numerous senior level personnel changes" (the Report of an Audit of The University of Adelaide, March 2003, p.5). The focus of each AUQA audit was to assess institutional performance against the objectives outlined in the university's Strategic Plan or strategy document, if the institution did not have a published Strategic Plan (Report of an Audit of Macquarie University, October 2002). The Dawkins reforms had been framed to allow "institutions to respond in their own way, and to determine their own missions, in response to the increased resources and the increased flexibility that came with the growth of the sector" (cited Croucher, Marginson et al, p.xii). However, in some respects it was conditional institutional autonomy which is not autonomy in a real sense:

> The Government will also ensure that institutions are free to manage their own resources without unnecessary intervention, (while at the same time remaining clearly accountable for their decisions and actions) (p.10) ... The Government's aim is to enhance the autonomy and capacity of institutions to direct their resources flexibly and effectively to meet their designated goals. It is not, as some respondents have suggested, to reduce that autonomy nor to limit the opportunities for staff to influence institutions decisions. As autonomy increases, however, so the need for accountability grows ('White' paper, p.101).

An examination of the second cycle AUQA Reports demonstrates that by 2008 all Australian universities, to a greater or lesser extent, were no longer traditional, collegial universities but academic-managerial institutions with corporate missions that were governed primarily by modern management practices. Carolyn Noble views the preparation required for an AUQA audit as "an opportunity to enact much of the ideological change that was occurring in the sector: primarily the implementation of managerialism, the anti-academic attitude held by management" (pp.249-250). Given the academic resistance and dissent expressed at a number of universities in the post-Dawkins period, some Vice-Chancellors perhaps did not give sufficient consideration to the Creative Engagement and Professional Community management archetype, which expects managerial leadership in Australian universities to be consultative and consistent with traditional collegial values (Sharrock, 2012, p.333).

Denise Bradley, Alan Robson and Peter Coaldrake describe

extensive consultation with their communities, while maintaining control of the strategic planning process. Alan Robson assumed this approach to avoid marginalising the academic community recommending that you "keep them involved but in a positive way if you can" (p.86). Both Alan Robson and Peter Coaldrake conducted wide-scale staff surveys, so they knew where the "hot spots" were which helped them manage dissent. Peter Coaldrake, for example, surveyed the university every three years and was relaxed about the criticism frequently expressed. "People become very cynical about these things, but over the years we sought to develop our capacity for self-criticism" (p.200). Ian Chubb stated that he consults others as required and has been "listening to clever people" (p.136) throughout his career. However, he also holds the view that senior leaders should not stand back "for fear of being labelled top-down people. You hold leadership positions to lead and that means that some of what you do is top-down" (p.134).

> I would describe my approach [to strategic planning] as a collegial process driven from the top. The decisions we made were not all made by me alone but ultimately the responsibility was mine. I would walk into a room and say, "today we are going to decide on X, Y, Z" and we would stay with it until we had agreed on the outcomes. But it might not be X as I took it in – it might be a substantial component of X with some variations which comes about when you incorporate input from people who in a lot of cases know a lot more than you about some topic or other (Ian Chubb, p.135).

The strategic planning process undertaken by Professor David Lloyd at the UniSA, the youngest Vice-Chancellor appointed in Australia, is the most comprehensive consultation exercise so far undertaken in an Australian university. The 38-hour Unijam event made possible by IBM technology enabled almost 8,000 people in 56 countries to contribute to the development of the 2013-2018 strategic plan *Crossing the Horizon* (Ross, 2019).

As the contributors' chapters demonstrate, the role of the Vice-Chancellor in the implementation of strategic planning in Australian universities was critical. Strategic planning may have been introduced to the sector by the Dawkins Reforms and a handful of entrepreneurial individuals, however it was implemented by Vice-Chancellors and their Senior Executives in universities throughout Australia during the post-Dawkins era. Similar findings on a global scale were shared by Professor Philip Altbach at an international gathering of higher education researchers, when he stated categorically that "... we are in the midst of a higher education revolution ... universities have been transformed since the end of the last century, there is no doubt about this ... there has also been a decline in Faculty power, there is no doubt about this ..." (Keynote Address, Society for Research into Higher Education, Annual Conference, Newport, Wales, UK, 11 December 2013).

Individuals who were enthusiastic about the opportunity to implement strategic planning and facilitate the transformation of their institution from a collegial academy to a modern complex mixed economy institution engaged productively with the process. Staff who held the opposite view were forced to make a choice to either become involved and try to shape the process so that it was more aligned with the traditional mode of collegial planning, engage the National Tertiary Education Union (NTEU) in an attempt to moderate some aspects of the process, or as Carolyn Noble suggests "to try to stop this madness" (pp.239-240), assume disruption tactics, such as the public protests documented in Connell (2017, 2013) or stand aside and let the process unfold without active involvement.

An alternative view is expressed by Ed Davis who was teaching business subjects and aspiring business leaders in a competitive business school. He suggests that strategy was frequently discussed as it was the "jargon of business leadership" (p.97) and had an impact on the strategic leadership and the teaching environment in the business school. Also, as Ed Davis taught Industrial Relations and Managing people which involved developing a strategic mindset, his leadership approach was "influenced by what I had read and taught" (p.102). The complexity of this situation is summarised by Simon Marginson:

> In my experience, there has been a wide range of approaches to strategic planning in Australian universities, with different levels of density in terms of detail and different kinds and rhythms of consultation. Some planning has a period of consultation at the start, some is entirely consultation driven, some planning involves continuing consultation as the plan is being implemented, and some doesn't have any consultation – there is a great deal of variation. One of the things that characterises Strategic Planning, in a sense of a capital S and capital P, is that the process of *post hoc* evaluation is not well developed. Perhaps reflects a weakness in the concept of strategic planning (p.214)

Therefore, we can conclude that it would not be possible for a single modern management process, strategic planning, to be all things to all the stakeholders in the sector – particularly when the philosophical perspectives of the individuals involved and the multiple and often contrasting shared meanings embodied in the construct are taken into account.

New leadership approaches

Part of the leadership complexity is because, as Ian Chubb reminds us, "academics are trained to critique … that's how academic work is conducted – deconstructing ideas and putting them back together in the same form or a different one" (p.136). Academic research outputs are evaluated competitively and frames the academic promotion process. Some interdisciplinary research is collaborative however it is often inter-institutional not intra-institutional. National research centres compete against each other in the Excellence in Research Australia (ERA) initiative which impacts on the willingness of competing research centres to collaborate and build national areas of research strength. Competition does not necessarily foster an interest in collaboration, teamwork or participative leadership approaches. There are numerous forms of individualism inherent in the collegial framework which require Vice-Chancellors to adopt a more nuanced leadership approach which will engage with the professoriate in a collaborative and meaningful way. Although, interestingly, Simon Marginson holds the view that universities are not "run on a collegial basis they are run by managers who work to budgets" (p.210).

A collegial academic environment therefore does not necessarily mean a cooperative or collaborative approach to planning and decision making. Alan Robson recalls attending Academic Board meetings as a young professor which seemed like "a very daunting, adversarial debating club" in which the "the Executive seemed to be constantly locked in debate with dissident professors" (p.69). Jim Ife recalls a "few pompous professors who liked the sound of their own voices and used to engage in quasi-scholarly debates quoting Latin at each other" (p.155). Later, as Vice-Chancellor, Alan Robson describes Executive meetings that featured "very robust and at times fierce – respectful, polite but very strong" disagreements (p.76). He maintains that it is possible to manage universities in a collegiate way, however this approach requires a different leadership mindset:

> I always say that universities are not businesses and have to be managed in a collegiate way and yes, I think

> you can manage universities in a collegiate way. You need to remember that you are managing people; highly educated, very talented, clever people ... in my view, you need to manage the voice of dissent and this requires you to have broad shoulders (p.87).

This was also the case if members of the executive, such as Jim Ife's Executive Dean, "respected the old traditions and although he took on that managerial role, he tried to do it in a collegial way, in a way that respected people's expertise and autonomy" (p.158).

Therefore, the question that needs to be addressed is how can executives in modern Australian universities lead their academic communities in more collegiate ways of planning that will position Australian universities for success in the 21st century? A starting point is in the recognition that academic work is intellectual and creative. This requires a fundamental shift in thinking and the implementation of policies and processes that foster and support academic innovation and intellectual creativity. Ian Chubb outlines some of the key leadership skills required for success:

> Universities are replete with people whose professional training is based on a finely-honed capacity to critique. That's how academic work is conducted – deconstructing ideas and putting them back together in the same form or a different one. So a university leader has to be able to operate in a particular environment ... It can be tricky, it can be hard, but it can be fantastic (p.136).

A shift in approach to leading strategic planning from an executive controlled to an inclusive approach will build more cohesive academic communities, increase the diversity of views contributing to the planning discussions, generate creative ideas and bring a generational eye to the process if students are more actively involved. This should ensure the strategic goals published in the Strategic Plan reflect the diverse values and aspirations held by all the stakeholders in the university.

Inclusive leadership is framed on the leadership traits of openness, accessibility, and availability, which research suggests are more likely to engage people in diverse organisations (Carmeli, Reiter-Palmon and Ziv, 2010). Universities are some of the most diverse, socio-political organisations in the world. Australian universities for example, are multi-cultural, multi-generational, globally mobile, technically sophisticated and hyper connected, characteristics indicative of diverse organisations (Shirley Davis n.d.) that would benefit from an inclusive leadership approach. While there is currently limited empirical leadership on the organisational benefits of inclusive leadership, connections can be made between inclusive leadership and organisational behaviour theory as research indicates that inclusive leadership is positively associated with employee engagement (Choi and Park, 2015), increases productivity and improves organisational efficiency (Hollander, 2009).

The six Cs of inclusive leadership proposed by Shirley Davis are: 1. Commitment; 2. Courage; 3. Cognizance of bias; 4. Curiosity; 5. Cultural intelligence; and 6. Collaboration (Shirley Davis, n.d.). This list of inclusive leadership characteristics is broader than those offered by traditional leadership paradigms and provides a framework that could be used to develop new models of leading strategic planning tailored for the Australian university sector. Applied research conducted by the Employers Network for Equality and Inclusion (ENEI) indicates that inclusive leadership is more effective in diverse contemporary organisational contexts. The findings suggest that if people are treated fairly, have a voice and an opportunity to participate in decision-making, they feel valued, appreciated and included. ENEI frames inclusive leadership around fifteen competencies, idealised influence, individualised consideration, inspirational motivation and intellectual stimulation – the 4I's of transformational leadership (Northouse,

2010, pp.176-180); plus unqualified acceptance, empathy, active listening, persuasion, confidence building, growth, foresight, conceptualisation, awareness, stewardship and healing.

All of these leadership competencies are either explicitly mentioned or implied in the preceding contributors' chapters. Therefore the following recommendations for leading strategic planning in Australian universities are proposed:

1. **Executive leaders should demonstrate characteristics from the transformational, inclusive, collaborative and participatory leadership paradigms.**

Executive leaders in Australian universities must understand that leadership, particularly strategic leadership, is situationally and contextually contingent. Therefore they should express leadership behaviours that are flexible, adaptive, inclusive, empathetic and collegial. This requires highly developed interpersonal skills and a willingness to engage positively with their diverse communities to motivate, inspire and energise staff and students to join them on the strategic planning journey. Particularly if the executive is leading strategic planning in a hostile internal environment as has been the case in some Australian universities over the last thirty years. "So, the first thing one would need to do in this type of context when seeking to lead strategically would be to persuade one's own colleagues to come along on the journey" (Peter Coaldrake, p.204). It is therefore critical that the strategic planning process is collaborative, participative, inclusive, respectful and responsive to the aspirations of a broad cross selection of stakeholders. "You need an enormous amount of engagement as you need to socialise these ideas" (Alan Robson, p.72). Executives should recognise that academic staff do not respond well to authoritarian or coercive approaches to leadership. Ian Chubb therefore recommends that executives adapt their leadership style to meet the unique challenges of the university sector:

> You can't be a leader if nobody wants to follow you. In a university you can't issue an edict and expect the line to form behind you. You have to work hard to earn the respect and the trust you need to lead. I think that good leaders have particular characteristics wherever they are. They have vision, courage, principles and values. Consistency. They are consultative, decisive, and are listeners who hear and are committed to evidence-based planning. You can earn, you have to earn trust, but you can't demand it. Leaders in universities need those characteristics … (p.136).

Engagement and commitment are not freely given, particularly by academics. These positive organisational dynamics are gains effective leaders are able to harness and bring to the strategic planning processes. Effective consultation will help generate commitment if it is meaningful, two-way consultation. Information sessions do not meet the genuine consultation test. Staff should also feel that their contributions are valued, respected and have the potential to influence the outcomes. "I would say that the planning process started off as top-down, but people will not engage with it unless they think they can influence it" (Peter Coaldrake, p.196). They should also see the draft plan change shape as this input is incorporated into the plan. Ed Davis positions staff engagement as a critical success factor in effective strategic planning. "I had also been employed as a consultant for many different organisations facilitating strategic planning and I knew that it needed to be an engaging process in which each staff member had the opportunity to contribute" (p.103). Consultation does not mean that every point of view is taken into account and written into the Strategic Plan. However, a mutually respectful negotiation process, led by a highly skilled leader, should be able to reconcile major points of disagreement. "The real question is how do you negotiate, discuss, debate and evolve broader agreement that if it was simply and purely top-down?" (Ian Chubb, p.134). Alan Robson recommends that you must also be " prepared to change the framework as you socialise it to fill in the gaps and add the detail" (p.73).

Academics are autonomous, intelligent and highly qualified individuals. They will not be persuaded using a command and control leadership approach. "Leadership is not about telling people what to do – if you just rely on this leadership approach you won't get anywhere" (Alan Robson, p.81). It may be possible to persuade others to engage in the process, if they are confident that the strategic goals they are working towards will reflect the outcomes of a genuine consultation process. If so, the final plan will represent issues the majority of staff are concerned about, which means that the Strategic Plan will be owned by the community as well as the Executive. If the new strategic vision is developed collaboratively, then coercive implementation tactics will not be necessary. The implementation process will be seamless. This will help build trust and confidence and increase the level of engagement in the next strategic planning stage.

> When we started strategic planning it was much more top-down because people were not as familiar with the process. Whereas with Blueprint 3, six years later, the process was more organic: it may have been initiated top-down, but from the outset a great deal of discussion came percolating from the community (Peter Coaldrake, p.195).

Decisions should also be made in accordance with the university's decision-making protocols to maintain legitimacy. These decisions should be communicated to the university community at planning reference points so that the next step of the process is based on these common areas of understanding. During periods of severe financial difficulties, and organisational instability due to amalgamations or mergers, decisions will need to be made that may not be popular with all the members of the university community. In these instances, the case for change needs to be articulated clearly and honestly, evinced in supporting documentation and agreed by a majority of participants who understand that the decisions will serve the best interests of the community. Alan Robson recommends supporting the planning decisions with data. "You cannot convince academics by rhetoric; this will not get you anywhere" (p.72). Denise Bradley further suggests that "although people didn't like what I said, they had to accept the power of the argument in the document"(p.50).

To achieve these aims, leaders should ensure productive relationships are established with the strategic planning participants (Dubrin and Dalglish, 2003, pp.197-199), that inspire enthusiasm (Dubrin and Dalglish, 2003. p.34; Kouzes and Posner, 2003, pp.31-32), commitment (Fullan and Scott, 2009, pp.226-227; Kouzes and Posner, 2003, pp.221-223); trust (Northouse, 2010, p.186; Dubrin and Dalglish, 2003, p.68; Kouzes and Posner, 2003, pp.244-247); and credibility (Kouzes and Posner, 2003, pp.367-368). Leaders must also be engaging and effective communicators (Northouse, 2010, pp.46-47; Dubrin and Dalglish, 2003, p 390; Kotter, 1996, p.87-100); willing to listen (Kouzes and Posner, 2003, pp.148-151; Kotter, 1996, pp.99-100); and enlist the support of others (Kouzes and Posner, 2003, pp. 141-170); to develop and share the strategic vision (Adair, 2010; pp.49-50; Dubrin and Dalglish, 2003, pp.382-383; Kouzes and Posner, 2003, pp. 141-170; Kotter, 1996, pp.67-83).

Executives leading strategic planning need effective communication skills that can motivate (Kouzes and Posner, 2003, pp.18-19); strengthen interpersonal relationships (Kouzes and Posner, 2003, 2003, pp.279-311); and empower others (Northouse, 2010, p.185-186). They must understand the importance of collaboration (Adair, 2010, pp.97-102; Kouzes and Posner, 2003, pp.241-277); the value of team building (Adair, 2010, pp.72-73; Northouse, 2010, p.348; Kotter, 1996, pp.57-59); in generating a new sense of purpose

(Northouse, 2010, p.212). This is essential to facilitate emerging strategy and imagine new possibilities (Kouzes and Posner, 2003, pp.114-115); and keep the participants involved in the process (Avery 2004, pp.96; Adair, 2010, p.17-19; Kouzes and Posner, 2003, pp.15-16).

Leading change relies on leaders who are able to establish an advocacy culture (Fullan and Scott, 2009, pp.30-31; Northouse, 2010, p.251); that envisions and shares a new future with all the stakeholders (Fullan and Scott, 2009, pp.86-90; Kouzes and Posner, 2003, pp.109-139); well developed skills in the art of persuasion (Northouse, 2010, pp.46-47), negotiation (Buchanan and Badham, 2004, p.176); and the communication skills to manage dissent to ensure the strategic planning process is not derailed (Fullan and Scott, 2009, p.77; Kouzes and Posner, 2003, p.83; Sharrock, 2014). Peter Coaldrake uses "non-formal communication channels rather than formal ones" (p.195) to engage extensively with as many of the stakeholders of the university as possible, personally negotiating with his constituents to resolve conflict and build institutional commitment … in an attempt to capture "hearts and minds" (p.202).

> To do all this is going to require systematic leadership in all quarters of the university. Postsecondary institutions are going to have to do something that they have never done. Instead of appointing the smartest people in the room to leadership … higher education institutions, like any of the top organizations in the world, *will have to deliberately cultivate leadership capabilities within their own ranks.* Turnaround must be brilliantly and sensitively led (Fullan and Scott, 2009, p.71).

2. **Executive leaders must have a comprehensive understanding of the university, stakeholder values and the internal dynamics to lead strategic planning**

effectively. This must be essentially collegial.

Effective executive leaders require a comprehensive understanding of all aspects of the university, including detailed knowledge of staff dynamics, internal challenges, areas of strength and areas of weakness, and able to respond to shifts in the external operating environment. They should also ensure the strategic planning approach respects academic staff autonomy and expertise, and that the strategic ambitions outlined in the new Strategic Plan reflect institutional values, not just the priorities of the executive. If the strategy and the university values are aligned, it is more likely that dissent can be minimised. If not, having a comprehensive understanding of the internal dynamics of the university will assist the leader to negotiate with disaffected individuals and/or organisational units to negotiate a compromise. "Universities are complex environments that can be manipulated but also have their own endogenous logic and things happen despite the wishes of all the participants, for good or bad" (Simon Marginson, p.212). Lynn Meek also suggests that leaders must value and "appreciate what makes a university different from other types of organisations which means developing an understanding of the culture and the organisational dynamics of the university" they are tasked to lead (p.190).

Executives also need to have a comprehensive understanding of the external planning environment to ensure the strategy is aligned with the external environment as Ian Chubb explains. "This is the conflict with local strategic planning. If you make it too rigid you can easily get out of step with plans being developed in agencies that influence your activities. It would be wonderful if the ANU could deliver 100% on its strategic plan because it had total control over everything, but it didn't (p.146). Maintaining connections with all the stakeholders provides a communication channel for concerns to be raised thus establishing an early alert system for problems or pockets of dissent developing in areas of the university.

Adjustments can then be made in the event unforeseen negative consequences become evident. Executives who are research active will have connections with research students and colleagues internal and external to the university. Executives who are able to factor some teaching commitments into their otherwise full diaries will maintain connections with the key university stakeholder – the students.

Simon Marginson warns that the "lack of engaged students is a problem for the sector" (p.226). This is wise advice as Lynn Meek reminds us that students are our primary stakeholder" (p.188). Yet, Carolyn Noble exclaimed when discussing the involvement or lack thereof of students in the strategic planning process, "I can't for the life of me think of what a Strategic Plan would have to look like to get students excited"! [48] (p.245). Maintaining connections with your colleagues will also help in this regard, advises Geoffrey Sherington. "The real difficulty for executive leaders will be trying to keep the connection between themselves and their colleagues, while remaining clear about the direction they are heading. In climbing the corporate ladder, you can easily lose connections with your peers … (p.127). Ed Davis agrees, suggesting that current Vice-Chancellors are also not as connected to their academic communities as they were in times past. "To some extent [they] have 'floated away' from their academic peers" (p.92). Jim Ife considers that "VCs became increasingly CEOs of businesses rather than leaders of universities" (p.157). Having a comprehensive understanding of the organisation, and strong connections to the stakeholders and external planning environments is critical to strategy development. As Simon Marginson suggests, strategy is also time critical and "these windows of opportunity are often very short term" (p.212). "The other variable is flexibility. The capacity to respond to changing events and the willingness to feed this information back

---

48 The topic of a conference presentation and paper currently in development.

into the plan to monitor unintended consequences, either positive or negative is critical" (p.215).

3. **There is no one 'right' way to lead strategic planning in Australian universities. Different planning contexts and different cohorts of stakeholders require different strategic planning approaches.**

> When I was younger and less experienced, I thought there was a right way to plan strategically but I no longer hold this view. There are different ways of doing it but what you need to do is get the balance between people having a sense of where they are going, and what they will be judged against, combined with a process that allows you to take a good idea and run with it. This is the great challenge of strategic planning and also of leadership (Denise Bradley, p.63).

It stands to reason, therefore, that there can be no simple formulaic, rational approach to strategic planning in Australian universities. It is not possible for one individual, or a small group of individuals, to know everything about the university and the external environment at any given point in time. That is why meaningful, effective consultation and situational analysis is critical. If Lynn Meek was tasked to lead strategic planning in the future he would attempt to generate ideas from the community. "I would try to put mechanisms in place to develop ideas much more from the bottom up … if you ignore the rank and file academic staff, or don't take their opinions seriously, those pockets of dissent are more likely to coalesce and become much more important than if you try to build a cohesive process. It is harder to do it that way, but I think you will produce a more enduring outcome" (p.177).

Universities are complex socio-political-educational institutions. The purpose of leading strategic planning, therefore, is to bring all this complexity together to develop a Strategic Plan that unites, not divides the community. Alan Robson also explains that the organisational culture needs to be receptive to new ideas to enable the strategic planning process to progress meaningfully. "A culture that enables strategic planning is a culture that is open, transparent, frank and communicative ... the other important thing that is important is that the message needs to be reinforced constantly ... and unless you were prepared to face people and argue your case, you will not win over their hearts and minds"(p.82). Peter Coaldrake also agrees that effective "strategic planning can take many forms. For example, I think the Melbourne Model was a very courageous model and I admire its innovative qualifies But, whether it would work was a very different matter. And obviously it was nuanced as it was rolled out. A plan needs to be tested by the reality of its context" (p.204).

A 'poor' strategic plan is described by the contributors as: one that is aligned too closely with the budget as this does not allow flexibility and limits the possibility of developing a Strategic Plan that is as visionary and inspirational as it could be; a process that is not in harmony with the culture and dynamics of the university; is too rigid which can result in the university being out of step with the external agencies; is not informed by genuine consultation; or is led too assertively which will not inspire or engage individual academics. "Strategic planning has to be almost by definition, led or initiated by the centre. But if it goes no further than that, it is probably not going to adequately serve the institution" (Lynn Meek, p.187).

> Successful strategic planning can vary a lot in terms of the degree of expertise required to develop a brilliant set of ideas which can then be sold successfully, because they are eminently good, so that people buy in despite the fact they weren't consulted. I don't think there is a hard and fast rule about the best way to lead strategic

planning" (Simon Marginson, pp.214-215).

A 'poor' Strategic Plan forced upon an unwilling community, that is not congruent with the culture and dynamics of the university, is rigid and inflexible, and "becomes a kind of ideology and that managers require everyone to adhere to, whether it is still working or not, whether the plan was well based or not and if it incorporated sufficient feedback" (Simon Marginson, p.231) will result in organisational dysfunction. There is therefore a high duty of care for executives leading strategic planning, as Denise Bradley warns that when strategic planning does not work "it can have a significant impact on innovation" (p.56). Carolyn Noble describes the impact poor strategic leadership has on academic staff from a therapeutic perspective. "In situations of poor leadership, staff burnout increased, and the educational results suffered. This negative impact would also cascade down for years, if not forever. In therapeutic terms, the workplace was constantly being retraumatized" (p.252).

So, what should an effective strategic plan for a modern Australian university look like?

A summation of the data provided by the contributors suggests a number of elements should be reflected in an 'effective' Strategic Plan[49]:

- It should be distinctive and reflect the unique institutional values and heritage of the university and developed in consultation with the university community.

- It should be a 'living', 'breathing' document.

- Is constantly recalibrated so that it remains relevant and situationally contingent.

- Is short, concise and directional providing clear strategic

---

49 The outline of proposed wide-scale research project funding permitting.

signals for the community, while relegating the detail to appendices or cascading plans.

- Is courageous and imagines new things – promises a new future, a new start.

- Is informed by forward thinking and is not merely a stylised representation of business as usual.

- Is strengthened by extensive collaboration, both internal and external.

- Reflects an understanding of the complex organisational communication and leadership connections and integrates related functions throughout the university.

- Identifies strategic objectives that will inspire the university community and is aligned with shifts in the external environment.

- Reflects key community aspirations and is owned by the university community, not just the Vice-Chancellor, Chancellor or the Executive.

When strategic planning was first implemented in the Australian university sector, although attempts were made by some individuals to be consultative and collaborative, the end result was more authoritarian. A contention of this publication is that this is because the model of strategic planning implemented in the Australian university sector was organisationally incompatible with academic collegial planning norms that were in place in most Australian universities at the time. Therefore, strategic planning needed to be implemented strongly by Vice-Chancellors and Senior Executive to achieve the Government's transformation objective. "If there is an **imperative in strategic planning, it is that the process be carefully thought out, that it be flexible, and that it result in expanding participation to broaden the base for acceptance,** [my emphasis]

(Rowley, Lujan and Dolence, 1997, p.280).

> The odd thing about management and leadership, especially leadership, is that different approaches can be successful. You can have a charismatic leader, a visionary, the first among equals; the extensive consulter, but also the person who goes off on their own and then comes up with a great idea and brings everyone along with them. Some people see their job as getting everyone on side, keeping them all motivated, protecting them and making them feel included and valued ... Successful leadership can take many forms (Simon Marginson, p.214).

There are many generational differences between the retired cohort of Vice-Chancellors and Executives, and the current generation of leaders who are perhaps more comfortable with the management responsibilities inherent in their academic leadership roles. Current generations of professional staff hold academic qualifications including doctorates, which means they have strong philosophical connections to academe. It is possible that the next generation of leaders may be able to traverse the 'us' and 'them' divide articulated in the preceding contributors' chapters, and develop mutually beneficial strategic partnerships that will engage the academic community, improve organisational cohesion and enable creativity and innovation to flourish. "I think we all know that unless the executives are in touch with their staff and find ways to resource them, inspire them, value them, reward them, train them and respect them, it will not work (Carolyn Noble, p.254).

The Australian university sector needs executive leaders who can reinvigorate strategic planning by leading the engagement of the professoriate, re-establishing connections with Academic Board, and increase the involvement of all the stakeholders in the strategic planning and strategy development processes, particularly the students. "If I was recruiting for leadership roles now, I would put more emphasis on the candidates leadership ability than on their research competence although there needs to be a balance ... they must also be highly skilled in how they communicate with, and lead, their peers, staff students and stakeholders. Getting this wrong can be disastrous (Ed Davis, p.105). Denise Bradley agrees implementing a recruitment strategy that looked for "people who had a history of performance-based management, and a history of playing nicely with others in that they were co-operators, not empire builders" (p.53).

It is therefore time to review, revise and develop new ways of leading strategic planning that rely less on a centrally driven, directional, rational-technical approach, and more on novel ways planning that will excite and inspire academic communities throughout Australia. "Leadership is not just about fancy talking. It is about getting to the destination, and the job done (p.202) ... a period outside university, outside the university sector, is very good for the head, for widening perspective, to collect a bit of lateral experience, as it were; and second, understand that none of these things is achieved by the guy or the girl at the top without a big team effort. Team is everything ..." (Peter Coaldrake, p.206).

> Two central things about leadership are developing strategy and exercising judgement and the judgement should always be about what to do, whether it is about people or activities, and it must be connected to your overall understanding of what the strategy is" (Denise Bradley, p.55).

Some of the contributors also took this opportunity to offer advice to Commonwealth and State Education Ministers, the Vice-Chancellors and members of university executive.

> I feel very, very concerned about [funding for the VET sector] because it does not bode well for Australia's social and economic future and there is a terrible disjunction

between the university and VET sectors which there should not be (p.60) … [and] of course, I would like more money to go into equity (p.61). There are [also] issues about the funding of the Australian Higher Education Sector and I personally don't think that it is in Australia's interest to return to a centralist model because it did not work. Anyone who has ever run an institution will tell you that – not necessarily publicly … Another key issue relating to funding is the fact that our entire system is being subsidised by International students which I don't agree with (Denise Bradley, p.63).

"In order for Australia to deliver and sustain a viable, quality, higher education system, policy must be evidence based and informed by the best higher education experts available. In my opinion, for this to happen, Australia needs an independent high-level policy structure that sits between the institutions and government. What it does not need is another review of higher education" (Lynn Meek, p.189).

Ian Chubb asks: "So, how do you get actual, real, quantitative, improvement in the sector? It is not by bringing the best down to some modest average level. What you need is a policy framework that encourages every university to aim to be better – and to be fit for its purpose. Some will be genuine international players on a big scale. Others have and should have a more regional focus. All have value and all have a role to make Australia and its place in the world better. Somehow we have got to work out a system that enables that to happen. It does mean a political process where there can be consultations, but the strategy has to be more than a rhetorical commitment to quality and excellence – and difference. It's got to be real" (Ian Chubb, p.148).

Academic communities should be able to look with optimism to 2050 and work together to lay the foundations of a more harmonious future. Academic work, teaching and research, are creative, intellectual pursuits that will not prosper under harsh authoritarian regimes. There should be no need to drive the strategy process through relentless cycles of implementation, governed by unforgiving strategic management regimes and performance metrics poorly applied across the institution. Coercion is not a substitute for cooperation. As the contributors attest, it is possible to manage universities in a collegial way, to win over the 'hearts and minds', build 'citizen communities', strengthening connections with academic staff and engaging our students while leading strategic planning.

These findings are more consistent with the "change-savvy leadership" for higher education proposed by Fullan and Scott (2009) than the modern management processes published in the North American modern management strategic planning and leadership literature:

> The essence of our conclusion was that effective leaders combine certain capabilities (personal, interpersonal and cognitive) and competencies (role-specific and generic skills) to manage change effectively ... Faced with demanding situations, they remain cool, empathize, understand differences, and work to find solutions through joint action. In particular, they listen, link, and lead, and model, teach and learn themselves. They hone these capabilities as continuous learners, and, above all, they foster these leading learning capacities in others, always generating leaders for the future" (pp.151-152).

As leaders of the future, our students should be at the centre of the transformation process. "Successful students, engaged students, will stimulate a positive learning, teaching and research culture which would be successful financially – rather than the other way around" (Simon Marginson, p.226).

SELECT BIBLIOGRAPHY

Adair, J. (2010) *Strategic Leadership*. London: Kogan Page.

Altbach, Philip (2013) Keynote Address, Society for Research into Higher Education, Annual Conference, Newport, Wales, UK, 11 December 2013.

Anderson, D., Johnson, R., Milligan, B. (1999) *Strategic Planning in Australian Universities.* Canberra: Department of Education Training and Youth Affairs.

Andrews, K. R. (2071) *The Concept of Corporate Strategy*. Homewood IL: Irwin.

Ansoff, H. I. (1984) *Implanting Strategic Management*. Englewood Cliffs, NJ: Prentice-Hall.

Ansoff, H. L. (1979) *Strategic Management*. London: Macmillan.

Ansoff, H. I. (1965) *Corporate Strategy*. New York: McGraw Hill.

Avery, G. C. (2004) *Understanding Leadership*. London: Sage Publications.

Becher, T., Trowler, P. (2001). *Academic Tribes and Territories*. Second edition. Buckingham: Open University Press.

Bessant, B. (1995) "Corporate management and its penetration of university administration and government", *The Australian Universities' Review*, 38 (1), pp.59-62.

Bessant, B. (2002) "A climate of fear': from collegiality to corporatisation", in J. Briggs & R. David (eds) *The Subversion of Australian Universities*. Wollongong: UOW, pp.52-84.

Biggs, J., Davis R. (2002) (eds) *The subversion of Australian Universities*. Wollongong: Fund for Intellectual Dissent.

Bosetti, L., Walker, K. (2010) "Perspectives of UK Vice-Chancellors on Leading Universities in a Knowledge-Based Economy", *Higher Education Quarterly*, 64 (1), January, pp.4-12.

Bourke, E. 'Australia's First Peoples: Identity and Population' in C Bourke et al. (eds) *Aboriginal Australia*, Second Edition, University of Queensland Press, St Lucia, Queensland, 1998.

Bradshaw, P. (2002) "Reframing board-staff relations: Exploring the governance funding using a storytelling metaphor", *Nonprofit*

Management & Leadership, 12 (4), pp.471-484.

Buchanan, D., Badham, R. (2004) *Power, Politics, and Organisational Change*: Winning the Turf Game. Sage: London.

Campbell, C. (2010) "Class and Competition", in Connell, R., Campbell, C., Vickers, M., Welch, A., Foley, D., Bagnall, N., Hayes, D., *Education, Change and Society,* Second Edition, South Melbourne: Oxford University Press.

Carmeli, A., Reiter-Palmon, R., & Ziv, E. (2010). Inclusive leadership and employee involvement in creative tasks in the workplace: The mediating role of psychological safety. *Creativity Research Journal*, 22, pp.250-260.

Carter, C., Clegg, S. R., and Kornberger, M. (2008) *A Very Short, Fairly Interesting and Reasonably Cheap Book About Studying Strategy*. Sage: London.

Coady, T. (2000) (ed). *Why Universities Matter*. Sydney: Allen & Unwin

Coaldrake, P. & Stedman, L. (2013) *Raising the Stakes: Gambling with the future of universities*. St Lucia: University of Queensland Press.

Connell, R. (2019). *The Good University*. Monash University Publishing.

Connell, R. (2013a) *Open Letter to the Vice-Chancellor – Raewyn Connell*, National Tertiary Education Union web site, http://www.nteu.org.ay/sydney/article/Open-Letter-to-the-Vice-Chancellor---Raewyn-Connell/

Connell, R. (2013b) "The neoliberal cascade and education: an essay on the market agenda and its consequences", *Critical Studies in Education*, 54 (2), pp.99-112.

Conway, T., Mackay, S., Yorke, D. "Strategic Planning in Higher Education: Who Are the Customers?" *International Journal of Educational Management*, 1994, 8 (6), pp.29-36.

Croucher, G., Marginson, S., Norton, A., Wells, J. (eds) (2013) *The Dawkins Revolution: 25 Years On*. Melbourne: Melbourne University Press.

Currie, J. Newson, J. (eds) (1998) *Universities and Globalization: Critical Perspectives*. Thousand Oaks, CA: Sage.

Daft R. L. (2016) *Organization Theory & Design*, 12th edition. Boston, MA: Cengage Learning.

Davis, G. (2017) *The Australian Idea of a University*. Melbourne University Press.

Davis, S. The business case for inclusive leadership https://www.

linkedin.com/learning/inclusive-leadership/the-business-case-for-inclusive-leadership?u=2126025

Davies, B. (2005) "The (im) possibility of intellectual work in neoliberal regimes". *Discourse: studies in the cultural politics of education*, 26 (1), pp.1-14.

Dawkins, J. S. (1987) *The Challenge for Higher Education in Australia.* Canberra, Australian Capital Territory: Australian Government Publishing Service,

Dawkins, J. S. (1987) *Higher Education: A policy discussion paper* (Green paper). Canberra, Australian Capital Territory: Australian Government Publishing Service,

Dawkins, J. S. (1988) *Higher Education: A policy statement* (White Paper). Canberra, Australian Capital Territory: Australian Government Publishing Service,

Dawkins, J. S. (1988b) *A New Commitment to Higher Education in Australia.* Canberra, Australian Capital Territory: Australian Government Publishing Service.

DiMaggio P. J., Powell, W. W., "Iron Cage Revisited: Institutional Isomorphism and Collective Rationality in Organizational Fields", *American Sociological Review*, 48, 1983, pp.147-160.

DuBrin, A. J., Dalglish, C. (2003) *Leadership: An Australian Focus.* Australian Edition. Milton, Qld: John Wiley & Sons.

Employers Network for equality and inclusion (ENEI). https://www.enei.org.uk/

French, S., Kelly, P., and James, R. (2017) "Futures for Australian Tertiary Education: Developing an integrated, coherent policy vision" in Richard James, Sarah French and Paula Kelly (eds) *Visions for Australian Tertiary Education.* Melbourne Centre for the Study of Higher Education, The University of Melbourne, pp.1-6,

Fullan, M., Scott, G. (2009) *Turnaround Leadership for Higher Education.* San Francisco, CA: Jossey Bass:

Golsorkhi, D., Rouleau, L. Seidl, D., Vaara, E. (2010) *Cambridge Handbook of Strategy as Practice.* Cambridge, NY: Cambridge University Press.

Hil, R. (2015) *Selling Students Short. Why you won't get the university education you deserve.* Allen & Unwin: Sydney, Australia.

Hil, R. (2012) *Whackademia: An insider's account of the troubled university.* Sydney: NewSouth.

Hoare, D. (Chair) (1995) *Higher Education management review: report of the committee of inquiry*. AGPS: Canberra.

Hollander, E. P. (2009). *Inclusive leadership: The essential leader-follower relationship*. New York: Routledge.

Howes, T. (2018) "Effective strategic planning in Australian universities: how good are we and how do we know?" *Journal of Higher Education Policy and Management,* 40 (5), pp.442-457.

Howes, T., Gonczi, A., Hayes, D. (2015). "The contested landscape of strategic planning in Australian universities from three perspectives: Participant observer, academic leader and vice-chancellor". In I. R. Dobson and R. Sharma (eds) *Proceedings of the Tertiary Education Management Conference Leading Locally Competing Globally* 31 Aug – 2 Sept (pp.145-159).

Hrebiniak L. G., and Joyce, W. F., "Organizational Adaptation: Strategic Choice and Environmental Determinism", *Administrative Science Quarterly,* Vol. 30, No. 3, September 1985, pp. 336-349.

James, R., French, S. and Kelly, P. (2017) (eds) *Visions for Australian Tertiary Education*. Melbourne Centre for the Study of Higher Education, The University of Melbourne,

Kaplan, R S., Norton, D. P. (1996) The *Balanced Scorecard: translating strategy into action*. Harvard Business School Press: Boston MA.

Keller, G. (1983) *Academic Strategy*. Baltimore: John Hopkins University Press.

Keller, G. (2008) *Higher Education and the New Society*. Baltimore: John Hopkins Press.

Kelly, N.H. and Shaw, R.N. (1987) "Strategic planning by academic institutions — following the corporate path?" *Higher Education,* Volume 16, pp.319–336.

Kotter, J.P. (1996) *Leading Change*. Boston MA: Harvard Business Review

Kotter, J.P. (2002) *The Heart of Change*. Boston MA: Harvard Business Review.

Kouzes, J. M., Posner, B. Z. (2003) *The Leadership Challenge,* 3rd Edition San Francisco, CA: Jossey-Bass.

Krause, K. L., Reid, J. (2013) "Chapter 7: The Student Experience" in Croucher, G., Marginson, S., Norton, A., Wells, J. (eds) (2013) *The Dawkins Revolution: 25 Years On*. Melbourne: Melbourne University Press.

Lelong, D., Shirley, R. (1990) "Planning: Identifying the Focal Points for

Action", *Planning for Higher Education*, 12 (4), 1990, pp.1-7.

Lowe, I. (1994) *Our Universities are turning us into the 'ignorant country'*. Kensington: NSW University Press.

Maassen, P.A.M, Potman, H.P. (1990) "Strategic decision making in higher education". *Higher Education*, December 1990, Volume 20 (4), pp.393-410.

Macintyre, S., Brett, A. and Croucher, G. (2017) *No End of a Lesson: Australia's United National System of Higher Education.* Melbourne University Press.

Macintyre, S., Croucher, G., Davis, G. and Marginson, S. (2013). "Chapter 1: Making the Unified National System" in Croucher, G., Marginson, S., Norton, A., Wells, J. (eds) (2013) *The Dawkins Revolution: 25 Years On.* Melbourne: Melbourne University Press.

Marginson, S. (2016a) *Higher Education and the Common Good.* Melbourne University Publishing.

Marginson, S. (2016b) *The Dream is Over: The crisis of Clark Kerr's California Idea of Higher Education,* University of California Press.

Marginson, S., Considine, M. (2000) *The Enterprise University: Power, Governance and Reinvention in Australia.* New York: Cambridge University Press.

Marshall, S. (2007) *Strategic Planning at University: what is new?* McGraw Hill.

Maslen, G., Slattery, L. (1994) *Why Our Universities are Failing: Crisis in the Clever Country,* Wilkinson Books, Melbourne.

Meek, V. L, Wood F. Q. (1998) "Higher education governance and management: Australia". *Higher Education Policy*, 11 (2-3), June 1998, pp.165-181.

Meyers, D. (2012) *Australian Universities: A Portrait of Decline.* AUPOD.

Mintzberg, H. (1994a) "The Fall and Rise of Strategic Planning", *Harvard Business Review*, 1994, 72 (1), pp.107-114

Mintzberg, H. (1994b, 2000 ed) *The Rise and Fall of Strategic Planning.* New York: Prentice Hall.

Mintzberg, H. (1973a) "Strategy-Making in Three Modes". *California Management Review*, 16 (2), Winter 1973, pp.44-53.

Mintzberg, J., & Waters, J. A. (1985). "Of strategies, deliberate and emergent", *Strategic Management Journal*, 6 (3), pp.257-272.

Murray, K. (Chair) (1957) *Report of the committee on Australian universities.*

Commonwealth Government Printer: Canberra.

Northouse, P. G. (2010). *Leadership: Theory and Practice*. Fifth Edition. Thousand Oaks, CA: Safe.

Parr, N. (2015) "Who goes to university? The changing profile of our students". *The Conversation*, May 25, 2015.

Pusey, M. (2003) *The Experience of Middle Australia: The Dark Side of Economic Reform*. Cambridge University Press.

Pusey, M. (1991) *Economic Rationalism in Canberra: A Nation-building State Changes its Mind*. Cambridge University Press.

Ross, J. "What is the point of a strategic plan?" Times Higher Education (THE) Feature https://www.timeshighereducation.com/features/what-point-strategic-plan

Rothschild, W. E. (1976) *Putting It All Together: A Guide to Strategic Thinking*. New York: AMACOM.

Rowlands, J. (2012) "Accountability, quality assurance and performativity: The changing role of the academic board", *Quality in Higher Education*, 18 (1), pp.97-110.

Rowley D. J., Sherman, H. (2001) *From Strategy to Change: Implementing the Plan in Higher Education*. San Francisco: Jossey-Bass.

Rowley, D. J., Lujan, H. D., Dolence, M. G. (1997) *Strategic Change in Colleges and Universities: Planning to Survive and Prosper*. San Francisco: Jossey-Bass.

Scott, G. (1999) *Change Matters: Making a difference in education and training*. Crows Nest, AUS: Allen & Unwin.

Sharrock, G. (2017) "Organising, Leading and Managing 21st Century Universities", in Richard James, Sarah French and Paula Kelly (eds) *Visions for Australian Tertiary Education*. Melbourne Centre for the Study of Higher Education, The University of Melbourne, pp.27-40,

Sharrock, G. (2014) "Communicating spending cuts: lessons for Australian university leaders. *Journal of Higher Education Policy and Management*, June 2014, Volume 36 (3), pp.338-354.

Sharrock, G. (2012). "Four management agendas for Australian universities". *Journal of Higher Education Policy and Management*, Volume 34 (3), June 2012, pp.323-337.

Shirley, R. C. (1988) "Strategic Planning: An Overview", in D. W. Steeples (ed). *Successful Strategic Planning: Case Studies. New Directions for Higher Education*, No. 64. San Francisco: Jossey-Bass.

Thomas, R. (1980) "Corporate Strategic Planning in a University", *Long*

SELECT BIBLIOGRAPHY

Range Planning, 13, pp.60-78.

Ward, J. "Strangulation by Regulation", *Australian*, 10 August 1988.

Welch, A. (2010) "Making Education Policy", in Connell, R., Campbell, C., Vickers, M., Welch, A., Foley, D., Bagnall, N., Hayes, D., *Education, Change and Society*, Second Edition, South Melbourne: Oxford University Press.

Welch, A. (2002) "Going Global? Internationalizing Australian Universities in a Time of Global Crisis", *Comparative Education Review*, 46 (4), pp.433-471.

Welch, A. (1998) "Education and the cult of efficiency. Comparative reflections on the reality and the rhetoric", *Comparative Education*, 34 (3), pp.157-176.

Welch, A. (1996) *Australian Education: Reform or Crisis?* Sydney: Allen & Unwin.

Yeatman, A. (1994) "The reform of public management: An overview". *Australian Journal of Public Administration*, 53(3), pp.287-295.

Yeatman, A. (1990) *Bureaucrats, Technocrats and Femocrats: Essays on the Contemporary Australian State*. Sydney: Allen & Unwin.

Zechlin, L. "Strategic Planning in Higher Education", *International Encyclopedia of Education*, 2010, pp.256-263.